Leaves of Grass.

Leaves

of

Grass.

150th Anniversary Edition

Edited and with a New Afterword
by David S. Reynolds

OXFORD
UNIVERSITY PRESS

2005

OXFORD
UNIVERSITY PRESS

Oxford University Press, Inc., publishes works that further
Oxford University's objective of excellence
in research, scholarship, and education.

Oxford   New York
Auckland   Cape Town   Dar es Salaam   Hong Kong   Karachi
Kuala Lumpur   Madrid   Melbourne   Mexico City   Nairobi
New Delhi   Shanghai   Taipei   Toronto

With offices in
Argentina   Austria   Brazil   Chile   Czech Republic   France   Greece
Guatemala   Hungary   Italy   Japan   Poland   Portugal   Singapore
South Korea   Switzerland   Thailand   Turkey   Ukraine   Vietnam

Published by Oxford University Press, Inc.
198 Madison Avenue, New York, New York 10016
www.oup.com

Oxford is a registered trademark of Oxford University Press

Library of Congress Cataloging-in-Publication Data
Whitman, Walt, 1819–1892
   [Leaves of grass]
   Walt Whitman's Leaves of grass /
   edited and with a new afterword by David S. Reynolds.
   —150th anniversary ed.
        p. cm.
   ISBN-13: 978-0-19-518342-9

I. Reynolds, David S., 1948–
II. Title.
PS3201 2005b
811'.3–dc22   2004026509

Every effort has been made to come as close to the font, pagination, punctuation,
and appearance of the original edition as possible. Line breaks and pagination of the
Preface are slightly different due to the constraints of space. The double-column layout
and font approximate the original Preface. Line breaks and pagination of the poetry
attempt to replicate the original text. Editorial insertions are contained in brackets.

10 11 12 13 14 15
Printed in the United States of America
on acid-free paper

Contents

Leaves of Grass.

[Walt Whitman in 1854, from daguerreotype by Gabriel
Harrison, copied by Samuel Hollyer onto a lithographic
plate and reprinted opposite title plate of the 1855
edition of *Leaves of Grass*. Library of Congress.]

Leaves

of

Grass.

———⟨◆⟩———

Brooklyn, New York:

1855.

Preface

AMERICA does not repel the past or what it has produced under its forms or amid other politics or the idea of castes or the old religions....accepts the lesson with calmness...is not so impatient as has been supposed that the slough still sticks to opinions and manners and literature while the life which served its requirements has passed into the new life of the new forms...perceives that the corpse is slowly borne from the eating and sleeping rooms of the house...perceives that it waits a little while in the door...that it was fittest for its days...that its action has descended to the stalwart and wellshaped heir who approaches...and that he shall be fittest for his days.

The Americans of all nations at any time upon the earth have probably the fullest poetical nature. The United States themselves are essentially the greatest poem. In the history of the earth hitherto the largest and most stirring appear tame and orderly to their ampler largeness and stir. Here at last is something in the doings of man that corresponds with the broadcast doings of the day and night. Here is not merely a nation but a teeming nation of nations. Here is action untied from strings necessarily blind to particulars and details magnificently moving in vast masses. Here is the hospitality which forever indicates heroes....Here are the roughs and beards and space and ruggedness and nonchalance that the soul loves. Here the performance disdaining the trivial unapproached in the tremendous audacity of its crowds and groupings and the push of its perspective spreads with crampless and flowing breadth and showers its prolific and splendid extravagance. One sees it must indeed own the riches of the summer and winter, and need never be bankrupt while corn grows from the ground or the orchards drop apples or the bays contain fish or men beget children upon women.

Other states indicate themselves in their deputies....but the genius of the United States is not best or most in its executives or legislatures, nor in its ambassadors or authors or colleges or churches or parlors, nor even in its newspapers or inventors...but always most in the common people. Their manners speech dress friendships — the freshness and candor of their physiognomy — the picturesque looseness of their carriage...their deathless attachment to freedom — their aversion to anything indecorous or soft or mean — the practical acknowledgment of the citizens of one state by the citizens of all other states — the fierceness of their roused resentment — their curiosity and welcome of novelty — their self-esteem and wonderful sympathy — their susceptibility to a slight — the air they have of persons who never knew how it felt to stand in the presence of superiors — the fluency of their speech — their delight in music, the sure symptom of manly tenderness and native elegance of soul...their good temper and openhandedness — the terrible significance of their elections — the President's taking off his hat to them not they to him — these too are unrhymed poetry. It awaits the gigantic and generous treatment worthy of it.

The largeness of nature or the nation were monstrous without a corresponding largeness and generosity of the spirit of the citizen. Not nature nor swarming states nor streets and steamships nor prosperous business nor farms nor capital nor learning may suffice for the ideal of man...nor suffice the poet. No reminiscences may suffice either. A live nation can always cut a deep mark and can have the best authority the cheapest...namely from its own soul. This is the sum of the profitable uses of individuals or states and of present action and grandeur and of the subjects of poets. — As if it were necessary to trot back generation after generation to the eastern records! As if the beauty and sacredness of the demonstrable must fall behind that of the mythical! As if men do not make their mark out of any times! As if the opening of the western continent by discovery and what has transpired since in North and South America were less than the small theatre of the antique or the aimless sleepwalking of the middle ages! The pride of the United States leaves the wealth and finesse of the cities and all returns of commerce and agriculture and all the magnitude of geography or shows of exterior victory to enjoy the breed of full-sized men or one full-sized man unconquerable and simple.

The American poets are to enclose old and new for America is the race of races. Of them a bard is to be commensurate with a people. To him the other continents arrive as contributions...he gives them reception for their sake and his own sake. His spirit responds to his country's spirit....he incarnates its geography and natural life and rivers and lakes. Mississippi with annual freshets and changing chutes, Missouri and Columbia and Ohio and Saint Lawrence with the falls and beautiful masculine Hudson, do not embouchure where they spend themselves more than they embouchure into him. The blue breadth over the inland sea of Virginia and Maryland and the sea off Massachusetts and Maine and over Manhattan bay and over Champlain and Erie and over Ontario and Huron and Michigan and Superior, and over the Texan and Mexican and Floridian and Cuban seas and over the seas off California and Or-

egon, is not tallied by the blue breadth of the waters below more than the breadth of above and below is tallied by him. When the long Atlantic coast stretches longer and the Pacific coast stretches longer he easily stretches with them north or south. He spans between them also from east to west and reflects what is between them. On him rise solid growths that offset the growths of pine and cedar and hemlock and liveoak and locust and chestnut and cypress and hickory and limetree and cottonwood and tuliptree and cactus and wildvine and tamarind and persimmon....and tangles as tangled as any canebrake or swamp....and forests coated with transparent ice and icicles hanging from the boughs and crackling in the wind....and sides and peaks of mountains....and pasturage sweet and free as savannah or upland or prairie....with flights and songs and screams that answer those of the wildpigeon and highhold and orchard-oriole and coot and surf-duck and redshouldered-hawk and fish-hawk and white-ibis and indian-hen and cat-owl and water-pheasant and qua-bird and pied-sheldrake and blackbird and mockingbird and buzzard and condor and night-heron and eagle. To him the hereditary countenance descends both mother's and father's. To him enter the essences of the real things and past and present events — of the enormous diversity of temperature and agriculture and mines — the tribes of red aborigines — the weather-beaten vessels entering new ports or making landings on rocky coasts — the first settlements north or south — the rapid stature and muscle — the haughty defiance of '76, and the war and peace and formation of the constitution....the union always surrounded by blatherers and always calm and impregnable — the perpetual coming of immigrants — the wharfhem'd cities and superior marine — the unsurveyed interior — the loghouses and clearings and wild animals and hunters and trappers....the free commerce —

the fisheries and whaling and gold-digging — the endless gestation of new states — the convening of Congress every December, the members duly coming up from all climates and the uttermost parts....the noble character of the young mechanics and of all free American workmen and workwomen....the general ardor and friendliness and enterprise — the perfect equality of the female with the male....the large amativeness — the fluid movement of the population — the factories and mercantile life and laborsaving machinery — the Yankee swap — the New York firemen and the target excursion — the southern plantation life — the character of the northeast and of the northwest and southwest — slavery and the tremulous spreading of hands to protect it, and the stern opposition to it which shall never cease till it ceases or the speaking of tongues and the moving of lips cease. For such the expression of the American poet is to be transcendant and new. It is to be indirect and not direct or descriptive or epic. Its quality goes through these to much more. Let the age and wars of other nations be chanted and their eras and characters be illustrated and that finish the verse. Not so the great psalm of the republic. Here the theme is creative and has vista. Here comes one among the wellbeloved stonecutters and plans with decision and science and sees the solid and beautiful forms of the future where there are now no solid forms.

Of all nations the United States with veins full of poetical stuff most need poets and will doubtless have the greatest and use them the greatest. Their Presidents shall not be their common referee so much as their poets shall. Of all mankind the great poet is the equable man. Not in him but off from him things are grotesque or eccentric or fail of their sanity. Nothing out of its place is good and nothing in its place is bad. He bestows on every object or quality its fit proportions neither more nor less. He is the ar-biter of the diverse and he is the key. He is the equalizer of his age and land....he supplies what wants supplying and checks what wants checking. If peace is the routine out of him speaks the spirit of peace, large, rich, thrifty, building vast and populous cities, encouraging agriculture and the arts and commerce — lighting the study of man, the soul, immortality — federal, state or municipal government, marriage, health, freetrade, intertravel by land and sea....nothing too close, nothing too far off...the stars not too far off. In war he is the most deadly force of the war. Who recruits him recruits horse and foot...he fetches parks of artillery the best that engineer ever knew. If the time becomes slothful and heavy he knows how to arouse it...he can make every word he speaks draw blood. Whatever stagnates in the flat of custom or obedience or legislation he never stagnates. Obedience does not master him, he masters it. High up out of reach he stands turning a concentrated light...he turns the pivot with his finger...he baffles the swiftest runners as he stands and easily overtakes and envelops them. The time straying toward infidelity and confections and persiflage he withholds by his steady faith...he spreads out his dishes...he offers the sweet firmfibred meat that grows men and women. His brain is the ultimate brain. He is no arguer...he is judgment. He judges not as the judge judges but as the sun falling around a helpless thing. As he sees the farthest he has the most faith. His thoughts are the hymns of the praise of things. In the talk on the soul and eternity and God off of his equal plane he is silent. He sees eternity less like a play with a prologue and denouement....he sees eternity in men and women...he does not see men and women as dreams or dots. Faith is the antiseptic of the soul...it pervades the common people and preserves them...they never give up believing and expecting and trusting. There is that indescribable freshness and unconsciousness about an illiterate person that humbles and mocks the power of the noblest expressive genius. The poet sees for a certainty how one not a great artist may be just as sacred and perfect as the greatest artist......The power to destroy or remould is freely used by him but never the power of attack. What is past is past. If he does not expose superior models and prove himself by every step he takes he is not what is wanted. The presence of the greatest poet conquers...not parleying or struggling or any prepared attempts. Now he has passed that way see after him! there is not left any vestige of despair or misanthropy or cunning or exclusiveness or the ignominy of a nativity or color or delusion of hell or the necessity of hell.....and no man thenceforward shall be degraded for ignorance or weakness or sin.

The greatest poet hardly knows pettiness or triviality. If he breathes into any thing that was before thought small it dilates with the grandeur and life of the universe. He is a seer....he is individual...he is complete in himself....the others are as good as he, only he sees it and they do not. He is not one of the chorus....he does not stop for any regulation...he is the president of regulation. What the eyesight does to the rest he does to the rest. Who knows the curious mystery of the eyesight? The other senses corroborate themselves, but this is removed from any proof but its own and foreruns the identities of the spiritual world. A single glance of it mocks all the investigations of man and all the instruments and books of the earth and all reasoning. What is marvellous? what is unlikely? what is impossible or baseless or vague? after you have once just opened the space of a peachpit and given audience to far and near and to the sunset and had all things enter with electric swiftness softly and duly without confusion or jostling or jam.

The land and sea, the animals fishes and birds, the sky of heaven and the orbs, the forests mountains and rivers, are not small themes...but folks expect of the poet to indicate more than the beauty and dignity which always attach to dumb real objects....they expect him to indicate the path between reality and their souls. Men and women perceive the beauty well enough..probably as well as he. The passionate tenacity of hunters, woodmen, early risers, cultivators of gardens and orchards and fields, the love of healthy women for the manly form, seafaring persons, drivers of horses, the passion for light and the open air, all is an old varied sign of the unfailing perception of beauty and of a residence of the poetic in outdoor people. They can never be assisted by poets to perceive...some may but they never can. The poetic quality is not marshalled in rhyme or uniformity or abstract addresses to things nor in melancholy complaints or good precepts, but is the life of these and much else and is in the soul. The profit of rhyme is that it drops seeds of a sweeter and more luxuriant rhyme, and of uniformity that it conveys itself into its own roots in the ground out of sight. The rhyme and uniformity of perfect poems show the free growth of metrical laws and bud from them as unerringly and loosely as lilacs or roses on a bush, and take shapes as compact as the shapes of chestnuts and oranges and melons and pears, and shed the perfume impalpable to form. The fluency and ornaments of the finest poems or music or orations or recitations are not independent but dependent. All beauty comes from beautiful blood and a beautiful brain. If the greatnesses are in conjunction in a man or woman it is enough....the fact will prevail through the universe....but the gaggery and gilt of a million years will not prevail. Who troubles himself about his ornaments or fluency is lost. This is what you shall do: Love the earth and sun and the animals, despise riches, give alms to every one that asks, stand up for the stupid and crazy, devote your income and labor to others, hate tyrants, argue not concerning God, have patience and indulgence toward the people, take off your hat to nothing known or unknown or to any man or number of men, go freely with powerful uneducated persons and with the young and with the mothers of families, read these leaves in the open air every season of every year of your life, re examine all you have been told at school or church or in any book, dismiss whatever insults your own soul, and your very flesh shall be a great poem and have the richest fluency not only in its words but in the silent lines of its lips and face and between the lashes of your eyes and in every motion and joint of your body........The poet shall not spend his time in unneeded work. He shall know that the ground is always ready ploughed and manured....others may not know it but he shall. He shall go directly to the creation. His trust shall master the trust of everything he touches....and shall master all attachment.

The known universe has one complete lover and that is the greatest poet. He consumes an eternal passion and is indifferent which chance happens and which possible contingency of fortune or misfortune and persuades daily and hourly his delicious pay. What balks or breaks others is fuel for his burning progress to contact and amorous joy. Other proportions of the reception of pleasure dwindle to nothing to his proportions. All expected from heaven or from the highest he is rapport with in the sight of the daybreak or a scene of the winter woods or the presence of children playing or with his arm round the neck of a man or woman. His love above all love has leisure and expanse....he leaves room ahead of himself. He is no irresolute or suspicious lover...he is sure...he scorns intervals. His experience and the showers and thrills are not for nothing. Nothing can jar him....suffering and darkness cannot — death and fear cannot. To him complaint and jealousy and envy are corpses buried and rotten in the earth....he saw them buried. The sea is not surer of the shore or the shore of the sea than he is of the fruition of his love and of all perfection and beauty.

The fruition of beauty is no chance of hit or miss...it is inevitable as life....it is exact and plumb as gravitation. From the eyesight proceeds another eyesight and from the hearing proceeds another hearing and from the voice proceeds another voice eternally curious of the harmony of things with man. To these respond perfections not only in the committees that were supposed to stand for the rest but in the rest themselves just the same. These understand the law of perfection in masses and floods...that its finish is to each for itself and onward from itself...that it is profuse and impartial...that there is not a minute of the light or dark nor an acre of the earth or sea without it — nor any direction of the sky nor any trade or employment nor any turn of events. This is the reason that about the proper expression of beauty there is precision and balance...one part does not need to be thrust above another. The best singer is not the one who has the most lithe and powerful organ...the pleasure of poems is not in them that take the handsomest measure and similes and sound.

Without effort and without exposing in the least how it is done the greatest poet brings the spirit of any or all events and passions and scenes and persons some more and some less to bear on your individual character as you hear or read. To do this well is to compete with the laws that pursue and follow time. What is the purpose must surely be there and the clue of it must be there....and the faintest indication is the indication of the best and then becomes the clearest indication. Past and present and future are not disjoined but joined. The greatest poet forms the consistence of what is to be from what has been and is. He drags the dead out of their coffins and stands them again on their feet....he says to the past, Rise and walk before me that I may realize you. He learns the lesson....he places himself where the future becomes present. The greatest poet does not only dazzle his rays over character and scenes and passions...he finally ascends and finishes all...he exhibits the pinnacles that no man can tell what they are for or what is beyond....he glows a moment on the extremest verge. He is most wonderful in his last half-hidden smile or frown...by that flash of the moment of parting the one that sees it shall be encouraged or terrified afterward for many years. The greatest poet does not moralize or make applications of morals...he knows the soul. The soul has that measureless pride which consists in never acknowledging any lessons but its own. But it has sympathy as measureless as its pride and the one balances the other and neither can stretch too far while it stretches in company with the other. The inmost secrets of art sleep with the twain. The greatest poet has lain close betwixt both and they are vital in his style and thoughts.

The art of art, the glory of expression and the sunshine of the light of letters is simplicity. Nothing is better than simplicity....nothing can make up for excess or for the lack of definiteness. To carry on the heave of impulse and pierce intellectual depths and give all subjects their articulations are powers neither common nor very uncommon. But to speak in literature with the perfect rectitude and insousiance of the movements of animals and the unimpeachableness of the sentiment of trees in the woods and grass by the roadside is the flawless triumph of art. If you have looked on him who has achieved it you have looked on one of the masters of the artists of all nations and times. You shall not contemplate the flight of the graygull over the bay or the mettlesome action of the blood horse or the tall leaning of sunflowers on their stalk or the appearance of the sun journeying through heaven or the appearance of the moon afterward with any more satisfaction than

you shall contemplate him. The greatest poet has less a marked style and is more the channel of thoughts and things without increase or diminution, and is the free channel of himself. He swears to his art, I will not be meddlesome, I will not have in my writing any elegance or effect or originality to hang in the way between me and the rest like curtains. I will have nothing hang in the way, not the richest curtains. What I tell I tell for precisely what it is. Let who may exalt or startle or fascinate or sooth I will have purposes as health or heat or snow has and be as regardless of observation. What I experience or portray shall go from my composition without a shred of my composition. You shall stand by my side and look in the mirror with me.

The old red blood and stainless gentility of great poets will be proved by their unconstraint. A heroic person walks at his ease through and out of that custom or precedent or authority that suits him not. Of the traits of the brotherhood of writers savans musicians inventors and artists nothing is finer than silent defiance advancing from new free forms. In the need of poems philosophy politics mechanism science behaviour, the craft of art, an appropriate native grand-opera, shipcraft, or any craft, he is greatest forever and forever who contributes the greatest original practical example. The cleanest expression is that which finds no sphere worthy of itself and makes one.

The messages of great poets to each man and woman are, Come to us on equal terms, Only then can you understand us, We are no better than you, What we enclose you enclose, What we enjoy you may enjoy. Did you suppose there could be only one Supreme? We affirm there can be unnumbered Supremes, and that one does not countervail another any more than one eyesight countervails another..and that men can be good or grand only of the consciousness of their supremacy within them. What do you

think is the grandeur of storms and dis-
memberments and the deadliest battles
and wrecks and the wildest fury of the
elements and the power of the sea and
the motion of nature and of the throes of
human desires and dignity and hate and
love? It is that something in the soul
which says, Rage on, Whirl on, I tread
master here and everywhere, Master of
the spasms of the sky and of the shatter
of the sea, Master of nature and passion
and death, And of all terror and all pain.

The American bards shall be marked
for generosity and affection and for en-
couraging competitors..They shall be kos-
mos..without monopoly or secresy..glad
to pass any thing to any one..hungry for
equals night and day. They shall not be
careful of riches and privilege....they shall
be riches and privilege....they shall per-
ceive who the most affluent man is. The
most affluent man is he that confronts all
the shows he sees by equivalents out of
the stronger wealth of himself. The Ameri-
can bard shall delineate no class of per-
sons nor one or two out of the strata of
interests nor love most nor truth most nor
the soul most nor the body most....and not
be for the eastern states more than the
western or the northern states more than
the southern.

Exact science and its practical move-
ments are no checks on the greatest poet
but always his encouragement and sup-
port. The outset and remembrance are
there..there the arms that lifted him first
and brace him best....there he returns af-
ter all his goings and comings. The sailor
and traveler..the anatomist chemist astrono-
mer geologist phrenologist spiritualist
mathematician historian and lexicographer
are not poets, but they are the lawgivers
of poets and their construction underlies
the structure of every perfect poem. No
matter what rises or is uttered they sent
the seed of the conception of it...of them
and by them stand the visible proofs of
souls.....always of their fatherstuff must
be begotten the sinewy races of bards. If

there shall be love and content between
the father and the son and if the great-
ness of the son is the exuding of the great-
ness of the father there shall be love
between the poet and the man of demon-
strable science. In the beauty of poems
are the tuft and final applause of science.

Great is the faith of the flush of knowl-
edge and of the investigation of the depths
of qualities and things. Cleaving and cir-
cling here swells the soul of the poet yet it
president of itself always. The depths are
fathomless and therefore calm. The inno-
cence and nakedness are resumed...they
are neither modest nor immodest. The
whole theory of the special and supernatu-
ral and all that was twined with it or
educed out of it departs as a dream. What
has ever happened....what happens and
whatever may or shall happen, the vital
laws enclose all....they are suffcient for
any case and for all cases...none to be
hurried or retarded....any miracle of af-
fairs or persons inadmissible in the vast
clear scheme where every motion and
every spear of grass and the frames and
spirits of men and women and all that
concerns them are unspeakably perfect
miracles all referring to all and each dis-
tinct and in its place. It is also not consis-
tent with the reality of the soul to admit
that there is anything in the known uni-
verse more divine than men and women.

Men and women and the earth and all
upon it are simply to be taken as they are,
and the investigation of their past and
present and future shall be unintermitted
and shall be done with perfect candor.
Upon this basis philosophy speculates
ever looking toward the poet, ever regard-
ing the eternal tendencies of all toward
happiness never inconsistent with what
is clear to the senses and to the soul. For
the eternal tendencies of all toward hap-
piness make the only point of sane phi-
losophy. Whatever comprehends less than
that...whatever is less than the laws of
light and of astronomical motion..or less
than the laws that follow the thief the liar

the glutton and the drunkard through this life and doubtless afterward.....or less than vast stretches of time or the slow formation of density or the patient up-heaving of strata — is of no account. Whatever would put God in a poem or system of philosophy as contending against some being or influence is also of no account. Sanity and ensemble char-acterise the great master...spoilt in one principle all is spoilt. The great master has nothing to do with miracles. He sees health for himself in being one of the mass....he sees the hiatus in singular emi-nence. To the perfect shape comes com-mon ground. To be under the general law is great for that is to correspond with it. The master knows that he is unspeakably great and that all are unspeakably great....that nothing for instance is greater than to conceive children and bring them up well...that to be is just as great as to per-ceive or tell.

In the make of the great masters the idea of political liberty is indispensible. Liberty takes the adherence of heroes wherever men and women exist....but never takes any adherence or welcome from the rest more than from poets. They are the voice and exposition of liberty. They out of ages are worthy the grand idea....to them it is confided and they must sustain it. Nothing has precedence of it and nothing can warp or degrade it. The attitude of great poets is to cheer up slaves and horrify despots. The turn of their necks, the sound of their feet, the motions of their wrists, are full of hazard to the one and hope to the other. Come nigh them awhile and though they neither speak or advise you shall learn the faith-ful American lesson. Liberty is poorly served by men whose good intent is quelled from one failure or two failures or any number of failures, or from the casual indifference or ingratitude of the people, or from the sharp show of the tushes of power, or the bringing to bear soldiers and cannon or any penal statutes.

Liberty relies upon itself, invites no one, promises nothing, sits in calmness and light, is positive and composed, and knows no discouragement. The battle rages with many a loud alarm and frequent advance and retreat....the enemy triumphs....the prison, the handcuffs, the iron necklace and anklet, the scaffold, garrote and lead-balls do their work....the cause is asleep ....the strong throats are choked with their own blood....the young men drop their eyelashes toward the ground when they pass each other....and is liberty gone out of that place? No never. When liberty goes it is not the first to go nor the sec-ond or third to go..it waits for all the rest to go..it is the last...When the memories of the old martyrs are faded utterly away ....when the large names of patriots are laughed at in the public halls from the lips of the orators....when the boys are no more christened after the same but chris-tened after tyrants and traitors instead ....when the laws of the free are grudg-ingly permitted and laws for informers and bloodmoney are sweet to the taste of the people....when I and you walk abroad upon the earth stung with compassion at the sight of numberless brothers answer-ing our equal friendship and calling no man master — and when we are elated with noble joy at the sight of slaves.... when the soul retires in the cool commun-ion of the night and surveys its experi-ence and has much extasy over the word and deed that put back a helpless inno-cent person into the gripe of the gripers or into any cruel inferiority....when those in all parts of these states who could easier realize the true American character but do not yet — when the swarms of cring-ers, suckers, doughfaces, lice of politics, planners of sly involutions for their own preferment to city offices or state legisla-tures or the judiciary or congress or the presidency, obtain a response of love and natural deference from the people whether they get the offices or no....when it is bet-ter to be a bound booby and rogue in office at a high salary than the poorest free mechanic or farmer with his hat unmoved from his head and firm eyes and a candid and generous heart....and when servility by town or state or the federal government or any oppression on a large scale or small scale can be tried on without its own punishment following duly after in exact proportion against the smallest chance of escape....or rather when all life and all the souls of men and women are discharged from any part of the earth — then only shall the instinct of liberty be discharged from that part of the earth.

As the attributes of the poets of the kosmos concentre in the real body and soul and in the pleasure of things they possess the superiority of genuineness over all fiction and romance. As they emit themselves facts are showered over with light....the daylight is lit with more volatile light....also the deep between the setting and rising sun goes deeper many fold. Each precise object or condition or combination or process exhibits a beauty....the multiplication table its — old age its — the carpenter's trade its — the grand-opera its....the hugehulled cleanshaped New York clipper at sea under steam or full sail gleams with unmatched beauty....the American circles and large harmonies of government gleam with theirs....and the commonest definite intentions and actions with theirs. The poets of the kosmos advance through all interpositions and coverings and turmoils and stratagems to first principles. They are of use....they dissolve poverty from its need and riches from its conceit. You large proprietor they say shall not realize or perceive more than any one else. The owner of the library is not he who holds a legal title to it having bought and paid for it. Any one and every one is owner of the library who can read the same through all the varieties of tongues and subjects and styles, and in whom they enter with ease and take residence and force toward paternity and

maternity, and make supple and powerful and rich and large.........These American states strong and healthy and accomplished shall receive no pleasure from violations of natural models and must not permit them. In paintings or mouldings or carvings in mineral or wood, or in the illustrations of books or newspapers, or in any comic or tragic prints, or in the patterns of woven stuffs or any thing to beautify rooms or furniture or costumes, or to put upon cornices or monuments or on the prows or sterns of ships, or to put anywhere before the human eye indoors or out, that which distorts honest shapes or which creates unearthly beings or places or contingencies is a nuisance and revolt. Of the human form especially it is so great it must never be made ridiculous. Of ornaments to a work nothing outre can be allowed..but those ornaments can be allowed that conform to the perfect facts of the open air and that flow out of the nature of the work and come irrepressibly from it and are necessary to the completion of the work. Most works are most beautiful without ornament...Exaggerations will be revenged in human physiology. Clean and vigorous children are jetted and conceived only in those communities where the models of natural forms are public every day.....Great genius and the people of these states must never be demeaned to romances. As soon as histories are properly told there is no more need of romances.

The great poets are also to be known by the absence in them of tricks and by the justification of perfect personal candor. Then folks echo a new cheap joy and a divine voice leaping from their brains: How beautiful is candor! All faults may be forgiven of him who has perfect candor. Henceforth let no man of us lie, for we have seen that openness wins the inner and outer world and that there is no single exception, and that never since our earth gathered itself in a mass have deceit or subterfuge or prevarication attracted its smallest particle or the faintest tinge of a shade — and that through the enveloping wealth and rank of a state or the whole republic of states a sneak or sly person shall be discovered and despised....and that the soul has never been once fooled and never can be fooled....and thrift without the loving nod of the soul is only a foetid puff....and there never grew up in any of the continents of the globe nor upon any planet or satellite or star, nor upon the asteroids, nor in any part of ethereal space, nor in the midst of density, nor under the fluid wet of the sea, nor in that condition which precedes the birth of babes, nor at any time during the changes of life, nor in that condition that follows what we term death, nor in any stretch of abeyance or action afterward of vitality, nor in any process of formation or reformation anywhere, a being whose instinct hated the truth.

Extreme caution or prudence, the soundest organic health, large hope and comparison and fondness for women and children, large alimentiveness and destructiveness and causality, with a perfect sense of the oneness of nature and the propriety of the same spirit applied to human affairs..these are called up of the flout of the brain of the world to be parts of the greatest poet from his birth out of his mother's womb and from her birth out of her mother's. Caution seldom goes far enough. It has been thought that the prudent citizen was the citizen who applied himself to solid going and did well for himself and his family and completed a lawful life without debt or crime. The greatest poet sees and admits these economics as he sees the economics of food and sleep, but has higher notions of prudence than to think he gives much when he gives a few slight attentions at the latch of the gate. The premises of the prudence of life are not the hospitality of it or the ripeness and harvest of it. Beyond the

independence of a little sum laid aside for burial-money, and of a few clapboards around and shingles overhead on a lot of American soil owned, and the easy dollars that supply the year's plain clothing and meals, the melancholy prudence of the abandonment of such a great being as a man is to the toss and pallor of years of moneymaking with all their scorching days and icy nights and all their stifling deceits and underhanded dodgings, or infinitessimals of parlors, or shameless stuffing while others starve, and all the loss of the bloom and odor of the earth and of the flowers and atmosphere and of the sea and of the true taste of the women and men you pass or have to do with in youth or middle age, and the issuing sickness and desperate revolt at the close of a life without elevation or naivete, and the ghastly chatter of a death without serenity or majesty, is the great fraud upon modern civilization and forethought, blotching the surface and system which civilization undeniably drafts, and moistening with tears the immense features it spreads and spreads with such velocity before the reached kisses of the soul...Still the right explanation remains to be made about prudence. The prudence of the mere wealth and respectability of the most esteemed life appears too faint for the eye to observe at all when little and large alike drop quietly aside at the thought of the prudence suitable for immortality. What is wisdom that fills the thinness of a year or seventy or eighty years to wisdom spaced out by ages and coming back at a certain time with strong reinforcements and rich presents and the clear faces of wedding-guests as far as you can look in every direction running gaily toward you? Only the soul is of itself....all else has reference to what ensues. All that a person does or thinks is of consequence. Not a move can a man or woman make that affects him or her in a day or a month or any part of the direct lifetime or the hour of death but the same affects him or her onward afterward through the indirect lifetime. The indirect is always as great and real as the direct. The spirit receives from the body just as much as it gives to the body. Not one name of word or deed..not of venereal sores or discolorations..not the privacy of the onanist..not of the putrid veins of gluttons or rumdrinkers...not peculation or cunning or betrayal or murder..no serpentine poison of those that seduce women..not the foolish yielding of women..not prostitution..not of any depravity of young men..not of the attainment of gain by discreditable means..not any nastiness of appetite..not any harshness of officers to men or judges to prisoners or fathers to sons or sons to fathers or of husbands to wives or bosses to their boys..not of greedy looks or malignant wishes...nor any of the wiles practised by people upon themselves...ever is or ever can be stamped on the programme but it is duly realized and returned, and that returned in further performances...and they returned again. Nor can the push of charity or personal force ever be any thing else than the profoundest reason, whether it bring arguments to hand or no. No specification is necessary..to add or subtract or divide is in vain. Little or big, learned or unlearned, white or black, legal or illegal, sick or well, from the first inspiration down the windpipe to the last expiration out of it, all that a male or female does that is rigorous and benevolent and clean is so much sure profit to him or her in the unshakable order of the universe and through the whole scope of it forever. If the savage or felon is wise it is well....if the greatest poet or savan is wise it is simply the same..if the President or chief justice is wise it is the same...if the young mechanic or farmer is wise it is no more or less..if the prostitute is wise it is no more nor less. The interest will come round..all will come round. All the best actions of war and peace...all help given to relatives and strangers and the poor and old and sorrowful and young children and widows and the sick, and to all shunned persons..all furtherance of fugitives and of the escape of slaves..all the self-denial that stood steady and aloof on wrecks and saw others take the seats of the boats...all offering of substance or life for the good old cause, or for a friend's sake or opinion's sake...all pains of enthusiasts scoffed at by their neighbors..all the vast sweet love and precious suffering of mothers...all honest men baffled in strifes recorded or unrecorded....all the grandeur and good of the few ancient nations whose fragments of annals we inherit..and all the good of the hundreds of far mightier and more ancient nations unknown to us by name or date or location....all that was ever manfully begun, whether it succeeded or no....all that has at any time been well suggested out of the divine heart of man or by the divinity of his mouth or by the shaping of his great hands..and all that is well thought or done this day on any part of the surface of the globe..or on any of the wandering stars or fixed stars by those there as we are here..or that is henceforth to be well thought or done by you whoever you are, or by any one — these singly and wholly inured at their time and inure now and will inure always to the identities from which they sprung or shall spring...Did you guess any of them lived only its moment? The world does not so exist..no parts palpable or impalpable so exist...no result exists now without being from its long antecedent result, and that from its antecedent, and so backward without the farthest mentionable spot coming a bit nearer the beginning than any other spot.....Whatever satisfies the soul is truth. The prudence of the greatest poet answers at last the craving and glut of the soul, is not contemptuous of less ways of prudence if they conform to its ways, puts off nothing, permits no let-up for its own case or any case, has no particular sabbath or judgment-day, divides not the living from the dead or the righteous from the unrighteous, is satisfied with the present, matches every thought or act by its correlative, knows no possible forgiveness or deputed atonement..knows that the young man who composedly periled his life and lost it has done exceeding well for himself, while the man who has not periled his life and retains it to old age in riches and ease has perhaps achieved nothing for himself worth mentioning..and that only that person has no great prudence to learn who has learnt to prefer real longlived things, and favors body and soul the same, and perceives the indirect assuredly following the direct, and what evil or good he does leaping onward and waiting to meet him again — and who in his spirit in any emergency whatever neither hurries or avoids death.

The direct trial of him who would be the greatest poet is today. If he does not flood himself with the immediate age as with vast oceanic tides.....and if he does not attract his own land body and soul to himself and hang on its neck with incomparable love and plunge his semitic muscle into its merits and demerits...and if he be not himself the age transfigured....and if to him is not opened the eternity which gives similitude to all periods and locations and processes and animate and inanimate forms, and which is the bond of time, and rises up from its inconceivable vagueness and infiniteness in the swimming shape of today, and is held by the ductile anchors of life, and makes the present spot the passage from what was to what shall be, and commits itself to the representation of this wave of an hour and this one of the sixty beautiful children of the wave — let him merge in the general run and wait his development ....Still the final test of poems or any character or work remains. The prescient poet projects himself centuries ahead and judges performer or performance after the changes of time. Does it live through them? Does it still hold on untired? Will the same style and the direction of genius to similar points be satisfactory now? Has no new discovery in science or arrival at superior planes of thought and judgment and behaviour fixed him or his so that either can be looked down upon? Have the marches of tens and hundreds and thousands of years made willing detours to the right hand and the left hand for his sake? Is he beloved long and long after he is buried? Does the young man think often of him? and the young woman think often of him? and do the middleaged and the old think of him?

A great poem is for ages and ages in common and for all degrees and complexions and all departments and sects and for a woman as much as a man and a man as much as a woman. A great poem is no finish to a man or woman but rather a beginning. Has any one fancied he could sit at last under some due authority and rest satisfied with explanation and realize and be content and full? To no such terminus does the greatest poet bring...he brings neither cessation or sheltered fatness and ease. The touch of him tells in action. Whom he takes he takes with firm sure grasp into live regions previously unattained....thenceforward is no rest....they see the space and ineffable sheen that turn the old spots and lights into dead vacuums. The companion of him beholds the birth and progress of stars and learns one of the meanings. Now there shall be a man cohered out of tumult and chaos....the elder encourages the younger and shows him how...they two shall launch off fearlessly together till the new world fits an orbit for itself and looks unabashed on the lesser orbits of the stars and sweeps through the ceaseless rings and shall never be quiet again.

There will soon be no more priests. Their work is done. They may wait awhile ..perhaps a generation or two..dropping off by degrees. A superior breed shall take their place....the gangs of kosmos and prophets en masse shall take their place. A new order shall arise and they shall be the priests of man, and every man shall be his own priest. The churches built under their umbrage shall be the churches of men and women. Through the divinity of themselves shall the kosmos and the new breed of poets be interpreters of men and women and of all events and things. They shall find their inspiration in real objects today, symptoms of the past and future....They shall not deign to defend immortality or God or the perfection of things or liberty or the exquisite beauty and reality of the soul. They shall arise in America and be responded to from the remainder of the earth.

The English language befriends the grand American expression....it is brawny enough and limber and full enough. On the tough stock of a race who through all change of circumstance was never without the idea of political liberty, which is the animus of all liberty, it has attracted the terms of daintier and gayer and subtler and more elegant tongues. It is the powerful language of resistance...it is the dialect of common sense. It is the speech of the proud and melancholy races and of all who aspire. It is the chosen tongue to express growth faith self-esteem freedom justice equality friendliness amplitude prudence decision and courage. It is the medium that shall well nigh express the inexpressible.

No great literature nor any like style of behaviour or oratory or social intercourse or household arrangements or public institutions or the treatment by bosses of employed people, nor executive detail or detail of the army or navy, nor spirit of legislation or courts or police or tuition or architecture or songs or amusements or the costumes of young men, can long elude the jealous and passionate instinct of American standards. Whether or no the sign appears from the mouths of the people, it throbs a live interrogation in

every freeman's and freewoman's heart after that which passes by or this built to remain. Is it uniform with my country? Are its disposals without ignominious distinctions? Is it for the evergrowing communes of brothers and lovers, large, well-united, proud beyond the old models, generous beyond all models? Is it something grown fresh out of the fields or drawn from the sea for use to me today here? I know that what answers for me an American must answer for any individual or nation that serves for a part of my materials. Does this answer? or is it without reference to universal needs? or sprung of the needs of the less developed society of special ranks? or old needs of pleasure overlaid by modern science and forms? Does this acknowledge liberty with audible and absolute acknowledgement, and set slavery at nought for life and death? Will it help breed one goodshaped and wellhung man, and a woman to be his perfect and independent mate? Does it improve manners? Is it for the nursing of the young of the republic? Does it solve readily with the sweet milk of the nipples of the breasts of the mother of many children? Has it too the old ever-fresh forbearance and impartiality? Does it look with the same love on the last born and on those hardening toward stature, and on the errant, and on those who disdain all strength of assault outside of their own?

The poems distilled from other poems will probably pass away. The coward will surely pass away. The expectation of the vital and great can only be satisfied by the demeanor of the vital and great. The swarms of the polished deprecating and reflectors and the polite float off and leave no remembrance. America prepares with composure and goodwill for the visitors that have sent word. It is not intellect that is to be their warrant and welcome. The talented, the artist, the ingenious, the editor, the statesman, the erudite..they are not unappreciated..they fall in their place and do their work. The soul of the nation also does its work. No disguise can pass on it..no disguise can conceal from it. It rejects none, it permits all. Only toward as good as itself and toward the like of itself will it advance half-way. An individual is as superb as a nation when he has the qualities which make a superb nation. The soul of the largest and wealthiest and proudest nation may well go half-way to meet that of its poets. The signs are effectual. There is no fear of mistake. If the one is true the other is true. The proof of a poet is that his country absorbs him as affectionately as he has absorbed it.

Leaves of Grass.

⇒◇⇐

[Song of Myself]

I CELEBRATE myself,
And what I assume you shall assume,
For every atom belonging to me as good belongs to you.

I loafe and invite my soul,
I lean and loafe at my ease....observing a spear of summer grass.

Houses and rooms are full of perfumes....the shelves are crowded with perfumes,
I breathe the fragrance myself, and know it and like it,
The distillation would intoxicate me also, but I shall not let it.

The atmosphere is not a perfume....it has no taste of the distillation....it is
   odorless,
It is for my mouth forever....I am in love with it,
I will go to the bank by the wood and become undisguised and naked,
I am mad for it to be in contact with me.

The smoke of my own breath,
Echos, ripples, and buzzed whispers....loveroot, silkthread, crotch and vine,
My respiration and inspiration....the beating of my heart....the passing of blood
   and air through my lungs,
The sniff of green leaves and dry leaves, and of the shore and darkcolored sea-
   rocks, and of hay in the barn,
The sound of the belched words of my voice....words loosed to the eddies of
   the wind,
A few light kisses....a few embraces....a reaching around of arms,
The play of shine and shade on the trees as the supple boughs wag,
The delight alone or in the rush of the streets, or along the fields and hillsides,
The feeling of health....the full-noon trill....the song of me rising from bed
   and meeting the sun.

Have you reckoned a thousand acres much? Have you reckoned the earth much?
Have you practiced so long to learn to read?
Have you felt so proud to get at the meaning of poems?

Stop this day and night with me and you shall possess the origin of all poems,
You shall possess the good of the earth and sun....there are millions of suns left,
You shall no longer take things at second or third hand....nor look through the
　　eyes of the dead....nor feed on the spectres in books,
You shall not look through my eyes either, nor take things from me,
You shall listen to all sides and filter them from yourself.

I have heard what the talkers were talking....the talk of the beginning and the end,
But I do not talk of the beginning or the end.

There was never any more inception than there is now,
Nor any more youth or age than there is now;
And will never be any more perfection than there is now,
Nor any more heaven or hell than there is now.

Urge and urge and urge,
Always the procreant urge of the world.

Out of the dimness opposite equals advance....Always substance and increase,
Always a knit of identity....always distinction....always a breed of life.

To elaborate is no avail....Learned and unlearned feel that it is so.

Sure as the most certain sure....plumb in the uprights, well entretied, braced in
　　the beams,
Stout as a horse, affectionate, haughty, electrical,
I and this mystery here we stand.

Clear and sweet is my soul....and clear and sweet is all that is not my soul.

Lack one lacks both....and the unseen is proved by the seen,
Till that becomes unseen and receives proof in its turn.

Showing the best and dividing it from the worst, age vexes age,
Knowing the perfect fitness and equanimity of things, while they discuss I am silent,
　　and go bathe and admire myself.

Welcome is every organ and attribute of me, and of any man hearty and clean,
Not an inch nor a particle of an inch is vile, and none shall be less familiar
　　than the rest.

I am satisfied....I see, dance, laugh, sing;

As God comes a loving bedfellow and sleeps at my side all night and close on the
    peep of the day,
And leaves for me baskets covered with white towels bulging the house with their
    plenty,
Shall I postpone my acceptation and realization and scream at my eyes,
That they turn from gazing after and down the road,
And forthwith cipher and show me to a cent,
Exactly the contents of one, and exactly the contents of two, and which is ahead?

Trippers and askers surround me,
People I meet.....the effect upon me of my early life....of the ward and city I
    live in....of the nation,
The latest news....discoveries, inventions, societies....authors old and new,
My dinner, dress, associates, looks, business, compliments, dues,
The real or fancied indifference of some man or woman I love,
The sickness of one of my folks — or of myself....or ill-doing....or loss or lack
    of money...: or depressions or exaltations,
They come to me days and nights and go from me again,
But they are not the Me myself.

Apart from the pulling and hauling stands what I am,
Stands amused, complacent, compassionating, idle, unitary,
Looks down, is erect, bends an arm on an impalpable certain rest,
Looks with its sidecurved head curious what will come next,
Both in and out of the game, and watching and wondering at it.

Backward I see in my own days where I sweated through fog with linguists and
    contenders,
I have no mockings or arguments....I witness and wait.

I believe in you my soul....the other I am must not abase itself to you,
And you must not be abased to the other.

Loafe with me on the grass....loose the stop from your throat,
Not words, not music or rhyme I want....not custom or lecture, not even the best,
Only the lull I like, the hum of your valved voice.

I mind how we lay in June, such a transparent summer morning;
You settled your head athwart my hips and gently turned over upon me.
And parted the shirt from my bosom-bone, and plunged your tongue to my barestript
    heart,
And reached till you felt my beard, and reached till you held my feet.

Swiftly arose and spread around me the peace and joy and knowledge that pass all
    the art and argument of the earth;
And I know that the hand of God is the elderhand of my own,

And I know that the spirit of God is the eldest brother of my own,
And that all the men ever born are also my brothers....and the women my sisters
    and lovers,
And that a kelson of the creation is love;
And limitless are leaves stiff or drooping in the fields,
And brown ants in the little wells beneath them,
And mossy scabs of the wormfence, and heaped stones, and elder and mullen and
    pokeweed.

A child said, What is the grass? fetching it to me with full hands;
How could I answer the child?....I do not know what it is any more than he.

I guess it must be the flag of my disposition, out of hopeful green stuff woven.

Or I guess it is the handkerchief of the Lord,
A scented gift and remembrancer designedly dropped,
Bearing the owner's name someway in the corners, that we may see and remark,
    and say Whose?

Or I guess the grass is itself a child....the produced babe of the vegetation.

Or I guess it is a uniform hieroglyphic,
And it means, Sprouting alike in broad zones and narrow zones,
Growing among black folks as among white,
Kanuck, Tuckahoe, Congressman, Cuff, I give them the same, I receive them the
    same.

And now it seems to me the beautiful uncut hair of graves.

Tenderly will I use you curling grass,
It may be you transpire from the breasts of young men,
It may be if I had known them I would have loved them;
It may be you are from old people and from women, and from offspring taken soon
    out of their mothers' laps,
And here you are the mothers' laps.

This grass is very dark to be from the white heads of old mothers,
Darker than the colorless beards of old men,
Dark to come from under the faint red roofs of mouths.

O I perceive after all so many uttering tongues!
And I perceive they do not come from the roofs of mouths for nothing.

I wish I could translate the hints about the dead young men and women,
And the hints about old men and mothers, and the offspring taken soon out of their
    laps.

What do you think has become of the young and old men?
And what do you think has become of the women and children?

They are alive and well somewhere;
The smallest sprout shows there is really no death,
And if ever there was it led forward life, and does not wait at the end to arrest it,
And ceased the moment life appeared.

All goes onward and outward....and nothing collapses,
And to die is different from what any one supposed, and luckier.

Has any one supposed it lucky to be born?
I hasten to inform him or her it is just as lucky to die, and I know it.

I pass death with the dying, and birth with the new-washed babe....and am not
    contained between my hat and boots,
And peruse manifold objects, no two alike, and every one good,
The earth good, and the stars good, and their adjuncts all good.

I am not an earth nor an adjunct of an earth,
I am the mate and companion of people, all just as immortal and fathomless as
    myself;
They do not know how immortal, but I know.

Every kind for itself and its own....for me mine male and female,
For me all that have been boys and that love women,
For me the man that is proud and feels how it stings to be slighted,
For me the sweetheart and the old maid....for me mothers and the mothers of
    mothers,
For me lips that have smiled, eyes that have shed tears,
For me children and the begetters of children.

Who need be afraid of the merge?
Undrape....you are not guilty to me, nor stale nor discarded,
I see through the broadcloth and gingham whether or no,
And am around, tenacious, acquisitive, tireless....and can never be shaken away.

The little one sleeps in its cradle,
I lift the gauze and look a long time, and silently brush away flies with my hand.

The youngster and the redfaced girl turn aside up the bushy hill,
I peeringly view them from the top.

The suicide sprawls on the bloody floor of the bedroom,
It is so....I witnessed the corpse....there the pistol had fallen.

The blab of the pave....the tires of carts and sluff of bootsoles and talk of the
    promenaders,
The heavy omnibus, the driver with his interrogating thumb, the clank of the shod
    horses on the granite floor,
The carnival of sleighs, the clinking and shouted jokes and pelts of snowballs;
The hurrahs for popular favorites....the fury of roused mobs,
The flap of the curtained litter — the sick man inside, borne to the hospital,
The meeting of enemies, the sudden oath, the blows and fall,
The excited crowd — the policeman with his star quickly working his passage to the
    centre of the crowd;
The impassive stones that receive and return so many echoes,
The souls moving along....are they invisible while the least atom of the stones is
    visible?
What groans of overfed or half-starved who fall on the flags sunstruck or in fits,
What exclamations of women taken suddenly, who hurry home and give birth to
    babes,
What living and buried speech is always vibrating here....what howls restrained
    by decorum,
Arrests of criminals, slights, adulterous offers made, acceptances, rejections with
    convex lips,
I mind them or the resonance of them....I come again and again.

The big doors of the country-barn stand open and ready,
The dried grass of the harvest-time loads the slow-drawn wagon,
The clear light plays on the brown gray and green intertinged,
The armfuls are packed to the sagging mow:
I am there....I help....I came stretched atop of the load,
I felt its soft jolts....one leg reclined on the other,
I jump from the crossbeams, and seize the clover and timothy,
And roll head over heels, and tangle my hair full of wisps.

Alone far in the wilds and mountains I hunt,
Wandering amazed at my own lightness and glee,
In the late afternoon choosing a safe spot to pass the night,
Kindling a fire and broiling the freshkilled game,
Soundly falling asleep on the gathered leaves, my dog and gun by my side.

The Yankee clipper is under her three skysails....she cuts the sparkle and scud,
My eyes settle the land....I bend at her prow or shout joyously from the deck.

The boatmen and clamdiggers arose early and stopped for me,
I tucked my trowser-ends in my boots and went and had a good time,
You should have been with us that day round the chowder-kettle.

I saw the marriage of the trapper in the open air in the far-west....the bride was
    a red girl,

Her father and his friends sat near by crosslegged and dumbly smoking....they
 had moccasins to their feet and large thick blankets hanging from their
 shoulders;
On a bank lounged the trapper....he was dressed mostly in skins....his luxuriant
 beard and curls protected his neck,
One hand rested on his rifle....the other hand held firmly the wrist of the red girl.
She had long eyelashes....her head was bare....her coarse straight locks
 descended upon her voluptuous limbs and reached to her feet.

The runaway slave came to my house and stopped outside,
I heard his motions crackling the twigs of the woodpile,
Through the swung half-door of the kitchen I saw him limpsey and weak,
And went where he sat on a log, and led him in and assured him,
And brought water and filled a tub for his sweated body and bruised feet,
And gave him a room that entered from my own, and gave him some coarse clean
 clothes,
And remember perfectly well his revolving eyes and his awkwardness,
And remember putting plasters on the galls of his neck and ankles;
He staid with me a week before he was recuperated and passed north,
I had him sit next me at table....my firelock leaned in the corner.

Twenty-eight young men bathe by the shore,
Twenty-eight young men, and all so friendly,
Twenty-eight years of womanly life, and all so lonesome.

She owns the fine house by the rise of the bank,
She hides handsome and richly drest aft the blinds of the window.

Which of the young men does she like the best?
Ah the homeliest of them is beautiful to her.

Where are you off to, lady? for I see you,
You splash in the water there, yet stay stock still in your room.

Dancing and laughing along the beach came the twenty-ninth bather,
The rest did not see her, but she saw them and loved them.

The beards of the young men glistened with wet, it ran from their long hair,
Little streams passed all over their bodies.

An unseen hand also passed over their bodies,
It descended tremblingly from their temples and ribs.

The young men float on their backs, their white bellies swell to the sun....they do
 not ask who seizes fast to them,

They do not know who puffs and declines with pendant and bending arch,
They do not think whom they souse with spray.

The butcher-boy puts off his killing-clothes, or sharpens his knife at the stall in the
     market,
I loiter enjoying his repartee and his shuffle and breakdown.
Blacksmiths with grimed and hairy chests environ the anvil,
Each has his main-sledge....they are all out....there is a great heat in the fire.

From the cinder-strewed threshold I follow their movements,
The lithe sheer of their waists plays even with their massive arms,
Overhand the hammers roll — overhand so slow — overhand so sure,
They do not hasten, each man hits in his place.

The negro holds firmly the reins of his four horses....the block swags underneath
     on its tied-over chain,
The negro that drives the huge dray of the stoneyard....steady and tall he stands
     poised on one leg on the stringpiece,
His blue shirt exposes his ample neck and breast and loosens over his hipband,
His glance is calm and commanding....he tosses the slouch of his hat away from
     his forehead,
The sun falls on his crispy hair and moustache....falls on the black of his polish'd
     and perfect limbs.

I behold the picturesque giant and love him....and I do not stop there,
I go with the team also.

In me the caresser of life wherever moving....backward as well as forward slue-
     ing,
To niches aside and junior bending.

Oxen that rattle the yoke or halt in the shade, what is that you express in your eyes?
It seems to me more than all the print I have read in my life.

My tread scares the wood-drake and wood-duck on my distant and daylong ramble,
They rise together, they slowly circle around.
....I believe in those winged purposes,
And acknowledge the red yellow and white playing within me,
And consider the green and violet and the tufted crown intentional;
And do not call the tortoise unworthy because she is not something else,
And the mockingbird in the swamp never studied the gamut, yet trills pretty well to
     me,
And the look of the bay mare shames silliness out of me.

The wild gander leads his flock through the cool night,

Ya-honk! he says, and sounds it down to me like an invitation;
The pert may suppose it meaningless, but I listen closer,
I find its purpose and place up there toward the November sky.

The sharphoofed moose of the north, the cat on the housesill, the chickadee, the
    prairie-dog,
The litter of the grunting sow as they tug at her teats,
The brood of the turkeyhen, and she with her halfspread wings,
I see in them and myself the same old law.

The press of my foot to the earth springs a hundred affections,
They scorn the best I can do to relate them.

I am enamoured of growing outdoors,
Of men that live among cattle or taste of the ocean or woods,
Of the builders and steerers of ships, of the wielders of axes and mauls, of the drivers
    of horses,
I can eat and sleep with them week in and week out.

What is commonest and cheapest and nearest and easiest is Me,
Me going in for my chances, spending for vast returns,
Adorning myself to bestow myself on the first that will take me,
Not asking the sky to come down to my goodwill,
Scattering it freely forever.

The pure contralto sings in the organloft,
The carpenter dresses his plank....the tongue of his foreplane whistles its wild
    ascending lisp,
The married and unmarried children ride home to their thanksgiving dinner,
The pilot seizes the king-pin, he heaves down with a strong arm,
The mate stands braced in the whaleboat, lance and harpoon are ready,
The duck-shooter walks by silent and cautious stretches,
The deacons are ordained with crossed hands at the altar,
The spinning-girl retreats and advances to the hum of the big wheel,
The farmer stops by the bars of a Sunday and looks at the oats and rye,
The lunatic is carried at last to the asylum a confirmed case,
He will never sleep any more as he did in the cot in his mother's bedroom;
The jour printer with gray head and gaunt jaws works at his case,
He turns his quid of tobacco, his eyes get blurred with the manuscript;
The malformed limbs are tied to the anatomist's table,
What is removed drops horribly in a pail;
The quadroon girl is sold at the stand....the drunkard nods by the barroom stove,
The machinist rolls up his sleeves....the policeman travels his beat....the gate-
    keeper marks who pass,

The young fellow drives the express-wagon....I love him though I do not know
    him;
The half-breed straps on his light boots to compete in the race,
The western turkey-shooting draws old and young....some lean on their rifles,
    some sit on logs,
Out from the crowd steps the marksman and takes his position and levels his piece;
The groups of newly-come immigrants cover the wharf or levee,
The woollypates hoe in the sugarfield, the overseer views them from his saddle;
The bugle calls in the ballroom, the gentlemen run for their partners, the dancers
    bow to each other;
The youth lies awake in the cedar-roofed garret and harks to the musical rain,
The Wolverine sets traps on the creek that helps fill the Huron,
The reformer ascends the platform, he spouts with his mouth and nose,
The company returns from its excursion, the darkey brings up the rear and bears the
    well-riddled target,
The squaw wrapt in her yellow-hemmed cloth is offering moccasins and beadbags for
    sale,
The connoisseur peers along the exhibition-gallery with halfshut eyes bent sideways,
The deckhands make fast the steamboat, the plank is thrown for the shoregoing
    passengers,
The young sister holds out the skein, the elder sister winds it off in a ball and stops
    now and then for the knots,
The one-year wife is recovering and happy, a week ago she bore her first child,
The cleanhaired Yankee girl works with her sewing-machine or in the factory or
    mill,
The nine months' gone is in the parturition chamber, her faintness and pains are ad-
    vancing;
The pavingman leans on his twohanded rammer — the reporter's lead flies swiftly
    over the notebook — the signpainter is lettering with red and gold,
The canal-boy trots on the towpath — the bookkeeper counts at his desk — the
    shoemaker waxes his thread,
The conductor beats time for the band and all the performers follow him,
The child is baptised — the convert is making the first professions,
The regatta is spread on the bay....how the white sails sparkle!
The drover watches his drove, he sings out to them that would stray,
The pedlar sweats with his pack on his back — the purchaser higgles about the odd
    cent,
The camera and plate are prepared, the lady must sit for her daguerreotype,
The bride unrumples her white dress, the minutehand of the clock moves slowly,
The opium eater reclines with rigid head and just-opened lips,
The prostitute draggles her shawl, her bonnet bobs on her tipsy and pimpled neck,
The crowd laugh at her blackguard oaths, the men jeer and wink to each other,
(Miserable! I do not laugh at your oaths nor jeer you,)
The President holds a cabinet council, he is surrounded by the great secretaries,

On the piazza walk five friendly matrons with twined arms;
The crow of the fish-smack pack repeated layers of halibut in the hold,
The Missourian crosses the plains toting his wares and his cattle,
The fare-collector goes through the train — he gives notice by the jingling of loose change,
The floormen are laying the floor — the tinners are tinning the roof — the masons are calling for mortar,
In single file each shouldering his hod pass onward the laborers;
Seasons pursuing each other the indescribable crowd is gathered....it is the Fourth of July....what salutes of cannon and small arms!
Seasons pursuing each other the plougher ploughs and the mower mows and the wintergrain falls in the ground;
Off on the lakes the pikefisher watches and waits by the hole in the frozen surface,
The stumps stand thick round the clearing, the squatter strikes deep with his axe,
The flatboatmen make fast toward dusk near the cottonwood or pekantrees,
The coon-seekers go now through the regions of the Red river, or through those drained by the Tennessee, or through those of the Arkansas,
The torches shine in the dark that hangs on the Chattahoochee or Altamahaw;
Patriarchs sit at supper with sons and grandsons and great grandsons around them,
In walls of abode, in canvass tents, rest hunters and trappers after their day's sport.
The city sleeps and the country sleeps,
The living sleep for their time....the dead sleep for their time,
The old husband sleeps by his wife and the young husband sleeps by his wife;
And these one and all tend inward to me, and I tend outward to them,
And such as it is to be of these more or less I am.

I am of old and young, of the foolish as much as the wise,
Regardless of others, ever regardful of others,
Maternal as well as paternal, a child as well as a man,
Stuffed with the stuff that is coarse, and stuffed with the stuff that is fine,
One of the great nation, the nation of many nations — the smallest the same and the largest the same,
A southerner soon as a northerner, a planter nonchalant and hospitable,
A Yankee bound my own way....ready for trade....my joints the limberest joints on earth and the sternest joints on earth,
A Kentuckian walking the vale of the Elkhorn in my deerskin leggings,
A boatman over the lakes or bays or along coasts....a Hoosier, a Badger, a Buckeye,
A Louisianian or Georgian, a poke-easy from sandhills and pines,
At home on Canadian snowshoes or up in the bush, or with fishermen off Newfoundland,
At home in the fleet of iceboats, sailing with the rest and tacking,
At home on the hills of Vermont or in the woods of Maine or the Texan ranch,
Comrade of Californians....comrade of free northwesterners, loving their big proportions,

Comrade of raftsmen and coalmen — comrade of all who shake hands and welcome
    to drink and meat;
A learner with the simplest, a teacher of the thoughtfulest,
A novice beginning experient of myriads of seasons,
Of every hue and trade and rank, of every caste and religion,
Not merely of the New World but of Africa Europe of Asia....a wandering
    savage,
A farmer, mechanic, or artist....a gentleman, sailor, lover or quaker,
A prisoner, fancy-man, rowdy, lawyer, physician or priest.

I resist anything better than my own diversity,
And breathe the air and leave plenty after me,
And am not stuck up, and am in my place.

The moth and the fisheggs are in their place,
The suns I see and the suns I cannot see are in their place,
The palpable is in its place and the impalpable is in its place.

These are the thoughts of all men in all ages and lands, they are not original with
    me,
If they are not yours as much as mine they are nothing or next to nothing,
If they do not enclose everything they are next to nothing,
If they are not the riddle and the untying of the riddle they are nothing,
If they are not just as close as they are distant they are nothing.

This is the grass that grows wherever the land is and the water is,
This is the common air that bathes the globe.

This is the breath of laws and songs and behaviour,
This is the tasteless water of souls....this is the true sustenance,
It is for the illiterate....it is for the judges of the supreme court....it is for the
    federal capitol and the state capitols,
It is for the admirable communes of literary men and composers and singers and
    lecturers and engineers and savans,
It is for the endless races of working people and farmers and seamen.

This is the trill of a thousand clear cornets and scream of the octave flute and strike
    of triangles.

I play not a march for victors only....I play great marches for conquered and
    slain persons.

Have you heard that it was good to gain the day?
I also say it is good to fall....battles are lost in the same spirit in which they are
    won.

I sound triumphal drums for the dead....I fling through my embouchures the
    loudest and gayest music to them,
Vivas to those who have failed, and to those whose war-vessels sank in the sea,
    and those themselves who sank in the sea,
And to all generals that lost engagements, and all overcome heroes, and the number-
    less unknown heroes equal to the greatest heroes known.

This is the meal pleasantly set....this is the meat and drink for natural hunger,
It is for the wicked just the same as the righteous....I make appointments with all,
I will not have a single person slighted or left away,
The keptwoman and sponger and thief are hereby invited....the heavy-lipped slave
    is invited....the venerealee is invited,
There shall be no difference between them and the rest.

This is the press of a bashful hand....this is the float and odor of hair,
This is the touch of my lips to yours....this is the murmur of yearning,
This is the far-off depth and height reflecting my own face,
This is the thoughtful merge of myself and the outlet again.

Do you guess I have some intricate purpose?
Well I have....for the April rain has, and the mica on the side of a rock has.

Do you take it I would astonish?
Does the daylight astonish? or the early redstart twittering through the woods?
Do I astonish more than they?

This hour I tell things in confidence,
I might not tell everybody but I will tell you.

Who goes there! hankering, gross, mystical, nude?
How is it I extract strength from the beef I eat?

What is a man anyhow? What am I? and what are you?
All I mark as my own you shall offset it with your own,
Else it were time lost listening to me.

I do not snivel that snivel the world over,
That months are vacuums and the ground but wallow and filth,
That life is a suck and a sell, and nothing remains at the end but threadbare crape
    and tears.

Whimpering and truckling fold with powders for invalids....conformity goes to
    the fourth-removed,
I cock my hat as I please indoors or out.

Shall I pray? Shall I venerate and be ceremonious

I have pried through the strata and analyzed to a hair,
And counselled with doctors and calculated close and found no sweeter fat than
     sticks to my own bones.

In all people I see myself, none more and not one a barleycorn less,
And the good or bad I say of myself I say of them.

And I know I am solid and sound,
To me the converging objects of the universe perpetually flow,
All are written to me, and I must get what the writing means.

And I know I am deathless,
I know this orbit of mine cannot be swept by a carpenter's compass,
I know I shall not pass like a child's carlacue cut with a burnt stick at night.

I know I am august,
I do not trouble my spirit to vindicate itself or be understood,
I see that the elementary laws never apologize,
I reckon I behave no prouder than the level I plant my house by after all.

I exist as I am, that is enough,
If no other in the world be aware I sit content,
And if each and all be aware I sit content.

One world is aware, and by far the largest to me, and that is myself,
And whether I come to my own today or in ten thousand or ten million years,
I can cheerfully take it now, or with equal cheerfulness I can wait.

My foothold is tenoned and mortised in granite,
I laugh at what you call dissolution,
And I know the amplitude of time.

I am the poet of the body,
And I am the poet of the soul.

The pleasures of heaven are with me, and the pains of hell are with me,
The first I graft and increase upon myself....the latter I translate into a new
     tongue.

I am the poet of the woman the same as the man,
And I say it is as great to be a woman as to be a man,
And I say there is nothing greater than the mother of men.

I chant a new chant of dilation or pride,
We have had ducking and deprecating about enough,
I show that size is only developement.

Have you outstript the rest? Are you the President?
It is a trifle....they will more than arrive there every one, and still pass on.

I am he that walks with the tender and growing night;
I call to the earth and sea half-held by the night.

Press close barebosomed night! Press close magnetic nourishing night!
Night of south winds! Night of the large few stars!
Still nodding night! Mad naked summer night!

Smile O voluptuous coolbreathed earth!
Earth of the slumbering and liquid trees!
Earth of departed sunset! Earth of the mountains misty-topt!
Earth of the vitreous pour of the full moon just tinged with blue!
Earth of shine and dark mottling the tide of the river!
Earth of the limpid gray of clouds brighter and clearer for my sake!
Far-swooping elbowed earth! Rich apple-blossomed earth!
Smile, for your lover comes!

Prodigal! you have given me love!....therefore I to you give love!
O unspeakable passionate love!

Thruster holding me tight and that I hold tight!
We hurt each other as the bridegroom and the bride hurt each other.

You sea! I resign myself to you also....I guess what you mean,
I behold from the beach your crooked inviting fingers,
I believe you refuse to go back without feeling of me;
We must have a turn together....I undress....hurry me out of sight of the land,
Cushion me soft....rock me in billowy drowse,
Dash me with amorous wet....I can repay you.

Sea of stretched ground-swells!
Sea breathing broad and convulsive breaths!
Sea of the brine of life! Sea of unshovelled and always-ready graves!
Howler and scooper of storms! Capricious and dainty sea!
I am integral with you....I too am of one phase and of all phases.

Partaker of influx and efflux....extoler of hate and conciliation,
Extoler of amies and those that sleep in each others' arms.

I am he attesting sympathy;
Shall I make my list of things in the house and skip the house that supports them?

I am the poet of commonsense and of the demonstrable and of immortality;
And am not the poet of goodness only....I do not decline to be the poet of wick-
edness also.

Washes and razors for foofoos....for me freckles and a bristling beard.

What blurt is it about virtue and about vice?
Evil propels me, and reform of evil propels me....I stand indifferent,
My gait is no faultfinder's or rejecter's gait,
I moisten the roots of all that has grown.

Did you fear some scrofula out of the unflagging pregnancy?
Did you guess the celestial laws are yet to be worked over and rectified?

I step up to say that what we do is right and what we affirm is right....and some
    is only the ore of right,
Witnesses of us....one side a balance and the antipodal side a balance,
Soft doctrine as steady help as stable doctrine,
Thoughts and deeds of the present our rouse and early start.

This minute that comes to me over the past decillions,
There is no better than it and now.

What behaved well in the past or behaves well today is not such a wonder,
The wonder is always and always how there can be a mean man or an infidel.

Endless unfolding of words of ages!
And mine a word of the modern....a word en masse.

A word of the faith that never balks,
One time as good as another time....here or henceforward it is all the same to
    me.

A word of reality....materialism first and last imbueing.

Hurrah for positive science! Long live exact demonstration!
Fetch stonecrop and mix it with cedar and branches of lilac;
This is the lexicographer or chemist....this made a grammar of the old
    cartouches,
These mariners put the ship through dangerous unknown seas,
This is the geologist, and this works with the scalpel, and this is a mathematician.

Gentlemen I receive you, and attach and clasp hands with you,
The facts are useful and real....they are not my dwelling....I enter by them to
    an area of the dwelling.

I am less the reminder of property or qualities, and more the reminder of life,
And go on the square for my own sake and for others' sakes,

And make short account of neuters and geldings, and favor men and women fully
    equipped,
And beat the gong of revolt, and stop with fugitives and them that plot and conspire.

Walt Whitman, an American, one of the roughs, a kosmos,
Disorderly fleshy and sensual....eating drinking and breeding,
No sentimentalist....no stander above men and women or apart from them....no
    more modest than immodest.

Unscrew the locks from the doors!
Unscrew the doors themselves from their jambs!

Whoever degrades another degrades me....and whatever is done or said returns
    at last to me,
And whatever I do or say I also return.

Through me the afflatus surging and surging....through me the current and index.

I speak the password primeval....I give the sign of democracy;
By God! I will accept nothing which all cannot have their counterpart of on the
    same terms.

Through me many long dumb voices,
Voices of the interminable generations of slaves,
Voices of prostitutes and of deformed persons,
Voices of the diseased and despairing, and of thieves and dwarfs,
Voices of cycles of preparation and accretion,
And of the threads that connect the stars — and of wombs, and of the fatherstuff,
And of the rights of them the others are down upon,
Of the trivial and flat and foolish and despised,
Of fog in the air and beetles rolling balls of dung.

Through me forbidden voices,
Voices of sexes and lusts....voices veiled, and I remove the veil,
Voices indecent by me clarified and transfigured.

I do not press my finger across my mouth,
I keep as delicate around the bowels as around the head and heart,
Copulation is no more rank to me than death is.

I believe in the flesh and the appetites,
Seeing hearing and feeling are miracles, and each part and tag of me is a miracle.

Divine am I inside and out, and I make holy whatever I touch or am touched from;
The scent of these arm-pits is aroma finer than prayer,
This head is more than churches or bibles or creeds.

If I worship any particular thing it shall be some of the spread of my body;
Translucent mould of me it shall be you,
Shaded ledges and rests, firm masculine coulter, it shall be you,
Whatever goes to the tilth of me it shall be you,
You my rich blood, your milky stream pale strippings of my life;
Breast that presses against other breasts it shall be you,
My brain it shall be your occult convolutions,
Root of washed sweet-flag, timorous pond-snipe, nest of guarded duplicate eggs, it
    shall be you,
Mixed tussled hay of head and beard and brawn it shall be you,
Trickling sap of maple, fibre of manly wheat, it shall be you;
Sun so generous it shall be you,
Vapors lighting and shading my face it shall be you,
You sweaty brooks and dews it shall be you,
Winds whose soft-tickling genitals rub against me it shall be you,
Broad muscular fields, branches of liveoak, loving lounger in my winding paths, it
    shall be you,
Hands I have taken, face I have kissed, mortal I have ever touched, it shall be you.

I dote on myself....there is that lot of me, and all so luscious,
Each moment and whatever happens thrills me with joy.

I cannot tell how my ankles bend....nor whence the cause of my faintest wish,
Nor the cause of the friendship I emit....nor the cause of the friendship I take
    again.

To walk up my stoop is unaccountable....I pause to consider if it really be,
That I eat and drink is spectacle enough for the great authors and schools,
A morning-glory at my window satisfies me more than the metaphysics of books.

To behold the daybreak!
The little light fades the immense and diaphanous shadows,
The air tastes good to my palate.

Hefts of the moving world at innocent gambols, silently rising, freshly exuding,
Scooting obliquely high and low.

Something I cannot see puts upward libidinous prongs,
Seas of bright juice suffuse heaven.

The earth by the sky staid with....the daily close of their junction,
The heaved challenge from the east that moment over my head,
The mocking taunt, See then whether you shall be master!

Dazzling and tremendous how quick the sunrise would kill me,
If I could not now and always send sunrise out of me.

We also ascend dazzling and tremendous as the sun,
We found our own my soul in the calm and cool of the daybreak.

My voice goes after what my eyes cannot reach,
With the twirl of my tongue I encompass worlds and volumes of worlds.

Speech is the twin of my vision....it is unequal to measure itself.

It provokes me forever,
It says sarcastically, Walt, you understand enough....why don't you let it out
    then?

Come now I will not be tantalized....you conceive too much of articulation.

Do you not know how the buds beneath are folded?
Waiting in gloom protected by frost,
The dirt receding before my prophetical screams,
I underlying causes to balance them at last,
My knowledge my live parts....it keeping tally with the meaning of things,
Happiness....which whoever hears me let him or her set out in search of this
    day.

My final merit I refuse you....I refuse putting from me the best I am.

Encompass worlds but never try to encompass me,
I crowd your noisiest talk by looking toward you.

Writing and talk do not prove me,
I carry the plenum of proof and every thing else in my face,
With the hush of my lips I confound the topmost skeptic.

I think I will do nothing for a long time but listen,
And accrue what I hear into myself....and let sounds contribute toward me.

I hear the bravuras of birds....the bustle of growing wheat....gossip of flames
    ....clack of sticks cooking my meals.

I hear the sound of the human voice....a sound I love,
I hear all sounds as they are tuned to their uses....sounds of the city and sounds
    out of the city....sounds of the day and night;
Talkative young ones to those that like them....the recitative of fish-pedlars and
    fruit-pedlars....the loud laugh of workpeople at their meals,
The angry base of disjointed friendship....the faint tones of the sick,
The judge with hands tight to the desk, his shaky lips pronouncing a death sentence,
The heave'e'yo of stevedores unlading ships by the wharves....the refrain of the
    anchor-lifters;

The ring of alarm-bells....the cry of fire....the whirr of swift-streaking engines
    and hose-carts with premonitory tinkles and colored lights,
The steam-whistle....the solid roll of the train of approaching cars;
The slow-march played at night at the head of the association,
They go to guard some corpse....the flag-tops are draped with black muslin.

I hear the violincello or man's heart's complaint,
And hear the keyed cornet or else the echo of sunset.

I hear the chorus....it is a grand-opera....this indeed is music!

A tenor large and fresh as the creation fills me,
The orbic flex of his mouth is pouring and filling me full.

I hear the trained soprano....she convulses me like the climax of my love-grip;
The orchestra whirls me wider than Uranus flies,
It wrenches unnamable ardors from my breast,
It throbs me to gulps of the farthest down horror,
It sails me....I dab with bare feet....they are licked by the indolent waves,
I am exposed....cut by bitter and poisoned hail,
Steeped amid honeyed morphine....my windpipe squeezed in the fakes of death,
Let up again to feel the puzzle of puzzles,
And that we call Being.

To be in any form, what is that?
If nothing lay more developed the quahaug and its callous shell were enough.

Mine is no callous shell,
I have instant conductors all over me whether I pass or stop,
They seize every object and lead it harmlessly through me.

I merely stir, press, feel with my fingers, and am happy,
To touch my person to some one else's is about as much as I can stand.

Is this then a touch?....quivering me to a new identity,
Flames and ether making a rush for my veins,
Treacherous tip of me reaching and crowding to help them,
My flesh and blood playing out lightning, to strike what is hardly different from
    myself,
On all sides prurient provokers stiffening my limbs,
Straining the udder of my heart for its withheld drip,
Behaving licentious toward me, taking no denial,
Depriving me of my best as for a purpose,
Unbuttoning my clothes and holding me by the bare waist,
Deluding my confusion with the calm of the sunlight and pasture fields,

Immodestly sliding the fellow-senses away,
They bribed to swap off with touch, and go and graze at the edges of me,
No consideration, no regard for my draining strength or my anger,
Fetching the rest of the herd around to enjoy them awhile,
Then all uniting to stand on a headland and worry me.

The sentries desert every other part of me,
They have left me helpless to a red marauder,
They all come to the headland to witness and assist against me.

I am given up by traitors;
I talk wildly....I have lost my wits....I and nobody else am the greatest
    traitor,
I went myself first to the headland....my own hands carried me there.

You villain touch! what are you doing?....my breath is tight in its throat;
Unclench your floodgates! you are too much for me.

Blind loving wrestling touch! Sheathed hooded sharptoothed touch!
Did it make you ache so leaving me?

Parting tracked by arriving....perpetual payment of the perpetual loan,
Rich showering rain, and recompense richer afterward.

Sprouts take and accumulate....stand by the curb prolific and vital,
Landscapes projected masculine full-sized and golden.

All truths wait in all things,
They neither hasten their own delivery nor resist it,
They do not need the obstetric forceps of the surgeon,
The insignificant is as big to me as any,
What is less or more than a touch?

Logic and sermons never convince,
The damp of the night drives deeper into my soul.

Only what proves itself to every man and woman is so,
Only what nobody denies is so.

A minute and a drop of me settle my brain;
I believe the soggy clods shall become lovers and lamps,
And a compend of compends is the meat of a man or woman,
And a summit and flower there is the feeling they have for each other,
And they are to branch boundlessly out of that lesson until it becomes omnific,
And until every one shall delight us, and we them.

I believe a leaf of grass is no less than the journeywork of the stars,
And the pismire is equally perfect, and a grain of sand, and the egg of the wren,
And the tree-toad is a chef-d'ouvre for the highest,
And the running blackberry would adorn the parlors of heaven,
And the narrowest hinge in my hand puts to scorn all machinery,
And the cow crunching with depressed head surpasses any statue,
And a mouse is miracle enough to stagger sextillions of infidels,
And I could come every afternoon of my life to look at the farmer's girl boiling her
    iron tea-kettle and baking shortcake.

I find I incorporate gneiss and coal and long-threaded moss and fruits and grains and
    esculent roots,
And am stucco'd with quadrupeds and birds all over,
And have distanced what is behind me for good reasons,
And call any thing close again when I desire it.

In vain the speeding or shyness,
In vain the plutonic rocks send their old heat against my approach,
In vain the mastadon retreats beneath its own powdered bones,
In vain objects stand leagues off and assume manifold shapes,
In vain the ocean settling in hollows and the great monsters lying low,
In vain the buzzard houses herself with the sky,
In vain the snake slides through the creepers and logs,
In vain the elk takes to the inner passes of the woods,
In vain the razorbilled auk sails far north to Labrador,
I follow quickly....I ascend to the nest in the fissure of the cliff.

I think I could turn and live awhile with the animals....they are so placid and self-
    contained,
I stand and look at them sometimes half the day long.

They do not sweat and whine about their condition,
They do not lie awake in the dark and weep for their sins,
They do not make me sick discussing their duty to God,
Not one is dissatisfied....not one is demented with the mania of owning things,
Not one kneels to another nor to his kind that lived thousands of years ago,
Not one is respectable or industrious over the whole earth.

So they show their relations to me and I accept them;
They bring me tokens of myself....they evince them plainly in their possession.

I do not know where they got those tokens,
I must have passed that way untold times ago and negligently dropt them,
Myself moving forward then and now and forever,
Gathering and showing more always and with velocity,

Infinite and omnigenous and the like of these among them;
Not too exclusive toward the reachers of my remembrancers,
Picking out here one that shall be my amie,
Choosing to go with him on brotherly terms.

A gigantic beauty of a stallion, fresh and responsive to my caresses,
Head high in the forehead and wide between the ears,
Limbs glossy and supple, tail dusting the ground,
Eyes well apart and full of sparkling wickedness....ears finely cut and flexibly
    moving.

His nostrils dilate....my heels embrace him....his well built limbs tremble with
    pleasure....we speed around and return.

I but use you a moment and then I resign you stallion....and do not need your
    paces, and outgallop them,
And myself as I stand or sit pass faster than you.

Swift wind! Space! My Soul! Now I know it is true what I guessed at;
What I guessed when I loafed on the grass,
What I guessed while I lay alone in my bed....and again as I walked the beach
    under the paling stars of the morning.

My ties and ballasts leave me....I travel....I sail....my elbows rest in the
    sea-gaps,
I skirt the sierras....my palms cover continents,
I am afoot with my vision.

By the city's quadrangular houses....in log-huts, or camping with lumbermen,
Along the ruts of the turnpike....along the dry gulch and rivulet bed,
Hoeing my onion-patch, and rows of carrots and parsnips....crossing savannas...
    trailing in forests,
Prospecting....gold-digging....girdling the trees of a new purchase,
Scorched ankle-deep by the hot sand....hauling my boat down the shallow river;
Where the panther walks to and fro on a limb overhead....where the buck turns
    furiously at the hunter,
Where the rattlesnake suns his flabby length on a rock....where the otter is
    feeding on fish,
Where the alligator in his tough pimples sleeps by the bayou,
Where the black bear is searching for roots or honey....where the beaver pats
    the mud with his paddle-tail;
Over the growing sugar....over the cottonplant....over the rice in its low
    moist field;
Over the sharp-peaked farmhouse with its scalloped scum and slender shoots from
    the gutters;

Over the western persimmon....over the longleaved corn and the delicate blue-
  flowered flax;
Over the white and brown buckwheat, a hummer and a buzzer there with the rest,
Over the dusky green of the rye as it ripples and shades in the breeze;
Scaling mountains....pulling myself cautiously up....holding on by low scrag-
  ged limbs,
Walking the path worn in the grass and beat through the leaves of the brush;
Where the quail is whistling betwixt the woods and the wheatlot,
Where the bat flies in the July eve....where the great goldbug drops through the
  dark;
Where the flails keep time on the barn floor,
Where the brook puts out of the roots of the old tree and flows to the meadow,
Where cattle stand and shake away flies with the tremulous shuddering of their
  hides,
Where the cheese-cloth hangs in the kitchen, and andirons straddle the hearth-slab,
  and cobwebs fall in festoons from the rafters;
Where triphammers crash....where the press is whirling its cylinders;
Wherever the human heart beats with terrible throes out of its ribs;
Where the pear-shaped balloon is floating aloft....floating in it myself and look-
  ing composedly down;
Where the life-car is drawn on the slipnoose....where the heat hatches pale-
  green eggs in the dented sand,
Where the she-whale swims with her calves and never forsakes them,
Where the steamship trails hindways its long pennant of smoke,
Where the ground-shark's fin cuts like a black chip out of the water,
Where the half-burned brig is riding on unknown currents,
Where shells grow to her slimy deck, and the dead are corrupting below;
Where the striped and starred flag is borne at the head of the regiments;
Approaching Manhattan, up by the long-stretching island,
Under Niagara, the cataract falling like a veil over my countenance;
Upon a door-step....upon the horse-block of hard wood outside,
Upon the race-course, or enjoying pic-nics or jigs or a good game of base-ball,
At he-festivals with blackguard jibes and ironical license and bull-dances and
  drinking and laughter,
At the cider-mill, tasting the sweet of the brown sqush....sucking the juice
  through a straw,
At apple-pealings, wanting kisses for all the red fruit I find,
At musters and beach-parties and friendly bees and huskings and house-raisings;
Where the mockingbird sounds his delicious gurgles, and cackles and screams and
  weeps,
Where the hay-rick stands in the barnyard, and the dry-stalks are scattered, and the
  brood cow waits in the hovel,
Where the bull advances to do his masculine work, and the stud to the mare, and the
  cock is treading the hen,
Where the heifers browse, and the geese nip their food with short jerks;

Where the sundown shadows lengthen over the limitless and lonesome prairie,
Where the herds of buffalo make a crawling spread of the square miles far and
near;
Where the hummingbird shimmers....where the neck of the longlived swan is
curving and winding;
Where the laughing-gull scoots by the slappy shore and laughs her near-human
laugh;
Where beehives range on a gray bench in the garden half-hid by the high weeds;
Where the band-necked partridges roost in a ring on the ground with their heads
out;
Where burial coaches enter the arched gates of a cemetery;
Where winter wolves bark amid wastes of snow and icicled trees;
Where the yellow-crowned heron comes to the edge of the marsh at night and feeds
upon small crabs;
Where the splash of swimmers and divers cools the warm noon;
Where the katydid works her chromatic reed on the walnut-tree over the well;
Through patches of citrons and cucumbers with silver-wired leaves,
Through the salt-lick or orange glade....or under conical furs;
Through the gymnasium....through the curtained saloon....through the office
or public hall;
Pleased with the native and pleased with the foreign....pleased with the new
and old,
Pleased with women, the homely as well as the handsome,
Pleased with the quakeress as she puts off her bonnet and talks melodiously,
Pleased with the primitive tunes of the choir of the whitewashed church,
Pleased with the earnest words of the sweating Methodist preacher, or any preacher
....looking seriously at the camp-meeting;
Looking in at the shop-windows in Broadway the whole forenoon....pressing the
flesh of my nose to the thick plate-glass,
Wandering the same afternoon with my face turned up to the clouds;
My right and left arms round the sides of two friends and I in the middle;
Coming home with the bearded and dark-cheeked bush-boy....riding behind him
at the drape of the day;
Far from the settlements studying the print of animals' feet, or the moccasin print;
By the cot in the hospital reaching lemonade to a feverish patient,
By the coffined corpse when all is still, examining with a candle;
Voyaging to every port to dicker and adventure;
Hurrying with the modern crowd, as eager and fickle as any,
Hot toward one I hate, ready in my madness to knife him;
Solitary at midnight in my back yard, my thoughts gone from me a long while,
Walking the old hills of Judea with the beautiful gentle god by my side;
Speeding through space....speeding through heaven and the stars,
Speeding amid the seven satellites and the broad ring and the diameter of eighty
thousand miles,

Speeding with tailed meteors....throwing fire-balls like the rest,
Carrying the crescent child that carries its own full mother in its belly:
Storming enjoying planning loving cautioning,
Backing and filling, appearing and disappearing,
I tread day and night such roads.

I visit the orchards of God and look at the spheric product,
And look at quintillions ripened, and look at quintillions green.

I fly the flight of the fluid and swallowing soul,
My course runs below the soundings of plummets.

I help myself to material and immaterial,
No guard can shut me off, no law can prevent me.

I anchor my ship for a little while only,
My messengers continually cruise away or bring their returns to me.

I go hunting polar furs and the seal....leaping chasms with a pike-pointed staff
    ....clinging to topples of brittle and blue.

I ascend to the foretruck....I take my place late at night in the crow's nest....
    we sail through the arctic sea....it is plenty light enough,
Through the clear atmosphere I stretch around on the wonderful beauty,
The enormous masses of ice pass me and I pass them....the scenery is plain in
    all directions,
The white-topped mountains point up in the distance....I fling out my fancies
    toward them;
We are about approaching some great battlefield in which we are soon to be
    engaged,
We pass the colossal outposts of the encampments....we pass with still feet and
    caution;
Or we are entering by the suburbs some vast and ruined city....the blocks and
    fallen architecture more than all the living cities of the globe.

I am a free companion....I bivouac by invading watchfires.

I turn the bridegroom out of bed and stay with the bride myself,
And tighten her all night to my thighs and lips.

My voice is the wife's voice, the screech by the rail of the stairs,
They fetch my man's body up dripping and drowned.

I understand the large hearts of heroes,
The courage of present times and all times;

How the skipper saw the crowded and rudderless wreck of the steamship, and death
    chasing it up and down the storm,
How he knuckled tight and gave not back one inch, and was faithful of days and
    faithful of nights,
And chalked in large letters on a board, Be of good cheer, We will not desert you;
How he saved the drifting company at last,
How the lank loose-gowned women looked when boated from the side of their
    prepared graves,
How the silent old-faced infants, and the lifted sick, and the sharp-lipped unshaved
    men;
All this I swallow and it tastes good....I like it well, and it becomes mine,
I am the man....I suffered....I was there.

The disdain and calmness of martyrs,
The mother condemned for a witch and burnt with dry wood, and her children
    gazing on;
The hounded slave that flags in the race and leans by the fence, blowing and
    covered with sweat,
The twinges that sting like needles his legs and neck,
The murderous buckshot and the bullets,
All these I feel or am.

I am the hounded slave....I wince at the bite of the dogs,
Hell and despair are upon me....crack and again crack the marksmen,
I clutch the rails of the fence....my gore dribs thinned with the ooze of my skin,
I fall on the weeds and stones,
The riders spur their unwilling horses and haul close,
They taunt my dizzy ears....they beat me violently over the head with their
    whip-stocks.

Agonies are one of my changes of garments;
I do not ask the wounded person how he feels....I myself become the wounded
    person,
My hurt turns livid upon me as I lean on a cane and observe.

I am the mashed fireman with breastbone broken....tumbling walls buried me in
    their debris,
Heat and smoke I inspired....I heard the yelling shouts of my comrades,
I heard the distant click of their picks and shovels;
They have cleared the beams away....they tenderly lift me forth.

I lie in the night air in my red shirt....the pervading hush is for my sake,
Painless after all I lie, exhausted but not so unhappy,
White and beautiful are the faces around me....the heads are bared of their fire-
    caps,
The kneeling crowd fades with the light of the torches.

Distant and dead resuscitate,
They show as the dial or move as the hands of me....and I am the clock myself.

I am an old artillerist, and tell of some fort's bombardment....and am there again.

Again the reveille of drummers....again the attacking cannon and mortars and
     howitzers,
Again the attacked send their cannon responsive.

I take part....I see and hear the whole,
The cries and curses and roar....the plaudits for well aimed shots,
The ambulanza slowly passing and trailing its red drip,
Workmen searching after damages and to make indispensible repairs,
The fall of grenades through the rent roof....the fan-shaped explosion,
The whizz of limbs heads stone wood and iron high in the air.

Again gurgles the mouth of my dying general....he furiously waves with his
     hand,
He gasps through the clot....Mind not me....mind....the entrenchments.

I tell not the fall of Alamo....not one escaped to tell the fall of Alamo,
The hundred and fifty are dumb yet at Alamo.

Hear now the tale of a jetblack sunrise,
Hear of the murder in cold blood of four hundred and twelve young men.

Retreating they had formed in a hollow square with their baggage for breastworks,
Nine hundred lives out of the surrounding enemy's nine times their number was the
     price they took in advance,
Their colonel was wounded and their ammunition gone,
They treated for an honorable capitulation, received writing and seal, gave up their
     arms, and marched back prisoners of war.

They were the glory of the race of rangers,
Matchless with a horse, a rifle, a song, a supper or a courtship,
Large, turbulent, brave, handsome, generous, proud and affectionate,
Bearded, sunburnt, dressed in the free costume of hunters,
Not a single one over thirty years of age.

The second Sunday morning they were brought out in squads and massacred....it
     was beautiful early summer,
The work commenced about five o'clock and was over by eight.

None obeyed the command to kneel,
Some made a mad and helpless rush....some stood stark and straight,
A few fell at once, shot in the temple or heart....the living and dead lay together,

The maimed and mangled dug in the dirt....the new-comers saw them there;
Some half-killed attempted to crawl away,
These were dispatched with bayonets or battered with the blunts of muskets;
A youth not seventeen years old seized his assassin till two more came to release
    him,
The three were all torn, and covered with the boy's blood.

At eleven o'clock began the burning of the bodies;
And that is the tale of the murder of the four hundred and twelve young men,
And that was a jetblack sunrise.

Did you read in the seabooks of the oldfashioned frigate-fight?
Did you learn who won by the light of the moon and stars?

Our foe was no skulk in his ship, I tell you,
His was the English pluck, and there is no tougher or truer, and never was, and
    never will be;
Along the lowered eve he came, horribly raking us.

We closed with him....the yards entangled....the cannon touched,
My captain lashed fast with his own hands.

We had received some eighteen-pound shots under the water,
On our lower-gun-deck two large pieces had burst at the first fire, killing all around
    and blowing up overhead.

Ten o'clock at night, and the full moon shining and the leaks on the gain, and five feet
    of water reported,
The master-at-arms loosing the prisoners confined in the after-hold to give them a
    chance for themselves.

The transit to and from the magazine was now stopped by the sentinels,
They saw so many strange faces they did not know whom to trust.

Our frigate was afire....the other asked if we demanded quarters? if our colors
    were struck and the fighting done?

I laughed content when I heard the voice of my little captain,
We have not struck, he composedly cried, We have just begun our part of the
    fighting.

Only three guns were in use,
One was directed by the captain himself against the enemy's mainmast,
Two well-served with grape and canister silenced his musketry and cleared his decks,

The tops alone seconded the fire of this little battery, especially the maintop,
They all held out bravely during the whole of the action.

Not a moment's cease,
The leaks gained fast on the pumps....the fire eat toward the powder-magazine,
One of the pumps was shot away....it was generally thought we were sinking.

Serene stood the little captain,
He was not hurried....his voice was neither high nor low,
His eyes gave more light to us than our battle-lanterns.

Toward twelve at night, there in the beams of the moon they surrendered to us.

Stretched and still lay the midnight,
Two great hulls motionless on the breast of the darkness,
Our vessel riddled and slowly sinking....preparations to pass to the one we had
    conquered,
The captain on the quarter deck coldly giving his orders through a countenance
    white as a sheet,
Near by the corpse of the child that served in the cabin,
The dead face of an old salt with long white hair and carefully curled whiskers,
The flames spite of all that could be done flickering aloft and below,
The husky voices of the two or three officers yet fit for duty,
Formless stacks of bodies and bodies by themselves....dabs of flesh upon the
    masts and spars,
The cut of cordage and dangle of rigging....the slight shock of the soothe of
    waves,
Black and impassive guns, and litter of powder-parcels, and the strong scent,
Delicate sniffs of the seabreeze....smells of sedgy grass and fields by the shore....
    death-messages given in charge to survivors,
The hiss of the surgeon's knife and the gnawing teeth of his saw,
The wheeze, the cluck, the swash of falling blood....the short wild scream, the
    long dull tapering groan,
These so....these irretrievable.

O Christ! My fit is mastering me!
What the rebel said gaily adjusting his throat to the rope-noose,
What the savage at the stump, his eye-sockets empty, his mouth spirting whoops
    and defiance,
What stills the traveler come to the vault at Mount Vernon,
What sobers the Brooklyn boy as he looks down the shores of the Wallabout and
    remembers the prison ships,
What burnt the gums of the redcoat at Saratoga when he surrendered his brigades,
These become mine and me every one, and they are but little,
I become as much more as I like.

I become any presence or truth of humanity here,
And see myself in prison shaped like another man,
And feel the dull unintermitted pain.

For me the keepers of convicts shoulder their carbines and keep watch,
It is I let out in the morning and barred at night.

Not a mutineer walks handcuffed to the jail, but I am handcuffed to him and walk
    by his side,
I am less the jolly one there, and more the silent one with sweat on my twitching
    lips.

Not a youngster is taken for larceny, but I go up too and am tried and sentenced.

Not a cholera patient lies at the last gasp, but I also lie at the last gasp,
My face is ash-colored, my sinews gnarl....away from me people retreat.

Askers embody themselves in me, and I am embodied in them,
I project my hat and sit shamefaced and beg.

I rise extatic through all, and sweep with the true gravitation,
The whirling and whirling is elemental within me.

Somehow I have been stunned. Stand back!
Give me a little time beyond my cuffed head and slumbers and dreams and gaping,
I discover myself on a verge of the usual mistake.

That I could forget the mockers and insults!
That I could forget the trickling tears and the blows of the bludgeons and hammers!
That I could look with a separate look on my own crucifixion and bloody crowning!

I remember....I resume the overstaid fraction,
The grave of rock multiplies what has been confided to it....or to any
    graves,
The corpses rise....the gashes heal....the fastenings roll away.

I troop forth replenished with supreme power, one of an average unending
    procession,
We walk the roads of Ohio and Massachusetts and Virginia and Wisconsin and
    New York and New Orleans and Texas and Montreal and San Francisco and
    Charleston and Savannah and Mexico,
Inland and by the seacoast and boundary lines....and we pass the boundary lines.

Our swift ordinances are on their way over the whole earth,
The blossoms we wear in our hats are the growth of two thousand years.

Eleves I salute you,
I see the approach of your numberless gangs....I see you understand yourselves
    and me,
And know that they who have eyes are divine, and the blind and lame are equally
    divine,
And that my steps drag behind yours yet go before them,
And are aware how I am with you no more than I am with everybody.

The friendly and flowing savage....Who is he?
Is he waiting for civilization or past it and mastering it?

Is he some southwesterner raised outdoors? Is he Canadian?
Is he from the Mississippi country? or from Iowa, Oregon or California? or from
    the mountains? or prairie life or bush-life? or from the sea?

Wherever he goes men and women accept and desire him,
They desire he should like them and touch them and speak to them and stay with
    them.

Behaviour lawless as snow-flakes....words simple as grass....uncombed head
    and laughter and naivete;
Slowstepping feet and the common features, and the common modes and emanations,
They descend in new forms from the tips of his fingers,
They are wafted with the odor of his body or breath....they fly out of the glance
    of his eyes.

Flaunt of the sunshine I need not your bask....lie over,
You light surfaces only....I force the surfaces and the depths also.

Earth! you seem to look for something at my hands,
Say old topknot! what do you want?

Man or woman! I might tell how I like you, but cannot,
And might tell what it is in me and what it is in you, but cannot,
And might tell the pinings I have....the pulse of my nights and days.

Behold I do not give lectures or a little charity,
What I give I give out of myself.

You there, impotent, loose in the knees, open your scarfed chops till I blow grit
    within you,
Spread your palms and lift the flaps of your pockets,
I am not to be denied....I compel....I have stores plenty and to spare,
And any thing I have I bestow,

I do not ask who you are....that is not important to me,
You can do nothing and be nothing but what I will infold you.

To a drudge of the cottonfields or emptier of privies I lean....on his right cheek
    I put the family kiss,
And in my soul I swear I never will deny him.

On women fit for conception I start bigger and nimbler babes,
This day I am jetting the stuff of far more arrogant republics.

To any one dying....thither I speed and twist the knob of the door,
Turn the bedclothes toward the foot of the bed,
Let the physician and the priest go home.

I seize the descending man....I raise him with resistless will.

O despairer, here is my neck,
By God! you shall not go down! Hang your whole weight upon me.

I dilate you with tremendous breath....I buoy you up;
Every room of the house do I fill with an armed force....lovers of me, bafflers
    of graves:
Sleep! I and they keep guard all night;
Not doubt, not decease shall dare to lay finger upon you,
I have embraced you, and henceforth possess you to myself,
And when you rise in the morning you will find what I tell you is so.

I am he bringing help for the sick as they pant on their backs,
And for strong upright men I bring yet more needed help.

I heard what was said of the universe,
Heard it and heard of several thousand years;
It is middling well as far as it goes....but is that all?

Magnifying and applying come I,
Outbidding at the start the old cautious hucksters,
The most they offer for mankind and eternity less than a spirt of my own seminal
    wet,
Taking myself the exact dimensions of Jehovah and laying them away,
Lithographing Kronos and Zeus his son, and Hercules his grandson,
Buying drafts of Osiris and Isis and Belus and Brahma and Adonai,
In my portfolio placing Manito loose, and Allah on a leaf, and the crucifix engraved,
With Odin, and the hideous-faced Mexitli, and all idols and images,
Honestly taking them all for what they are worth, and not a cent more,
Admitting they were alive and did the work of their day,

Admitting they bore mites as for unfledged birds who have now to rise and fly and
    sing for themselves,
Accepting the rough deific sketches to fill out better in myself....bestowing them
    freely on each man and woman I see,
Discovering as much or more in a framer framing a house,
Putting higher claims for him there with his rolled-up sleeves, driving the mallet and
    chisel;
Not objecting to special revelations....considering a curl of smoke or a hair on
    the back of my hand as curious as any revelation;
Those ahold of fire-engines and hook-and-ladder ropes more to me than the gods of
    the antique wars,
Minding their voices peal through the crash of destruction,
Their brawny limbs passing safe over charred laths....their white foreheads whole
    and unhurt out of the flames;
By the mechanic's wife with her babe at her nipple interceding for every person
    born;
Three scythes at harvest whizzing in a row from three lusty angels with shirts
    bagged out at their waists;
The snag-toothed hostler with red hair redeeming sins past and to come,
Selling all he possesses and traveling on foot to fee lawyers for his brother and sit
    by him while he is tried for forgery:
What was strewn in the amplest strewing the square rod about me, and not filling
    the square rod then;
The bull and the bug never worshipped half enough,
Dung and dirt more admirable than was dreamed,
The supernatural of no account....myself waiting my time to be one of the
    supremes,
The day getting ready for me when I shall do as much good as the best, and be as
    prodigious,
Guessing when I am it will not tickle me much to receive puffs out of pulpit or
    print;
By my life-lumps! becoming already a creator!
Putting myself here and now to the ambushed womb of the shadows!

....A call in the midst of the crowd,
My own voice, orotund sweeping and final.

Come my children,
Come my boys and girls, and my women and household and intimates,
Now the performer launches his nerve....he has passed his prelude on the reeds
    within.

Easily written loosefingered chords! I feel the thrum of their climax and close.

My head evolves on my neck,

Music rolls, but not from the organ....folks are around me, but they are no
    household of mine.

Ever the hard and unsunk ground,
Ever the eaters and drinkers....ever the upward and downward sun....ever the
    air and the ceaseless tides,
Ever myself and my neighbors, refreshing and wicked and real,
Ever the old inexplicable query....ever that thorned thumb — that breath of itches
    and thirsts,
Ever the vexer's hoot! hoot! till we find where the sly one hides and bring him
    forth;
Ever love....ever the sobbing liquid of life,
Ever the bandage under the chin....ever the tressels of death.

Here and there with dimes on the eyes walking,
To feed the greed of the belly the brains liberally spooning,
Tickets buying or taking or selling, but in to the feast never once going;
Many sweating and ploughing and thrashing, and then the chaff for payment re-
    ceiving,
A few idly owning, and they the wheat continually claiming.

This is the city....and I am one of the citizens;
Whatever interests the rest interests me....politics, churches, newspapers,
    schools,
Benevolent societies, improvements, banks, tariffs, steamships, factories, markets,
Stocks and stores and real estate and personal estate.

They who piddle and patter here in collars and tailed coats....I am aware who
    they are....and that they are not worms or fleas,
I acknowledge the duplicates of myself under all the scrape-lipped and pipe-legged
    concealments.

The weakest and shallowest is deathless with me,
What I do and say the same waits for them,
Every thought that flounders in me the same flounders in them.

I know perfectly well my own egotism,
And know my omniverous words, and cannot say any less,
And would fetch you whoever you are flush with myself.

My words are words of a questioning, and to indicate reality;
This printed and bound book....but the printer and the printing-office boy?
The marriage estate and settlement....but the body and mind of the bridegroom?
    also those of the bride?
The panorama of the sea....but the sea itself?

The well-taken photographs....but your wife or friend close and solid in your
    arms?
The fleet of ships of the line and all the modern improvements....but the craft
    and pluck of the admiral?
The dishes and fare and furniture....but the host and hostess, and the look out of
    their eyes?
The sky up there....yet here or next door or across the way?
The saints and sages in history....but you yourself?
Sermons and creeds and theology....but the human brain, and what is called
    reason, and what is called love, and what is called life?

I do not despise you priests;
My faith is the greatest of faiths and the least of faiths,
Enclosing all worship ancient and modern, and all between ancient and modern,
Believing I shall come again upon the earth after five thousand years,
Waiting responses from oracles....honoring the gods....saluting the sun,
Making a fetish of the first rock or stump....powowing with sticks in the circle of
    obis,
Helping the lama or brahmin as he trims the lamps of the idols,
Dancing yet through the streets in a phallic procession....rapt and austere in the
    woods, a gymnosophist,
Drinking mead from the skull-cup....to shasta and vedas admirant....minding
    the koran,
Walking the teokallis, spotted with gore from the stone and knife — beating the
    serpent-skin drum;
Accepting the gospels, accepting him that was crucified, knowing assuredly that he
    is divine,
To the mass kneeling — to the puritan's prayer rising — sitting patiently in a pew,
Ranting and frothing in my insane crisis — waiting dead-like till my spirit arouses me;
Looking forth on pavement and land, and outside of pavement and land,
Belonging to the winders of the circuit of circuits.

One of that centripetal and centrifugal gang,
I turn and talk like a man leaving charges before a journey.

Down-hearted doubters, dull and excluded,
Frivolous sullen moping angry affected disheartened atheistical,
I know every one of you, and know the unspoken interrogatories,
By experience I know them.

How the flukes splash!
How they contort rapid as lightning, with spasms and spouts of blood!

Be at peace bloody flukes of doubters and sullen mopers,
I take my place among you as much as among any;

The past is the push of you and me and all precisely the same,
And the day and night are for you and me and all,
And what is yet untried and afterward is for you and me and all.

I do not know what is untried and afterward,
But I know it is sure and alive and sufficient.

Each who passes is considered, and each who stops is considered, and not a single
    one can it fail.

It cannot fail the young man who died and was buried,
Nor the young woman who died and was put by his side,
Nor the little child that peeped in at the door and then drew back and was never
    seen again,
Nor the old man who has lived without purpose, and feels it with bitterness worse
    than gall,
Nor him in the poorhouse tubercled by rum and the bad disorder,
Nor the numberless slaughtered and wrecked....nor the brutish koboo, called the
    ordure of humanity,
Nor the sacs merely floating with open mouths for food to slip in,
Nor any thing in the earth, or down in the oldest graves of the earth,
Nor any thing in the myriads of spheres, nor one of the myriads of myriads that in-
    habit them,
Nor the present, nor the least wisp that is known.

It is time to explain myself....let us stand up.

What is known I strip away....I launch all men and women forward with me into
    the unknown.

The clock indicates the moment....but what does eternity indicate?

Eternity lies in bottomless reservoirs....its buckets are rising forever and ever,
They pour and they pour and they exhale away.

We have thus far exhausted trillions of winters and summers;
There are trillions ahead, and trillions ahead of them.

Births have brought us richness and variety,
And other births will bring us richness and variety.

I do not call one greater and one smaller,
That which fills its period and place is equal to any.

Were mankind murderous or jealous upon you my brother or my sister?

I am sorry for you....they are not murderous or jealous upon me;
All has been gentle with me......I keep no account with lamentation;
What have I to do with lamentation?

I am an acme of things accomplished, and I an encloser of things to be.

My feet strike an apex of the apices of the stairs,
On every step bunches of ages, and larger bunches between the steps,
All below duly traveled — and still I mount and mount.

Rise after rise bow the phantoms behind me,
Afar down I see the huge first Nothing, the vapor from the nostrils of death,
I know I was even there....I waited unseen and always,
And slept while God carried me through the lethargic mist,
And took my time....and took no hurt from the foetid carbon.

Long I was hugged close....long and long.

Immense have been the preparations for me,
Faithful and friendly the arms that have helped me.

Cycles ferried my cradle, rowing and rowing like cheerful boatmen;
For room to me stars kept aside in their own rings,
They sent influences to look after what was to hold me.

Before I was born out of my mother generations guided me,
My embryo has never been torpid....nothing could overlay it;
For it the nebula cohered to an orb....the long slow strata piled to rest it on
      ....vast vegetables gave it sustenance,
Monstrous sauroids transported it in their mouths and deposited it with care.

All forces have been steadily employed to complete and delight me,
Now I stand on this spot with my soul.

Span of youth! Ever-pushed elasticity! Manhood balanced and florid and full!

My lovers suffocate me!
Crowding my lips, and thick in the pores of my skin,
Jostling me through streets and public halls....coming naked to me at night,
Crying by day Ahoy from the rocks of the river....swinging and chirping over my
      head,
Calling my name from flowerbeds or vines or tangled underbrush,
Or while I swim in the bath....or drink from the pump at the corner....or the
      curtain is down at the opera....or I glimpse at a woman's face in the
      railroad car;

Lighting on every moment of my life,
Bussing my body with soft and balsamic busses,
Noiselessly passing handfuls out of their hearts and giving them to be mine.

Old age superbly rising! Ineffable grace of dying days!

Every condition promulges not only itself....it promulges what grows after and out
of itself,
And the dark hush promulges as much as any.

I open my scuttle at night and see the far-sprinkled systems,
And all I see, multiplied as high as I can cipher, edge but the rim of the farther
systems.

Wider and wider they spread, expanding and always expanding,
Outward and outward and forever outward.

My sun has his sun, and round him obediently wheels,
He joins with his partners a group of superior circuit,
And greater sets follow, making specks of the greatest inside them.

There is no stoppage, and never can be stoppage;
If I and you and the worlds and all beneath or upon their surfaces, and all the
palpable life, were this moment reduced back to a pallid float, it would not
avail in the long run,
We should surely bring up again where we now stand,
And as surely go as much farther, and then farther and farther.

A few quadrillions of eras, a few octillions of cubic leagues, do not hazard the span,
or make it impatient,
They are but parts....any thing is but a part.

See ever so far....there is limitless space outside of that,
Count ever so much....there is limitless time around that.

Our rendezvous is fitly appointed....God will be there and wait till we come.

I know I have the best of time and space — and that I was never measured, and
never will be measured.

I tramp a perpetual journey,
My signs are a rain-proof coat and good shoes and a staff cut from the woods;
No friend of mine takes his case in my chair,
I have no chair, nor church nor philosophy;
I lead no man to a dinner-table or library or exchange,

But each man and each woman of you I lead upon a knoll,
My left hand hooks you round the waist,
My right hand points to landscapes of continents, and a plain public road.

Not I, not any one else can travel that road for you,
You must travel it for yourself.

It is not far....it is within reach,
Perhaps you have been on it since you were born, and did not know,
Perhaps it is every where on water and on land.

Shoulder your duds, and I will mine, and let us hasten forth;
Wonderful cities and free nations we shall fetch as we go.

If you tire, give me both burdens, and rest the chuff of your hand on my hip,
And in due time you shall repay the same service to me;
For after we start we never lie by again.

This day before dawn I ascended a hill and looked at the crowded heaven,
And I said to my spirit, When we become the enfolders of those orbs and the plea-
    sure and knowledge of every thing in them, shall we be filled and satisfied then?
And my spirit said No, we level that lift to pass and continue beyond.

You are also asking me questions, and I hear you;
I answer that I cannot answer....you must find out for yourself.

Sit awhile wayfarer,
Here are biscuits to eat and here is milk to drink,
But as soon as you sleep and renew yourself in sweet clothes I will certainly kiss you
    with my goodbye kiss and open the gate for your egress hence.

Long enough have you dreamed contemptible dreams,
Now I wash the gum from your eyes,
You must habit yourself to the dazzle of the light and of every moment of your
    life.

Long have you timidly waded, holding a plank by the shore,
Now I will you to be a bold swimmer,
To jump off in the midst of the sea, and rise again and nod to me and shout, and
    laughingly dash with your hair.

I am the teacher of athletes,
He that by me spreads a wider breast than my own proves the width of my own,
He most honors my style who learns under it to destroy the teacher.

The boy I love, the same becomes a man not through derived power but in his own
    right,
Wicked, rather than virtuous out of conformity or fear,
Fond of his sweetheart, relishing well his steak,
Unrequited love or a slight cutting him worse than a wound cuts,
First rate to ride, to fight, to hit the bull's eye, to sail a skiff, to sing a song or play
    on the banjo,
Preferring scars and faces pitted with smallpox over all latherers and those that
    keep out of the sun.

I teach straying from me, yet who can stray from me?
I follow you whoever you are from the present hour;
My words itch at your ears till you understand them.

I do not say these things for a dollar, or to fill up the time while I wait for a boat;
It is you talking just as much as myself....I act as the tongue of you,
It was tied in your mouth....in mine it begins to be loosened.

I swear I will never mention love or death inside a house,
And I swear I never will translate myself at all, only to him or her who privately
    stays with me in the open air.

If you would understand me go to the heights or water-shore,
The nearest gnat is an explanation and a drop or the motion of waves a key,
The maul the oar and the handsaw second my words.

No shuttered room or school can commune with me,
But roughs and little children better than they.

The young mechanic is closest to me....he knows me pretty well,
The woodman that takes his axe and jug with him shall take me with him all day,
The farmboy ploughing in the field feels good at the sound of my voice,
In vessels that sail my words must sail....I go with fishermen and seamen, and
    love them,
My face rubs to the hunter's face when he lies down alone in his blanket,
The driver thinking of me does not mind the jolt of his wagon,
The young mother and old mother shall comprehend me,
The girl and the wife rest the needle a moment and forget where they are,
They and all would resume what I have told them.

I have said that the soul is not more than the body,
And I have said that the body is not more than the soul,
And nothing, not God, is greater to one than one's-self is,
And whoever walks a furlong without sympathy walks to his own funeral, dressed in
    his shroud,

And I or you pocketless of a dime may purchase the pick of the earth,
And to glance with an eye or show a bean in its pod confounds the learning of all
    times,
And there is no trade or employment but the young man following it may become a
    hero,
And there is no object so soft but it makes a hub for the wheeled universe,
And any man or woman shall stand cool and supercilious before a million universes.

And I call to mankind, Be not curious about God,
For I who am curious about each am not curious about God,
No array of terms can say how much I am at peace about God and about death.

I hear and behold God in every object, yet I understand God not in the least,
Nor do I understand who there can be more wonderful than myself.

Why should I wish to see God better than this day?
I see something of God each hour of the twenty-four, and each moment then,
In the faces of men and women I see God, and in my own face in the glass;
I find letters from God dropped in the street, and every one is signed by God's name,
And I leave them where they are, for I know that others will punctually come for-
    ever and ever.

And as to you death, and you bitter hug of mortality....it is idle to try to alarm
    me.

To his work without flinching the accoucheur comes,
I see the elderhand pressing receiving supporting,
I recline by the sills of the exquisite flexible doors....and mark the outlet, and
    mark the relief and escape.

And as to you corpse I think you are good manure, but that does not offend me,
I smell the white roses sweetscented and growing,
I reach to the leafy lips....I reach to the polished breasts of melons.

And as to you life, I reckon you are the leavings of many deaths,
No doubt I have died myself ten thousand times before.

I hear you whispering there O stars of heaven,
O suns....O grass of graves....O perpetual transfers and promotions....if
    you do not say anything how can I say anything?

Of the turbid pool that lies in the autumn forest,
Of the moon that descends the steeps of the soughing twilight,
Toss, sparkles of day and dusk....toss on the black stems that decay in the muck,
Toss to the moaning gibberish of the dry limbs.

I ascend from the moon....I ascend from the night,
And perceive of the ghastly glitter the sunbeams reflected,
And debouch to the steady and central from the offspring great or small.

There is that in me....I do not know what it is....but I know it is in me.

Wrenched and sweaty....calm and cool then my body becomes;
I sleep....I sleep long.

I do not know it....it is without name....it is a word unsaid,
It is not in any dictionary or utterance or symbol.

Something it swings on more than the earth I swing on,
To it the creation is the friend whose embracing awakes me.

Perhaps I might tell more....Outlines! I plead for my brothers and sisters.

Do you see O my brothers and sisters?
It is not chaos or death....it is form and union and plan....it is eternal life....
    it is happiness.

The past and present wilt....I have filled them and emptied them,
And proceed to fill my next fold of the future.

Listener up there! Here you....what have you to confide to me?
Look in my face while I snuff the sidle of evening,
Talk honestly, for no one else hears you, and I stay only a minute longer.

Do I contradict myself?
Very well then....I contradict myself;
I am large....I contain multitudes.

I concentrate toward them that are nigh....I wait on the door-slab.

Who has done his day's work and will soonest be through with his supper?
Who wishes to walk with me?

Will you speak before I am gone? Will you prove already too late?

The spotted hawk swoops by and accuses me....he complains of my gab and my
    loitering.

I too am not a bit tamed....I too am untranslatable,
I sound my barbaric yawp over the roofs of the world.

The last scud of day holds back for me,

It flings my likeness after the rest and true as any on the shadowed wilds,
It coaxes me to the vapor and the dusk.

I depart as air....I shake my white locks at the runaway sun,
I effuse my flesh in eddies and drift it in lacy jags.

I bequeath myself to the dirt to grow from the grass I love,
If you want me again look for me under your bootsoles.

You will hardly know who I am or what I mean,
But I shall be good health to you nevertheless,
And filter and fibre your blood.

Failing to fetch me me at first keep encouraged,
Missing me one place search another,
I stop some where waiting for you.

Leaves of Grass.

⫸◆⫷

[A Song for Occupations]

COME closer to me,
Push close my lovers and take the best I possess,
Yield closer and closer and give me the best you possess.

This is unfinished business with me....how is it with you?
I was chilled with the cold types and cylinder and wet paper between us.

I pass so poorly with paper and types....I must pass with the contact of bodies
and souls.

I do not thank you for liking me as I am, and liking the touch of me....I know that
it is good for you to do so.

Were all educations practical and ornamental well displayed out of me, what would
it amount to?
Were I as the head teacher or charitable proprietor or wise statesman, what would
it amount to?
Were I to you as the boss employing and paying you, would that satisfy you?

The learned and virtuous and benevolent, and the usual terms;
A man like me, and never the usual terms.

Neither a servant nor a master am I,
I take no sooner a large price than a small price....I will have my own whoever
enjoys me,
I will be even with you, and you shall be even with me.

If you are a workman or workwoman I stand as high as the highest that works in
the same shop,
If you bestow gifts on your brother or dearest friend, I demand as good as your
brother or dearest friend,
If your lover or husband or wife is welcome by day or night, I must be personally as
welcome;

If you have become degraded or ill, then I will become so for your sake;
If you remember your foolish and outlawed deeds, do you think I cannot remember
    my foolish and outlawed deeds?
If you carouse at the table I say I will carouse at the opposite side of the table;
If you meet some stranger in the street and love him or her, do I not often meet
    strangers in the street and love them?
If you see a good deal remarkable in me I see just as much remarkable in you.

Why what have you thought of yourself?
Is it you then that thought yourself less?
Is it you that thought the President greater than you? or the rich better off than
    you? or the educated wiser than you?

Because you are greasy or pimpled — or that you was once drunk, or a thief, or
    diseased, or rheumatic, or a prostitute — or are so now — or from frivolity or
    impotence — or that you are no scholar, and never saw your name in print....
    do you give in that you are any less immortal?

Souls of men and women! it is not you I call unseen, unheard, untouchable and
    untouching;
It is not you I go argue pro and con about, and to settle whether you are alive or
    no;
I own publicly who you are, if nobody else owns....and see and hear you, and
    what you give and take;
What is there you cannot give and take?

I see not merely that you are polite or whitefaced....married or single....
    citizens of old states or citizens of new states....eminent in some profession
    ....a lady or gentleman in a parlor....or dressed in the jail uniform....
    or pulpit uniform,
Not only the free Utahan, Kansian, or Arkansian....not only the free Cuban...
    not merely the slave....not Mexican native, or Flatfoot, or negro from
    Africa,
Iroquois eating the warflesh — fishtearer in his lair of rocks and sand....
    Esquimaux in the dark cold snowhouse....Chinese with his transverse eyes
    ....Bedowee — or wandering nomad — or tabounschik at the head of his
    droves,
Grown, half-grown, and babe — of this country and every country, indoors and out-
    doors I see....and all else is behind or through them.

The wife — and she is not one jot less than the husband,
The daughter — and she is just as good as the son,
The mother — and she is every bit as much as the father.

Offspring of those not rich — boys apprenticed to trades,

Young fellows working on farms and old fellows working on farms;
The naive....the simple and hardy....he going to the polls to vote....he
    who has a good time, and he who has a bad time;
Mechanics, southerners, new arrivals, sailors, mano'warsmen, merchantmen, coast-
    ers,
All these I see....but nigher and farther the same I see;
None shall escape me, and none shall wish to escape me.

I bring what you much need, yet always have,
I bring not money or amours or dress or eating....but I bring as good;
And send no agent or medium....and offer no representative of value — but offer
    the value itself.

There is something that comes home to one now and perpetually,
It is not what is printed or preached or discussed....it eludes discussion and
    print,
It is not to be put in a book....it is not in this book,
It is for you whoever you are....it is no farther from you than your hearing and
    sight are from you,
It is hinted by nearest and commonest and readiest....it is not them, though it is
    endlessly provoked by them....What is there ready and near you now?

You may read in many languages and read nothing about it;
You may read the President's message and read nothing about it there,
Nothing in the reports from the state department or treasury department....or in
    the daily papers, or the weekly papers,
Or in the census returns or assessors' returns or prices current or any accounts of
    stock.

The sun and stars that float in the open air....the appleshaped earth and we upon
    it....surely the drift of them is something grand;
I do not know what it is except that it is grand, and that it is happiness,
And that the enclosing purport of us here is not a speculation, or bon-mot or
    reconnoissance,
And that it is not something which by luck may turn out well for us, and without
    luck must be a failure for us,
And not something which may yet be retracted in a certain contingency.

The light and shade — the curious sense of body and identity — the greed that
    with perfect complaisance devours all things — the endless pride and out-
    stretching of man — unspeakable joys and sorrows,
The wonder every one sees in every one else he sees....and the wonders that fill
    each minute of time forever and each acre of surface and space forever,

Have you reckoned them as mainly for a trade or farmwork! or for the profits of
    a store? or to achieve yourself a position? or to fill a gentleman's leisure or a
    lady's leisure?

Have you reckoned the landscape took substance and form that it might be painted
    in a picture?
Or men and women that they might be written of, and songs sung?
Or the attraction of gravity and the great laws and harmonious combinations and
    the fluids of the air as subjects for the savans?
Or the brown land and the blue sea for maps and charts?
Or the stars to be put in constellations and named fancy names?
Or that the growth of seeds is for agricultural tables or agriculture itself?

Old institutions....these arts libraries legends collections — and the practice
    handed along in manufactures....will we rate them so high?
Will we rate our prudence and business so high?....I have no objection,
I rate them as high as the highest....but a child born of a woman and man I rate
    beyond all rate.

We thought our Union grand and our Constitution grand;
I do not say they are not grand and good — for they are,
I am this day just as much in love with them as you,
But I am eternally in love with you and with all my fellows upon the earth.

We consider the bibles and religions divine....I do not say they are not divine,
I say they have all grown out of you and may grow out of you still,
It is not they who give the life....it is you who give the life;
Leaves are not more shed from the trees or trees from the earth than they are shed
    out of you.

The sum of all known value and respect I add up in you whoever you are;
The President is up there in the White House for you....it is not you who are
    here for him,
The Secretaries act in their bureaus for you....not you here for them,
The Congress convenes every December for you,
Laws, courts, the forming of states, the charters of cities, the going and coming of
    commerce and mails are all for you.

All doctrines, all politics and civilization exurge from you,
All sculpture and monuments and anything inscribed anywhere are tallied in you,
The gist of histories and statistics as far back as the records reach is in you this
    hour — and myths and tales the same;
If you were not breathing and walking here where would they all be?
The most renowned poems would be ashes....orations and plays would be
    vacuums.

All architecture is what you do to it when you look upon it;
Did you think it was in the white or gray stone? or the lines of the arches and
    cornices?

All music is what awakens from you when you are reminded by the instruments,
It is not the violins and the cornets....it is not the oboe nor the beating drums —
    nor the notes of the baritone singer singing his sweet romanza....nor those
    of the men's chorus, nor those of the women's chorus,
It is nearer and further than they.

Will the whole come back then?
Can each see the signs of the best by a look in the lookingglass? Is there nothing
    greater or more?
Does all sit there with you and here with me?

The old forever now things....you foolish child!....the closest simplest things
    — this moment with you,
Your person and every particle that relates to your person,
The pulses of your brain waiting their chance and encouragement at every deed
    or sight;
Anything you do in public by day, and anything you do in secret betweendays,
What is called right and what is called wrong....what you behold or touch....
    what causes your anger or wonder,
The anklechain of the slave, the bed of the bedhouse, the cards of the gambler, the
    plates of the forger;
What is seen or learned in the street, or intuitively learned,
What is learned in the public school — spelling, reading, writing and ciphering....
    the blackboard and the teacher's diagrams:
The panes of the windows and all that appears through them....the going forth
    in the morning and the aimless spending of the day;
(What is it that you made money? what is it that you got what you wanted?)
The usual routine....the workshop, factory, yard, office, store, or desk;
The jaunt of hunting or fishing, or the life of hunting or fishing,
Pasturelife, foddering, milking and herding, and all the personnel and usages;
The plum-orchard and apple-orchard....gardening..seedlings, cuttings, flowers
    and vines,
Grains and manures..marl, clay, loam..the subsoil plough..the shovel and pick
    and rake and hoe..irrigation and draining;
The currycomb..the horse-cloth..the halter and bridle and bits..the very wisps
    of straw,
The barn and barn-yard..the bins and mangers..the mows and racks:
Manufactures..commerce..engineering..the building of cities, and every trade
    carried on there..and the implements of every trade,
The anvil and tongs and hammer..the axe and wedge..the square and mitre and
    jointer and smoothingplane;

The plumbob and trowel and level..the wall-scaffold, and the work of walls and
    ceilings..or any mason-work:
The ship's compass..the sailor's tarpaulin..the stays and lanyards, and the ground-
    tackle for anchoring or mooring,
The sloop's tiller..the pilot's wheel and bell..the yacht or fish-smack..the great
    gay-pennanted three-hundred-foot steamboat under full headway, with her proud
    fat breasts and her delicate swift-flashing paddles;
The trail and line and hooks and sinkers..the seine, and hauling the seine;
Smallarms and rifles....the powder and shot and caps and wadding....the
    ordnance for war....the carriages:
Everyday objects....the housechairs, the carpet, the bed and the counterpane of
    the bed, and him or her sleeping at night, and the wind blowing, and the indefi-
    nite noises:
The snowstorm or rainstorm....the tow-trowsers....the lodge-hut in the woods,
    and the still-hunt:
City and country..fireplace and candle..gaslight and heater and aqueduct;
The message of the governor, mayor, or chief of police....the dishes of breakfast
    or dinner or supper;
The bunkroom, the fire-engine, the string-team, and the car or truck behind;
The paper I write on or you write on..and every word we write..and every
    cross and twirl of the pen..and the curious way we write what we think....
    yet very faintly;
The directory, the detector, the ledger....the books in ranks or the bookshelves
    ....the clock attached to the wall,
The ring on your finger..the lady's wristlet..the hammers of stonebreakers or
    coppersmiths..the druggist's vials and jars;
The etui of surgical instruments, and the etui of oculist's or aurist's instruments, or
    dentist's instruments;
Glassblowing, grinding of wheat and corn..casting, and what is cast..tinroofing,
    shingledressing,
Shipcarpentering, flagging of sidewalks by floggers..dockbuilding, fishcuring, ferry-
    ing;
The pump, the piledriver, the great derrick..the coalkiln and brickkiln,
Ironworks or whiteleadworks..the sugarhouse..steam-saws, and the great mills
    and factories;
The cottonbale..the stevedore's book..the saw and buck of the sawyer..the
    screen of the coalscreener..the mould of the moulder..the workingknife of
    the butcher;
The cylinder press..the handpress..the frisket and tympan..the compositor's
    stick and rule,
The implements for daguerreotyping....the tools of the rigger or grappler or sail-
    maker or blockmaker,
Goods of guttapercha or papiermache....colors and brushes....glaziers' im-
    plements,

The veneer and gluepot..the confectioner's ornaments..the decanter and glasses
..the shears and flatiron;

The awl and kneestrap..the pint measure and quart measure..the counter and
stool..the writingpen of quill or metal;

Billiards and tenpins....the ladders and hanging ropes of the gymnasium, and the
manly exercises;

The designs for wallpapers or oilcloths or carpets....the fancies for goods for
women....the bookbinder's stamps;

Leatherdressing, coachmaking, boilermaking, ropetwisting, distilling, signpainting,
limeburning, coopering, cottonpicking,

The walkingbeam of the steam-engine..the throttle and governors, and the up and
down rods,

Stavemachines and plainingmachines....the cart of the carman..the omnibus..
the ponderous dray;

The snowplough and two engines pushing it....the ride in the express train of
only one car....the swift go through a howling storm:

The bearhunt or coonhunt....the bonfire of shavings in the open lot in the city
..the crowd of children watching;

The blows of the fighting-man..the upper cut and one-two-three;

The shopwindows....the coffins in the sexton's wareroom....the fruit on the
fruitstand....the beef on the butcher's stall,

The bread and cakes in the bakery....the white and red pork in the pork-store;

The milliner's ribbons..the dressmaker's patterns....the tea-table..the home-
made sweetmeats:

The column of wants in the one-cent paper..the news by telegraph....the
amusements and operas and shows:

The cotton and woolen and linen you wear....the money you make and spend;

Your room and bedroom....your piano-forte....the stove and cookpans,

The house you live in....the rent....the other tenants....the deposite in the
savings-bank....the trade at the grocery,

The pay on Saturday night....the going home, and the purchases;

In them the heft of the heaviest....in them far more than you estimated, and far
less also,

In them, not yourself....you and your soul enclose all things, regardless of estima-
tion,

In them your themes and hints and provokers..if not, the whole earth has no
themes or hints or provokers, and never had.

I do not affirm what you see beyond is futile....I do not advise you to stop,
I do not say leadings you thought great are not great,
But I say that none lead to greater or sadder or happier than those lead to.

Will you seek afar off? You surely come back at last,
In things best known to you finding the best or as good as the best,

In folks nearest to you finding also the sweetest and strongest and lovingest,
Happiness not in another place, but this place..not for another hour, but this hour,
Man in the first you see or touch....always in your friend or brother or nighest
　　neighbor....Woman in your mother or lover or wife,
And all else thus far known giving place to men and women.

When the psalm sings instead of the singer,
When the script preaches instead of the preacher,
When the pulpit descends and goes instead of the carver that carved the supporting
　　desk,
When the sacred vessels or the bits of the eucharist, or the lath and plast, procreate
　　as effectually as the young silversmiths or bakers, or the masons in their
　　overalls,
When a university course convinces like a slumbering woman and child convince,
When the minted gold in the vault smiles like the nightwatchman's daughter,
When warrantee deeds loafe in chairs opposite and are my friendly companions,
I intend to reach them my hand and make as much of them as I do of men and
　　women.

Leaves of Grass.

≡►◆◄≡

[To Think of Time]

To think of time....to think through the retrospection,
To think of today..and the ages continued henceforward.

Have you guessed you yourself would not continue? Have you dreaded those
earth-beetles?
Have you feared the future would be nothing to you?

Is today nothing? Is the beginningless past nothing?
If the future is nothing they are just as surely nothing.

To think that the sun rose in the east....that men and women were flexible and
real and alive....that every thing was real and alive;
To think that you and I did not see feel think nor bear our part,
To think that we are now here and bear our part.

Not a day passes..not a minute or second without an accouchement;
Not a day passes..not a minute or second without a corpse.

When the dull nights are over, and the dull days also,
When the soreness of lying so much in bed is over,
When the physician, after long putting off, gives the silent and terrible look for an
answer,
When the children come hurried and weeping, and the brothers and sisters have
been sent for,
When medicines stand unused on the shelf, and the camphor-smell has pervaded the
rooms,
When the faithful hand of the living does not desert the hand of the dying,
When the twitching lips press lightly on the forehead of the dying,
When the breath ceases and the pulse of the heart ceases,
Then the corpse-limbs stretch on the bed, and the living look upon them,
They are palpable as the living are palpable.

The living look upon the corpse with their eyesight,
But without eyesight lingers a different living and looks curiously on the corpse.

To think that the rivers will come to flow, and the snow fall, and fruits ripen..and
    act upon others as upon us now....yet not act upon us;
To think of all these wonders of city and country..and others taking great interest
    in them..and we taking small interest in them.

To think how eager we are in building our houses,
To think others shall be just as eager..and we quite indifferent.

I see one building the house that serves him a few years....or seventy or eighty
    years at most;
I see one building the house that serves him longer than that.

Slowmoving and black lines creep over the whole earth....they never cease....
    they are the burial lines,
He that was President was buried, and he that is now President shall surely be
    buried.

Cold dash of waves at the ferrywharf,
Posh and ice in the river....half-frozen mud in the streets,
A gray discouraged sky overhead....the short last daylight of December,
A hearse and stages....other vehicles give place,
The funeral of an old stagedriver....the cortege mostly drivers.

Rapid the trot to the cemetery,
Duly rattles the deathbell....the gate is passed....the grave is halted at....
    the living alight....the hearse uncloses,
The coffin is lowered and settled....the whip is laid on the coffin,
The earth is swiftly shovelled in....a minute..no one moves or speaks....it is
    done,
He is decently put away....is there anything more?

He was a goodfellow,
Freemouthed, quicktempered, not badlooking, able to take his own part,
Witty, sensitive to a slight, ready with life or death for a friend,
Fond of women,..played some..eat hearty and drank hearty,
Had known what it was to be flush..grew lowspirited toward the last..sickened
    ..was helped by a contribution,
Died aged forty-one years..and that was his funeral.

Thumb extended or finger uplifted,
Apron, cape, gloves, strap....wetweather clothes....whip carefully chosen....
    boss, spotter, starter, and hostler,

Somebody loafing on you, or you loafing on somebody....headway....man
    before and man behind,
Good day's work or bad day's work....pet stock or mean stock....first out or
    last out....turning in at night,
To think that these are so much and so nigh to other drivers..and he there takes
    no interest in them.

The markets, the government, the workingman's wages....to think what account
    they are through our nights and days;
To think that other workingmen will make just as great account of them..yet we
    make little or no account.

The vulgar and the refined....what you call sin and what you call goodness..to
    think how wide a difference;
To think the difference will still continue to others, yet we lie beyond the difference.

To think how much pleasure there is!
Have you pleasure from looking at the sky? Have you pleasure from poems?
Do you enjoy yourself in the city? or engaged in business? or planning a nomina-
    tion and election? or with your wife and family?
Or with your mother and sisters? or in womanly housework? or the beautiful ma-
    ternal cares?

These also flow onward to others....you and I flow onward;
But in due time you and I shall take less interest in them.

Your farm and profits and crops....to think how engrossed you are;
To think there will still be farms and profits and crops..yet for you of what avail?

What will be will be well — for what is is well,
To take interest is well, and not to take interest shall be well.

The sky continues beautiful....the pleasure of men with women shall never be
    sated..nor the pleasure of women with men..nor the pleasure from poems;
The domestic joys, the daily housework or business, the building of houses — they
    are not phantasms..they have weight and form and location;
The farms and profits and crops..the markets and wages and government..they
    also are not phantasms;
The difference between sin and goodness is no apparition;
The earth is not an echo....man and his life and all the things of his life are well-
    considered.

You are not thrown to the winds..you gather certainly and safely around yourself,
Yourself! Yourself! Yourself forever and ever!

It is not to diffuse you that you were born of your mother and father — it is to
     identify you,
It is not that you should be undecided, but that you should be decided;
Something long preparing and formless is arrived and formed in you,
You are thenceforth secure, whatever comes or goes.

The threads that were spun are gathered....the weft crosses the warp....
     the pattern is systematic.

The preparations have every one been justified;
The orchestra have tuned their instruments sufficiently....the baton has given the
     signal.

The guest that was coming....he waited long for reasons....he is now housed,
He is one of those who are beautiful and happy....he is one of those that to look
     upon and be with is enough.

The law of the past cannot be eluded,
The law of the present and future cannot be eluded,
The law of the living cannot be eluded....it is eternal,
The law of promotion and transformation cannot be eluded,
The law of heroes and good-doers cannot be eluded,
The law of drunkards and informers and mean persons cannot be eluded.

Slowmoving and black lines go ceaselessly over the earth,
Northerner goes carried and southerner goes carried....and they on the Atlantic
     side and they on the Pacific, and they between, and all through the Mississippi
     country....and all over the earth.

The great masters and kosmos are well as they go....the heroes and good-doers
     are well,
The known leaders and inventors and the rich owners and pious and distinguished
     may be well,
But there is more account than that....there is strict account of all.

The interminable hordes of the ignorant and wicked are not nothing,
The barbarians of Africa and Asia are not nothing,
The common people of Europe are not nothing....the American aborigines are
     not nothing,
A zambo or a foreheadless Crowfoot or a Camanche is not nothing,
The infected in the immigrant hospital are not nothing....the murderer or mean
     person is not nothing,
The perpetual succession of shallow people are not nothing as they go,
The prostitute is not nothing....the mocker of religion is not nothing as he goes.

I shall go with the rest....we have satisfaction:

I have dreamed that we are not to be changed so much....nor the law of us
    changed;
I have dreamed that heroes and good-doers shall be under the present and past law,
And that murderers and drunkards and liars shall be under the present and past law;
For I have dreamed that the law they are under now is enough.

And I have dreamed that the satisfaction is not so much changed....and that there
    is no life without satisfaction;
What is the earth? what are body and soul without satisfaction?

I shall go with the rest,
We cannot be stopped at a given point....that is no satisfaction;
To show us a good thing or a few good things for a space of time — that is no satis-
    faction;
We must have the indestructible breed of the best, regardless of time.

If otherwise, all these things came but to ashes of dung;
If maggots and rats ended us, then suspicion and treachery and death.

Do you suspect death? If I were to suspect death I should die now,
Do you think I could walk pleasantly and well-suited toward annihilation?

Pleasantly and well-suited I walk,
Whither I walk I cannot define, but I know it is good,
The whole universe indicates that it is good,
The past and the present indicate that it is good.

How beautiful and perfect are the animals! How perfect is my soul!
How perfect the earth, and the minutest thing upon it!
What is called good is perfect, and what is called sin is just as perfect;
The vegetables and minerals are all perfect..and the imponderable fluids are
    perfect;
Slowly and surely they have passed on to this, and slowly and surely they will yet
    pass on.

O my soul! if I realize you I have satisfaction,
Animals and vegetables! if I realize you I have satisfaction,
Laws of the earth and air! if I realize you I have satisfaction.

I cannot define my satisfaction..yet it is so,
I cannot define my life..yet it is so.

I swear I see now that every thing has an eternal soul!
The trees have, rooted in the ground....the weeds of the sea have....the
    animals.

I swear I think there is nothing but immortality!
That the exquisite scheme is for it, and the nebulous float is for it, and the cohering
    is for it,
And all preparation is for it..and identity is for it..and life and death are for it.

Leaves of Grass.

[The Sleepers]

I WANDER all night in my vision,
Stepping with light feet....swiftly and noiselessly stepping and stopping,
Bending with open eyes over the shut eyes of sleepers;
Wandering and confused....lost to myself....ill-assorted....contradictory,
Pausing and gazing and bending and stopping.

How solemn they look there, stretched and still;
How quiet they breathe, the little children in their cradles.

The wretched features of ennuyees, the white features of corpses, the livid faces of
    drunkards, the sick-gray faces of onanists,
The gashed bodies on battlefields, the insane in their strong-doored rooms, the
    sacred idiots,
The newborn emerging from gates and the dying emerging from gates,
The night pervades them and enfolds them.

The married couple sleep calmly in their bed, he with his palm on the hip of the
    wife, and she with her palm on the hip of the husband,
The sisters sleep lovingly side by side in their bed,
The men sleep lovingly side by side in theirs,
And the mother sleeps with her little child carefully wrapped.

The blind sleep, and the deaf and dumb sleep,
The prisoner sleeps well in the prison....the runaway son sleeps,

The murderer that is to be hung next day....how does he sleep?
And the murdered person....how does he sleep?

The female that loves unrequited sleeps,
And the male that loves unrequited sleeps;
The head of the moneymaker that plotted all day sleeps,
And the enraged and treacherous dispositions sleep.

I stand with drooping eyes by the worstsuffering and restless,
I pass my hands soothingly to and fro a few inches from them;
The restless sink in their beds....they fitfully sleep.

The earth recedes from me into the night,
I saw that it was beautiful....and I see that what is not the earth is beautiful.

I go from bedside to bedside....I sleep close with the other sleepers, each
    in turn;
I dream in my dream all the dreams of the other dreamers,
And I become the other dreamers.

I am a dance....Play up there! the fit is whirling me fast.

I am the everlaughing....it is new moon and twilight,
I see the hiding of douceurs....I see nimble ghosts whichever way I look,
Cache and cache again deep in the ground and sea, and where it is neither ground or
    sea.

Well do they do their jobs, those journeymen divine,
Only from me can they hide nothing and would not if they could;
I reckon I am their boss, and they make me a pet besides,
And surround me, and lead me and run ahead when I walk,
And lift their cunning covers and signify me with stretched arms, and resume the
    way;
Onward we move, a gay gang of blackguards with mirthshouting music and wild-
    flapping pennants of joy.

I am the actor and the actress....the voter..the politician,
The emigrant and the exile..the criminal that stood in the box,
He who has been famous, and he who shall be famous after today,
The stammerer....the wellformed person..the wasted or feeble person.

I am she who adorned herself and folded her hair expectantly;
My truant lover has come and it is dark.

Double yourself and receive me darkness,
Receive me and my lover too....he will not let me go without him.

I roll myself upon you as upon a bed....I resign myself to the dusk;

He whom I call answers me and takes the place of my lover,
He rises with me silently from the bed.

Darkness you are gentler than my lover....his flesh was sweaty and panting,
I feel the hot moisture yet that he left me.

My hands are spread forth..I pass them in all directions,
I would sound up the shadowy shore to which you are journeying.

Be careful, darkness....already, what was it touched me?
I thought my lover had gone....else darkness and he are one,
I hear the heart-beat....I follow..I fade away.

O hotcheeked and blushing! O foolish hectic!
O for pity's sake, no one must see me now!....my clothes were stolen while I
    was abed,
Now I am thrust forth, where shall I run?

Pier that I saw dimly last night when I looked from the windows,
Pier out from the main, let me catch myself with you and stay....I will not chafe
    you;
I feel ashamed to go naked about the world,
And am curious to know where my feet stand....and what is this flooding
    me, childhood or manhood....and the hunger that crosses the bridge
    between.

The cloth laps a first sweet eating and drinking,
Laps life-swelling yolks....laps ear of rose-corn, milky and just ripened:
The white teeth stay, and the boss-tooth advances in darkness,
And liquor is spilled on lips and bosoms by touching glasses, and the best liquor
    afterward.

I descend my western course....my sinews are flaccid,
Perfume and youth course through me, and I am their wake.

It is my face yellow and wrinkled instead of the old woman's,
I sit low in a strawbottom chair and carefully darn my grandson's stockings.

It is I too....the sleepless widow looking out on the winter midnight,
I see the sparkles of starshine on the icy and pallid earth.

A shroud I see — and I am the shroud....I wrap a body and lie in the coffin;
It is dark here underground....it is not evil or pain here....it is blank here, for
    reasons.

It seems to me that everything in the light and air ought to be happy;
Whoever is not in his coffin and the dark grave, let him know he has enough.

I see a beautiful gigantic swimmer swimming naked through the eddies of the sea,
His brown hair lies close and even to his head....he strikes out with courageous
   arms....he urges himself with his legs.

I see his white body....I see his undaunted eyes;
I hate the swift-running eddies that would dash him headforemost on the rocks.

What are you doing you ruffianly red-trickled waves?
Will you kill the courageous giant? Will you kill him in the prime of his middle age?

Steady and long he struggles;
He is baffled and banged and bruised....he holds out while his strength holds out,
The slapping eddies are spotted with his blood....they bear him away....they
   roll him and swing him and turn him:
His beautiful body is borne in the circling eddies....it is continually bruised on
   rocks,
Swiftly and out of sight is borne the brave corpse.

I turn but do not extricate myself;
Confused....a pastreading....another, but with darkness yet.

The beach is cut by the razory ice-wind....the wreck-guns sound,
The tempest lulls and the moon comes floundering through the drifts.

I look where the ship helplessly heads end on....I hear the burst as she strikes..
   I hear the howls of dismay....they grow fainter and fainter.

I cannot aid with my wringing fingers;
I can but rush to the surf and let it drench me and freeze upon me.

I search with the crowd....not one of the company is washed to us alive;
In the morning I help pick up the dead and lay them in rows in a barn.

Now of the old war-days..the defeat at Brooklyn;
Washington stands inside the lines..he stands on the entrenched hills amid a crowd
   of officers,
His face is cold and damp....he cannot repress the weeping drops....he lifts
   the glass perpetually to his eyes....the color is blanched from his cheeks,
He sees the slaughter of the southern braves confided to him by their parents.

The same at last and at last when peace is declared,
He stands in the room of the old tavern....the wellbeloved soldiers all past
   through,

The officers speechless and slow draw near in their turns,
The chief encircles their necks with his arm and kisses them on the cheek,
He kisses lightly the wet cheeks one after another....he shakes hands and bids
    goodbye to the army.

Now I tell what my mother told me today as we sat at dinner together,
Of when she was a nearly grown girl living home with her parents on the old home-
    stead.

A red squaw came one breakfasttime to the old homestead,
On her back she carried a bundle of rushes for rushbottoming chairs;
Her hair straight shiny coarse black and profuse halfenveloped her face,
Her step was free and elastic....her voice sounded exquisitely as she spoke.

My mother looked in delight and amazement at the stranger,
She looked at the beauty of her tallborne face and full and pliant limbs,
The more she looked upon her she loved her,
Never before had she seen such wonderful beauty and purity;
She made her sit on a bench by the jamb of the fireplace....she cooked food for
    her,
She had no work to give her but she gave her remembrance and fondness.

The red squaw staid all the forenoon, and toward the middle of the afternoon she
    went away;
O my mother was loth to have her go away,
All the week she thought of her....she watched for her many a month,
She remembered her many a winter and many a summer,
But the red squaw never came nor was heard of there again.

Now Lucifer was not dead....or if he was I am his sorrowful terrible heir;
I have been wronged....I am oppressed....I hate him that oppresses me,
I will either destroy him, or he shall release me.

Damn him! how he does defile me,
How he informs against my brother and sister and takes pay for their blood,
How he laughs when I look down the bend after the steamboat that carries away my
    woman.

Now the vast dusk bulk that is the whale's bulk....it seems mine,
Warily, sportsman! though I lie so sleepy and sluggish, my tap is death.

A show of the summer softness....a contact of something unseen....an amour
    of the light and air;
I am jealous and overwhelmed with friendliness,
And will go gallivant with the light and the air myself,
And have an unseen something to be in contact with them also.

O love and summer! you are in the dreams and in me,
Autumn and winter are in the dreams....the farmer goes with his thrift,
The droves and crops increase....the barns are wellfilled.

Elements merge in the night....ships make tacks in the dreams....the sailor
    sails....the exile returns home,
The fugitive returns unharmed....the immigrant is back beyond months and years;
The poor Irishman lives in the simple house of his childhood, with the wellknown
    neighbors and faces,
They warmly welcome him....he is barefoot again....he forgets he is welloff;
The Dutchman voyages home, and the Scotchman and Welchman voyage home..
    and the native of the Mediterranean voyages home;
To every port of England and France and Spain enter wellfilled ships;
The Swiss foots it toward his hills....the Prussian goes his way, and the
    Hungarian his way, and the Pole goes his way,
The Swede returns, and the Dane and Norwegian return.

The homeward bound and the outward bound,
The beautiful lost swimmer, the ennuyee, the onanist, the female that loves unre-
    quited, the moneymaker,
The actor and actress..those through with their parts and those waiting to
    commence,
The affectionate boy, the husband and wife, the voter, the nominee that is chosen
    and the nominee that has failed,
The great already known, and the great anytime after to day,
The stammerer, the sick, the perfectformed, the homely,
The criminal that stood in the box, the judge that sat and sentenced him, the fluent
    lawyers, the jury, the audience,
The laugher and weeper, the dancer, the midnight widow, the red squaw,
The consumptive, the erysipalite, the idiot, he that is wronged,
The antipodes, and every one between this and them in the dark,
I swear they are averaged now....one is no better than the other,
The night and sleep have likened them and restored them.

I swear they are all beautiful,
Every one that sleeps is beautiful....every thing in the dim night is beautiful,
The wildest and bloodiest is over and all is peace.

Peace is always beautiful,
The myth of heaven indicates peace and night.

The myth of heaven indicates the soul;
The soul is always beautiful....it appears more or it appears less....it comes or
    lags behind,

It comes from its embowered garden and looks pleasantly on itself and encloses the
    world;
Perfect and clean the genitals previously jetting, and perfect and clean the womb
    cohering,
The head wellgrown and proportioned and plumb, and the bowels and joints
    proportioned and plumb.

The soul is always beautiful,
The universe is duly in order....every thing is in its place,
What is arrived is in its place, and what waits is in its place;
The twisted skull waits....the watery or rotten blood waits,
The child of the glutton or venerealee waits long, and the child of the drunkard
    waits long, and the drunkard himself waits long,
The sleepers that lived and died wait....the far advanced are to go on in their
    turns, and the far behind are to go on in their turns,
The diverse shall be no less diverse, but they shall flow and unite....they unite
    now.

The sleepers are very beautiful as they lie unclothed,
They flow hand in hand over the whole earth from east to west as they lie un-
    clothed;
The Asiatic and African are hand in hand....the European and American are
    hand in hand,
Learned and unlearned are hand in hand..and male and female are hand in hand;
The bare arm of the girl crosses the bare breast of her lover....they press close
    without lust....his lips press her neck,
The father holds his grown or ungrown son in his arms with measureless love....
    and the son holds the father in his arms with measureless love,
The white hair of the mother shines on the white wrist of the daughter,
The breath of the boy goes with the breath of the man....friend is inarmed by
    friend,
The scholar kisses the teacher and the teacher kisses the scholar....the wronged
    is made right,
The call of the slave is one with the master's call..and the master salutes the slave,
The felon steps forth from the prison....the insane becomes sane....the suffer-
    ing of sick persons is relieved,
The sweatings and fevers stop..the throat that was unsound is sound..the lungs
    of the consumptive are resumed..the poor distressed head is free,
The joints of the rheumatic move as smoothly as ever, and smoother than ever,
Stiflings and passages open....the paralysed become supple,
The swelled and convulsed and congested awake to themselves in condition,
They pass the invigoration of the night and the chemistry of the night and awake.

I too pass from the night;
I stay awhile away O night, but I return to you again and love you;

Why should I be afraid to trust myself to you?
I am not afraid....I have been well brought forward by you;
I love the rich running day, but I do not desert her in whom I lay so long:
I know not how I came of you, and I know not where I go with you....but I
    know I came well and shall go well.

I will stop only a time with the night....and rise betimes.

I will duly pass the day O my mother and duly return to you;
Not you will yield forth the dawn again more surely than you will yield forth me
    again,
Not the womb yields the babe in its time more surely than I shall be yielded from
    you in my time.

Leaves of Grass.

[I Sing the Body Electric]

THE bodies of men and women engirth me, and I engirth them,
    They will not let me off nor I them till I go with them and respond to them
and love them.

Was it dreamed whether those who corrupted their own live bodies could conceal
    themselves?
And whether those who defiled the living were as bad as they who defiled the
    dead?

The expression of the body of man or woman balks account,
The male is perfect and that of the female is perfect.

The expression of a wellmade man appears not only in his face,
It is in his limbs and joints also....it is curiously in the joints of his hips and wrists,
It is in his walk..the carriage of his neck..the flex of his waist and knees....
    dress does not hide him,

The strong sweet supple quality he has strikes through the cotton and flannel;
To see him pass conveys as much as the best poem..perhaps more,
You linger to see his back and the back of his neck and shoulderside.

The sprawl and fulness of babes....the bosoms and heads of women....the
    folds of their dress....their style as we pass in the street....the contour of
    their shape downwards;
The swimmer naked in the swimmingbath..seen as he swims through the salt
    transparent greenshine, or lies on his back and rolls silently with the heave of
    the water;
Framers bare-armed framing a house..hoisting the beams in their places..or
    using the mallet and mortising-chisel,
The bending forward and backward of rowers in rowboats....the horseman in his
    saddle;
Girls and mothers and housekeepers in all their exquisite offices,
The group of laborers seated at noontime with their open dinnerkettles, and their
    wives waiting,
The female soothing a child....the farmer's daughter in the garden or cowyard,
The woodman rapidly swinging his axe in the woods....the young fellow hoeing
    corn....the sleighdriver guiding his six horses through the crowd,
The wrestle of wrestlers..two apprentice-boys, quite grown, lusty, goodnatured,
    nativeborn, out on the vacant lot at sundown after work,
The coats vests and caps thrown down..the embrace of love and resistance,
The upperhold and underhold — the hair rumpled over and blinding the eyes;
The march of firemen in their own costumes — the play of the masculine muscle
    through cleansetting trowsers and waistbands,
The slow return from the fire....the pause when the bell strikes suddenly again —
    the listening on the alert,
The natural perfect and varied attitudes....the bent head, the curved neck, the
    counting:
Suchlike I love....I loosen myself and pass freely....and am at the mother's
    breast with the little child,
And swim with the swimmer, and wrestle with wrestlers, and march in line with the
    firemen, and pause and listen and count.

I knew a man....he was a common farmer....he was the father of five sons...
    and in them were the fathers of sons...and in them were the fathers of sons.

This man was of wonderful vigor and calmness and beauty of person;
The shape of his head, the richness and breadth of his manners, the pale yellow
    and white of his hair and beard, the immeasurable meaning of his black eyes,
These I used to go and visit him to see....He was wise also,
He was six feet tall....he was over eighty years old....his sons were massive
    clean bearded tanfaced and handsome,

They and his daughters loved him...all who saw him loved him...they did not
love him by allowance...they loved him with personal love;
He drank water only....the blood showed like scarlet through the clear brown
skin of his face;
He was a frequent gunner and fisher...he sailed his boat himself...he had a fine
one presented to him by a shipjoiner....he had fowling-pieces, presented to
him by men that loved him;
When he went with his five sons and many grandsons to hunt or fish you would pick
him out as the most beautiful and vigorous of the gang,
You would wish long and long to be with him:...you would wish to sit by him in
the boat that you and he might touch each other.

I have perceived that to be with those I like is enough,
To stop in company with the rest at evening is enough,
To be surrounded by beautiful curious breathing laughing flesh is enough,
To pass among them..to touch any one....to rest my arm ever so lightly round
his or her neck for a moment....what is this then?
I do not ask any more delight....I swim in it as in a sea.

There is something in staying close to men and women and looking on them and in
the contact and odor of them that pleases the soul well,
All things please the soul, but these please the soul well.

This is the female form,
A divine nimbus exhales from it from head to foot,
It attracts with fierce undeniable attraction,
I am drawn by its breath as if I were no more than a helpless vapor....all falls
aside but myself and it,
Books, art, religion, time..the visible and solid earth..the atmosphere and the
fringed clouds..what was expected of heaven or feared of hell are now
consumed,
Mad filaments, ungovernable shoots play out of it..the response likewise ungovern-
able,
Hair, bosom, hips, bend of legs, negligent falling hands — all diffused....mine too
diffused,
Ebb stung by the flow, and flow stung by the ebb....loveflesh swelling and
deliciously aching,
Limitless limpid jets of love hot and enormous....quivering jelly of love...white-
blow and delirious juice,
Bridegroom-night of love working surely and softly into the prostrate dawn,
Undulating into the willing and yielding day,
Lost in the cleave of the clasping and sweetfleshed day.

This is the nucleus...after the child is born of woman the man is born of woman,
This is the bath of birth...this is the merge of small and large and the outlet again.

Be not ashamed women..your privilege encloses the rest..it is the exit of the rest,
You are the gates of the body and you are the gates of the soul.

The female contains all qualities and tempers them....she is in her place....
    she moves with perfect balance,
She is all things duly veiled....she is both passive and active....she is to con-
    ceive daughters as well as sons and sons as well as daughters.

As I see my soul reflected in nature....as I see through a mist one with inexpress-
    ible completeness and beauty....see the bent head and arms folded over the
    breast....the female I see,
I see the bearer of the great fruit which is immortality....the good thereof is
    not tasted by roues, and never can be.

The male is not less the soul, nor more....he too is in his place,
He too is all qualities....he is action and power....the flush of the known
    universe is in him,
Scorn becomes him well and appetite and defiance become him well,
The fiercest largest passions..bliss that is utmost and sorrow that is utmost be-
    come him well....pride is for him,
The fullspread pride of man is calming and excellent to the soul;
Knowledge becomes him....he likes it always....he brings everything to the
    test of himself,
Whatever the survey..whatever the sea and the sail, he strikes soundings at last
    only here,
Where else does he strike soundings except here?

The man's body is sacred and the woman's body is sacred....it is no matter who,
Is it a slave? Is it one of the dullfaced immigrants just landed on the wharf?

Each belongs here or anywhere just as much as the welloff....just as much as
    you,
Each has his or her place in the procession.

All is a procession,
The universe is a procession with measured and beautiful motion.

Do you know so much that you call the slave or the dullface ignorant?
Do you suppose you have a right to a good sight...and he or she has no
    right to a sight?
Do you think matter has cohered together from its diffused float, and the soil is
    on the surface and water runs and vegetation sprouts for you..and not for
    him and her?

A slave at auction!
I help the auctioneer....the sloven does not half know his business.

Gentlemen look on this curious creature,
Whatever the bids of the bidders they cannot be high enough for him,
For him the globe lay preparing quintillions of years without one animal or plant,
For him the revolving cycles truly and steadily rolled.

In that head the allbaffling brain,
In it and below it the making of the attributes of heroes.

Examine these limbs, red black or white....they are very cunning in tendon and
    nerve;
They shall be stript that you may see them.

Exquisite senses, lifelit eyes, pluck, volition,
Flakes of breastmuscle, pliant backbone and neck, flesh not flabby, goodsized arms
    and legs,
And wonders within there yet.

Within there runs his blood....the same old blood..the same red running blood;
There swells and jets his heart....There all passions and desires..all reachings
    and aspirations:
Do you think they are not there because they are not expressed in parlors and
    lecture-rooms?

This is not only one man....he is the father of those who shall be fathers in their
    turns,
In him the start of populous states and rich republics,
Of him countless immortal lives with countless embodiments and enjoyments.

How do you know who shall come from the offspring of his offspring through the
    centuries?
Who might you find you have come from yourself if you could trace back through
    the centuries?

A woman at auction,
She too is not only herself....she is the teeming mother of mothers,
She is the bearer of them that shall grow and be mates to the mothers.

Her daughters or their daughters' daughters..who knows who shall mate with
    them?
Who knows through the centuries what heroes may come from them?

In them and of them natal love....in them the divine mystery....the same old
    beautiful mystery.

Have you ever loved a woman?

Your mother....is she living?....Have you been much with her? and has she
   been much with you?
Do you not see that these are exactly the same to all in all nations and times all
   over the earth?

If life and the soul are sacred the human body is sacred;
And the glory and sweet of a man is the token of manhood untainted,
And in man or woman a clean strong firmfibred body is beautiful as the most
   beautiful face.

Have you seen the fool that corrupted his own live body? or the fool that corrupted
   her own live body?
For they do not conceal themselves, and cannot conceal themselves.

Who degrades or defiles the living human body is cursed,
Who degrades or defiles the body of the dead is not more cursed.

Leaves of Grass.

[Faces]

S AUNTERING the pavement or riding the country byroad here then are
   faces,
Faces of friendship, precision, caution, suavity, ideality,
The spiritual prescient face, the always welcome common benevolent face,
The face of the singing of music, the grand faces of natural lawyers and judges
   broad at the backtop,
The faces of hunters and fishers, bulged at the brows....the shaved blanched
   faces of orthodox citizens,
The pure extravagant yearning questioning artist's face,
The welcome ugly face of some beautiful soul....the handsome detested or
   despised face,
The sacred faces of infants....the illuminated face of the mother of many children,

The face of an amour....the face of veneration,
The face as of a dream....the face of an immobile rock,
The face withdrawn of its good and bad..a castrated face,
A wild hawk..his wings clipped by the clipper,
A stallion that yielded at last to the thongs and knife of the gelder.

Sauntering the pavement or crossing the ceaseless ferry, here then are faces;
I see them and complain not and am content with all.

Do you suppose I could be content with all if I thought them their own finale?

This now is too lamentable a face for a man;
Some abject louse asking leave to be..cringing for it,
Some milknosed maggot blessing what lets it wrig to its hole.

This face is a dog's snout sniffing for garbage;
Snakes nest in that mouth..I hear the sibilant threat.

This face is a haze more chill than the arctic sea,
Its sleepy and wobbling icebergs crunch as they go.

This is a face of bitter herbs....this an emetic....they need no label,
And more of the drugshelf..laudanum, caoutchouc, or hog's lard.

This face is an epilepsy advertising and doing business....its wordless tongue
    gives out the unearthly cry,
Its veins down the neck distend....its eyes roll till they show nothing but their
    whites,
Its teeth grit..the palms of the hands are cut by the turned-in nails,
The man falls struggling and foaming to the ground while he speculates well.

This face is bitten by vermin and worms,
And this is some murderer's knife with a halfpulled scabbard.

This face owes to the sexton his dismalest fee,
An unceasing deathbell tolls there.

Those are really men!....the bosses and tufts of the great round globe!

Features of my equals, would you trick me with your creased and cadaverous
    march?
Well then you cannot trick me.

I see your rounded never-erased flow,
I see neath the rims of your haggard and mean disguises.

Splay and twist as you like....poke with the tangling fores of fishes or rats,
You'll be unmuzzled....you certainly will.

I saw the face of the most smeared and slobbering idiot they had at the asylum,
And I knew for my consolation what they knew not;
I knew of the agents that emptied and broke my brother,
The same wait to clear the rubbish from the fallen tenement;
And I shall look again in a score or two of ages,
And I shall meet the real landlord perfect and unharmed, every inch as good as
    myself.

The Lord advances and yet advances;
Always the shadow in front....always the reached hand bringing up the laggards.

Out of this face emerge banners and horses....O superb!....I see what is
    coming,
I see the high pioneercaps....I see the staves of runners clearing the way,
I have victorious drums.

This face is a lifeboat;
This is the face commanding and bearded....it asks no odds of the rest;
This face is flavored fruit ready for eating;
This face of a healthy honest boy is the programme of all good.

These faces bear testimony slumbering or awake,
They show their descent from the Master himself.

Off the word I have spoken I except not one....red white or black, all are deific,
In each house is the ovum....it comes forth after a thousand years.

Spots or cracks at the windows do not disturb me,
Tall and sufficient stand behind and make signs to me;
I read the promise and patiently wait.

This is a fullgrown lily's face,
She speaks to the limber-hip'd man near the garden pickets,
Come here, she blushingly cries....Come nigh to me limber-hip'd man and give me
    your finger and thumb,
Stand at my side till I lean as high as I can upon you,
Fill me with albescent honey....bend down to me,
Rub to me with your chafing beard..rub to my breast and shoulders.

The old face of the mother of many children:
Whist! I am fully content.

Lulled and late is the smoke of the Sabbath morning,
It hangs low over the rows of trees by the fences,
It hangs thin by the sassafras, the wildcherry and the catbrier under them.

I saw the rich ladies in full dress at the soiree,
I heard what the run of poets were saying so long,
Heard who sprang in crimson youth from the white froth and the water-blue.

Behold a woman!
She looks out from her quaker cap....her face is clearer and more beautiful than
    the sky.

She sits in an armchair under the shaded porch of the farmhouse,
The sun just shines on her old white head.

Her ample gown is of creamhued linen,
Her grandsons raised the flax, and her granddaughters spun it with the distaff and
    the wheel.

The melodious character of the earth!
The finish beyond which philosophy cannot go and does not wish to go!
The justified mother of men!

Leaves of Grass.

[Song of the Answerer]

A YOUNG man came to me with a message from his brother,
How should the young man know the whether and when of his brother?
Tell him to send me the signs.

And I stood before the young man face to face, and took his right hand in my left
    hand and his left hand in my right hand,
And I answered for his brother and for men....and I answered for the poet, and
    sent these signs.

Him all wait for....him all yield up to....his word is decisive and final,
Him they accept....in him lave....in him perceive themselves as amid light,
Him they immerse, and he immerses them.

Beautiful women, the haughtiest nations, laws, the landscape, people and animals,
The profound earth and its attributes, and the unquiet ocean,

All enjoyments and properties, and money, and whatever money will buy,
The best farms.....others toiling and planting, and he unavoidably reaps,
The noblest and costliest cities....others grading and building, and he domiciles
    there;
Nothing for any one but what is for him....near and far are for him,
The ships in the offing....the perpetual shows and marches on land are for him if
    they are for any body.

He puts things in their attitudes,
He puts today out of himself with plasticity and love,
He places his own city, times, reminiscences, parents, brothers and sisters, associ-
    ations employment and politics, so that the rest never shame them afterward,
    nor assume to command them.

He is the answerer,
What can be answered he answers, and what cannot be answered he shows how it
    cannot be answered.

A man is a summons and challenge,
It is vain to skulk....Do you hear that mocking and laughter? Do you hear the
    ironical echoes?

Books friendships philosophers priests action pleasure pride beat up and down
    seeking to give satisfaction;
He indicates the satisfaction, and indicates them that beat up and down also.

Whichever the sex...whatever the season or place he may go freshly and gently
    and safely by day or by night,
He has the passkey of hearts....to him the response of the prying of hands on the
    knobs.

His welcome is universal....the flow of beauty is not more welcome or universal
    than he is,
The person he favors by day or sleeps with at night is blessed.

Every existence has its idiom....every thing has an idiom and tongue;
He resolves all tongues into his own, and bestows it upon men..and any man
    translates..and any man translates himself also:
One part does not counteract another part....He is the joiner..he sees how they
    join.

He says indifferently and alike, How are you friend? to the President at his levee,
And he says Good day my brother, to Cudge that hoes in the sugarfield;
And both understand him and know that his speech is right.

He walks with perfect ease in the capitol,

He walks among the Congress....and one representative says to another, Here is
  our equal appearing and new.

Then the mechanics take him for a mechanic,
And the soldiers suppose him to be a captain....and the sailors that he has
  followed the sea,
And the authors take him for an author....and the artists for an artist,
And the laborers perceive he could labor with them and love them;
No matter what the work is, that he is one to follow it or has followed it,
No matter what the nation, that he might find his brothers and sisters there.

The English believe he comes of their English stock,
A Jew to the Jew he seems....a Russ to the Russ....usual and near..
  removed from none.

Whoever he looks at in the traveler's coffeehouse claims him,
The Italian or Frenchman is sure, and the German is sure, and the Spaniard is
  sure....and the island Cuban is sure.

The engineer, the deckhand on the great lakes or on the Mississippi or St Law-
  rence or Sacramento or Hudson or Delaware claims him.

The gentleman of perfect blood acknowledges his perfect blood,
The insulter, the prostitute, the angry person, the beggar, see themselves in the ways
  of him....he strangely transmutes them,
They are not vile any more....they hardly know themselves, they are so grown.

You think it would be good to be the writer of melodious verses,
Well it would be good to be the writer of melodious verses;
But what are verses beyond the flowing character you could have?....or
  beyond beautiful manners and behaviour?
Or beyond one manly or affectionate deed of an apprenticeboy?..or old woman?..
  or man that has been in prison or is likely to be in prison?

Leaves of Grass.

[Europe the 72d and 73d Years of These States]

SUDDENLY out of its stale and drowsy lair, the lair of slaves,
Like lightning Europe le'pt forth....half startled at itself,
Its feet upon the ashes and the rags....Its hands tight to the throats of kings.

O hope and faith! O aching close of lives! O many a sickened heart!
Turn back unto this day, and make yourselves afresh.

And you, paid to defile the People....you liars mark:
Not for numberless agonies, murders, lusts,
For court thieving in its manifold mean forms,
Worming from his simplicity the poor man's wages;
For many a promise sworn by royal lips, And broken, and laughed at in the breaking,
Then in their power not for all these did the blows strike of personal revenge..or
    the heads of the nobles fall;
The People scorned the ferocity of kings.

But the sweetness of mercy brewed bitter destruction, and the frightened rulers come
    back:
Each comes in state with his train....hangman, priest and tax-gatherer....
    soldier, lawyer, jailer and sycophant.

Yet behind all, lo, a Shape,
Vague as the night, draped interminably, head front and form in scarlet folds,
Whose face and eyes none may see,
Out of its robes only this....the red robes, lifted by the arm,
One finger pointed high over the top, like the head of a snake appears.

Meanwhile corpses lie in new-made graves....bloody corpses of young men:
The rope of the gibbet hangs heavily....the bullets of princes are flying....
    the creatures of power laugh aloud,
And all these things bear fruits....and they are good.

Those corpses of young men,
Those martyrs that hang from the gibbets...those hearts pierced by the gray lead,
Cold and motionless as they seem..live elsewhere with unslaughter'd vitality.

They live in other young men, O kings,
They live in brothers, again ready to defy you:
They were purified by death....They were taught and exalted.

Not a grave of the murdered for freedom but grows seed for freedom....in its
    turn to bear seed,
Which the winds carry afar and re-sow, and the rains and the snows nourish.

Not a disembodied spirit can the weapons of tyrants let loose,
But it stalks invisibly over the earth..whispering counseling cautioning.

Liberty let others despair of you....I never despair of you.

Is the house shut? Is the master away?
Nevertheless be ready....be not weary of watching,
He will soon return....his messengers come anon.

Leaves of Grass.

[A Boston Ballad]

C LEAR the way there Jonathan!
　Way for the President's marshal! Way for the government cannon!
Way for the federal foot and dragoons....and the phantoms afterward.

I rose this morning early to get betimes in Boston town;
Here's a good place at the corner....I must stand and see the show.

I love to look on the stars and stripes....I hope the fifes will play Yankee Doodle.

How bright shine the foremost with cutlasses,
Every man holds his revolver....marching stiff through Boston town.

A fog follows....antiques of the same come limping,
Some appear wooden-legged and some appear bandaged and bloodless.

Why this is a show! It has called the dead out of the earth,
The old graveyards of the hills have hurried to see;
Uncountable phantoms gather by flank and rear of it,
Cocked hats of mothy mould and crutches made of mist,
Arms in slings and old men leaning on young men's shoulders.

What troubles you, Yankee phantoms? What is all this chattering of bare gums?
Does the ague convulse your limbs? Do you mistake your crutches for firelocks,
　and level them?

If you blind your eyes with tears you will not see the President's marshal,
If you groan such groans you might balk the government cannon.

For shame old maniacs!....Bring down those tossed arms, and let your white
　hair be;
Here gape your smart grandsons....their wives gaze at them from the windows,
See how well-dressed....see how orderly they conduct themselves.

Worse and worse....Can't you stand it? Are you retreating?
Is this hour with the living too dead for you?

Retreat then! Pell-mell!....Back to the hills, old limpers!
I do not think you belong here anyhow.

But there is one thing that belongs here....Shall I tell you what it is, gentlemen of
　Boston?

I will whisper it to the Mayor....he shall send a committee to England,
They shall get a grant from the Parliament, and go with a cart to the royal vault.

Dig out King George's coffin....unwrap him quick from the graveclothes....
     box up his bones for a journey:
Find a swift Yankee clipper....here is freight for you blackbellied clipper,
Up with your anchor! shake out your sails!....steer straight toward Boston bay.

Now call the President's marshal again, and bring out the government cannon,
And fetch home the roarers from Congress, and make another procession and guard
     it with foot and dragoons.

Here is a centrepiece for them:
Look! all orderly citizens....look from the windows women.

The committee open the box and set up the regal ribs and glue those that will not
     stay,
And clap the skull on top of the ribs, and clap a crown on top of the skull.

You have got your revenge old buster!....The crown is come to its own and more
     than its own.

Stick your hands in your pockets Jonathan....you are a made man from this day,
You are mighty cute....and here is one of your bargains.

Leaves of Grass.

—➤•◆•◄—

[There Was a Child Went Forth]

THERE was a child went forth every day,
     And the first object he looked upon and received with wonder or pity or love
     or dread, that object he became,
And that object became part of him for the day or a certain part of the day....or
     for many years or stretching cycles of years.

The early lilacs became part of this child,
And grass, and white and red morningglories, and white and red clover, and the song
     of the phoebe-bird,
And the March-born lambs, and the sow's pink-faint litter, and the mare's foal, and
     the cow's calf, and the noisy brood of the barnyard or by the mire of the pond-
     side..and the fish suspending themselves so curiously below there..and the
     beautiful curious liquid..and the water-plants with their graceful flat heads..
     all became part of him.

And the field-sprouts of April and May became part of him....wintergrain sprouts,
     and those of the light-yellow corn, and of the esculent roots of the garden,
And the appletrees covered with blossoms, and the fruit afterward....and wood-
     berries..and the commonest weeds by the road;

And the old drunkard staggering home from the outhouse of the tavern whence he
   had lately risen,
And the schoolmistress that passed on her way to the school..and the friendly boys
   that passed..and the quarrelsome boys..and the tidy and freshcheeked girls..
   and the barefoot negro boy and girl,
And all the changes of city and country wherever he went.

His own parents..he that had propelled the fatherstuff at night, and fathered him..
   and she that conceived him in her womb and birthed him....they gave this
   child more of themselves than that,
They gave him afterward every day....they and of them became part of him.

The mother at home quietly placing the dishes on the suppertable,
The mother with mild words....clean her cap and gown....a wholesome odor
   falling off her person and clothes as she walks by:
The father, strong, selfsufficient, manly, mean, angered, unjust,
The blow, the quick loud word, the tight bargain, the crafty lure,
The family usages, the language, the company, the furniture....the yearning and
   swelling heart,
Affection that will not be gainsayed....The sense of what is real....the thought
   if after all it should prove unreal,
The doubts of daytime and the doubts of nighttime...the curious whether and how,
Whether that which appears so is so....Or is it all flashes and specks?
Men and women crowding fast in the streets..if they are not flashes and specks
   what are they?
The streets themselves, and the facades of houses....the goods in the windows,
Vehicles..teams..the tiered wharves, and the huge crossing at the ferries;
The village on the highland seen from afar at sunset....the river between,
Shadows..aurcola and mist..light falling on roofs and gables of white or brown,
   three miles off,
The schooner near by sleepily dropping down the tide..the little boat slacktowed
   astern,
The hurrying tumbling waves and quickbroken crests and slapping;
The strata of colored clouds....the long bar of maroontint away solitary by
   itself....the spread of purity it lies motionless in,
The horizon's edge, the flying seacrow, the fragrance of saltmarsh and shoremud;
These became part of that child who went forth every day, and who now goes and
   will always go forth every day,
And these become of him or her that peruses them now.

Leaves of Grass.

[Who Learns My Lesson Complete]

WHO learns my lesson complete?
    Boss and journeyman and apprentice?....churchman and atheist?
The stupid and the wise thinker....parents and offspring....merchant and clerk
    and porter and customer....editor, author, artist and schoolboy?

Draw nigh and commence,
It is no lesson....it lets down the bars to a good lesson,
And that to another....and every one to another still.

The great laws take and effuse without argument,
I am of the same style, for I am their friend,
I love them quits and quits....I do not halt and make salaams.

I lie abstracted and hear beautiful tales of things and the reasons of things,
They are so beautiful I nudge myself to listen.

I cannot say to any person what I hear....I cannot say it to myself....it is
    very wonderful.

It is no little matter, this round and delicious globe, moving so exactly in its orbit
    forever and ever, without one jolt or the untruth of a single second;
I do not think it was made in six days, nor in ten thousand years, nor ten decillions
    of years,
Nor planned and built one thing after another, as an architect plans and builds a house.

I do not think seventy years is the time of a man or woman,
Nor that seventy millions of years is the time of a man or woman,
Nor that years will ever stop the existence of me or any one else.

Is it wonderful that I should be immortal? as every one is immortal,
I know it is wonderful....but my eyesight is equally wonderful....and how I was
    conceived in my mother's womb is equally wonderful,
And how I was not palpable once but am now....and was born on the last day of
    May 1819....and passed from a babe in the creeping trance of three summers
    and three winters to articulate and walk....are all equally wonderful.

And that I grew six feet high....and that I have become a man thirty-six years old
    in 1855....and that I am here anyhow — are all equally wonderful;
And that my soul embraces you this hour, and we affect each other without ever
    seeing each other, and never perhaps to see each other, is every bit as
    wonderful:
And that I can think such thoughts as these is just as wonderful,
And that I can remind you, and you think them and know them to be true is just as
    wonderful,

And that the moon spins round the earth and on with the earth is equally wonderful,
And that they balance themselves with the sun and stars is equally wonderful.

Come I should like to hear you tell me what there is in yourself that is not just as
    wonderful,
And I should like to hear the name of anything between Sunday morning and
    Saturday night that is not just as wonderful.

Leaves of Grass.

[Great Are the Myths]

G REAT are the myths....I too delight in them,
Great are Adam and Eve....I too look back and accept them;
Great the risen and fallen nations, and their poets, women, sages, inventors, rulers,
    warriors and priests.

Great is liberty! Great is equality! I am their follower,
Helmsmen of nations, choose your craft....where you sail I sail,
Yours is the muscle of life or death....yours is the perfect science....in you I
    have absolute faith.

Great is today, and beautiful,
It is good to live in this age....there never was any better.

Great are the plunges and throes and triumphs and falls of democracy,
Great the reformers with their lapses and screams,
Great the daring and venture of sailors on new explorations.

Great are yourself and myself,
We are just as good and bad as the oldest and youngest or any,
What the best and worst did we could do,
What they felt..do not we feel it in ourselves?
What they wished..do we not wish the same?

Great is youth, and equally great is old age....great are the day and night;
Great is wealth and great is poverty....great is expression and great is silence.

Youth large lusty and loving....youth full of grace and force and fascination,
Do you know that old age may come after you with equal grace and force and
    fascination?

Day fullblown and splendid....day of the immense sun, and action and ambition
    and laughter,
The night follows close, with millions of suns, and sleep and restoring darkness.

Wealth with the flush hand and fine clothes and hospitality:

But then the soul's wealth — which is candor and knowledge and pride and enfolding
   love:
Who goes for men and women showing poverty richer than wealth?

Expression of speech..in what is written or said forget not that silence is also
   expressive,
That anguish as hot as the hottest and contempt as cold as the coldest may be with-
   out words,
That the true adoration is likewise without words and without kneeling.

Great is the greatest nation..the nation of clusters of equal nations.

Great is the earth, and the way it became what it is,
Do you imagine it is stopped at this?....and the increase abandoned?
Understand then that it goes as far onward from this as this is from the times when
   it lay in covering waters and gases.

Great is the quality of truth in man,
The quality of truth in man supports itself through all changes,
It is inevitably in the man....He and it are in love, and never leave each other.

The truth in man is no dictum....it is vital as eyesight,
If there be any soul there is truth....if there be man or woman there is truth....
   If there be physical or moral there is truth,
If there be equilibrium or volition there is truth....if there be things at all upon the
   earth there is truth.

O truth of the earth! O truth of things! I am determined to press the whole way
   toward you,
Sound your voice! I scale mountains or dive in the sea after you.

Great is language....it is the mightiest of the sciences,
It is the fulness and color and form and diversity of the earth....and of men and
   women....and of all qualities and processes;
It is greater than wealth....it is greater than buildings or ships or religions or
   paintings or music.

Great is the English speech....What speech is so great as the English?
Great is the English brood....What brood has so vast a destiny as the English?
It is the mother of the brood that must rule the earth with the new rule,
The new rule shall rule as the soul rules, and as the love and justice and equality
   that are in the soul rule.

Great is the law....Great are the old few landmarks of the law....they are the
   same in all times and shall not be disturbed.

Great are marriage, commerce, newspapers, books, freetrade, railroads, steamers,
    international mails and telegraphs and exchanges.

Great is Justice;
Justice is not settled by legislators and laws....it is in the soul,
It cannot be varied by statutes any more than love or pride or the attraction of
    gravity can,
It is immutable..it does not depend on majorities....majorities or what not come
    at last before the same passionless and exact tribunal.

For justice are the grand natural lawyers and perfect judges....it is in their souls,
It is well assorted....they have not studied for nothing....the great includes the
    less,
They rule on the highest grounds....they oversee all eras and states and
    administrations,

The perfect judge fears nothing....he could go front to front before God,
Before the perfect judge all shall stand back....life and death shall stand back
    ....heaven and hell shall stand back.

Great is goodness;
I do not know what it is any more than I know what health is....but I know it is
    great.

Great is wickedness....I find I often admire it just as much as I admire good-
    ness:
Do you call that a paradox? It certainly is a paradox.

The eternal equilibrium of things is great, and the eternal overthrow of things is
    great,
And there is another paradox.

Great is life..and real and mystical..wherever and whoever,
Great is death....Sure as life holds all parts together, death holds all parts
    together;
Sure as the stars return again after they merge in the light, death is great as life.

Afterword

David S. Reynolds

The publication of Walt Whitman's *Leaves of Grass* in July 1855 was a landmark event in literary history. Ralph Waldo Emerson judged the book "the most extraordinary piece of wit and wisdom America has yet contributed," saying that it had "the best merits, namely, of fortifying and encouraging."[1] Many have seconded this opinion. Whitman himself, after years of expanding and revising *Leaves of Grass*, looked back fondly on the 1855 edition. He commented that it had "an immediateness, . . . an incisive directness," absent from other editions, adding: "We miss that ecstasy of statement in some of the after-work."[2]

One need not discount his later poetry in order to recognize the specialness of the first edition. This was the *original* Whitman; this was Whitman at his freshest and, arguably, his most experimental. Nothing like the volume had ever appeared before. Everything about it—the unusual jacket and title page, the exuberant preface, the twelve free-flowing, untitled poems embracing every realm of experience—was new.

The current volume celebrates the 150th anniversary of the 1855 edition by reproducing that volume much the way it originally appeared. Here approximated are the title page, typeface, page layout, and even the arrangement of the poetic lines, which wrap around where they did originally. It is useful for today's readers to get a full sense of what may be called the "ur-text" of *Leaves of Grass*, the first version of this historic volume, before it went through many revisions of both format and style.

We learn much about Whitman's initial intentions when we read his volume in its earliest form. Whitman, an ex-printer and newspaper editor, left nothing to chance in the production of his poetry volumes. Unlike most authors, he had a hand in every step of the publication process. "I like to supervise the production of my own books," he explained. "My theory is that the author might be the maker even of the body of his work—set the type, print the book on a press, put a cover on it, with his own hands: learning his trade from A to Z—all there is of it."[3]

He carried out this theory in putting together the 1855 edition, which he helped typeset. Having written scraps of poems for years—"without deliberation," he later said, "in the gush, the throb, the flood, of the moment"[4]—Whitman spent the early months of 1855 seeing his volume through publication in Brooklyn, where he walked daily from his small frame house on Prince Street to the redbrick printing office of the Scottish immigrants Andrew and James Rome on the corner of Cranberry and Fulton streets. Sitting on a stool near a corner table, Whitman wrote careful instructions about particulars of the volume: its overall structure, the order of the poems, the estimated page length, and so forth. Some of these instructions he later ignored—for instance, he abandoned his original plan of including the picture of a ship at sail—but most of them he followed.

The volume's physical layout suggested his interest in attracting as wide an audience as possible. As his journalism shows, he was aware that the American public feasted on two main kinds of literature: the sentimental-domestic genre, produced largely by women writers and by the Fireside Poets; and sensational writings, ranging from penny newspapers to yellow-covered pamphlet novels. The former genre, often elegantly produced, was designed for the parlor. The latter, produced cheaply and crudely, was hawked on the sidewalks and in street-corner bookstalls.

Whitman evidently designed the 1855 edition to appeal to both audiences. The ornate jacket—dark green with an inlaid design, stamped gold lettering, gold borders, and marbled end papers inside—was aimed at the parlor-table readership. He once commented, "People as a rule like to open books on center tables, in parlors, and so on and so on."[5] His benign title, *Leaves of Grass*, reflected, among other things, this desire to make it into the middle-class parlor. Elegantly bound volume of "leaves" were very popular: there had been Mary A. Spooner's *Gathered Leaves* (1848), Meta V. Fuller's *Leaves from Nature* (1852), and, most notably, Fanny Fern's *Fern Leaves from Fanny's Portfolio* (1853), which sold more than 100,000 copies.

But *Leaves of Grass* was a parlor-table book with a difference. Its exterior announced elegance, but its interior radiated utter democracy and rough simplicity. Opening the volume, one met a stripped-down title page, with "Leaves of Grass" in large black letters, "Brooklyn, New York: 1855" below it, and the picture of the casually dressed Whitman opposite. Then came the double-column preface and the twelve untitled poems, presented with typographical simplicity, almost primitivism. If the jacket was designed for the parlor, the interior had resonances of the street. Whitman would say that he found democracy only in "the cheap mass-papers," and the typeface of the first edition gave it a newspaper look.[6]

Whitman expected a large readership: even after the first edition had failed to sell well, he wrote to Emerson (included in this volume) that soon there would be a demand for tens of thousands of copies, "more, quite likely."[7] He tried to gain a wide following by dissolving boundaries between competing readerships and between many cultural and social currents. In his effort to challenge boundaries, he sacrificed normal punctuation. Through the preface and much of the poetry he used ellipses instead of commas, periods, or semicolons. Lines never seemed to stop but flowed onward without interruption. Sometimes punctuation was dropped altogether. The interblending of cultural levels was syntactically enforced, for instance, by his statement in the preface that "the anatomist chemist astronomer geologist phrenologist spiritualist mathematician historian and lexicographer are not poets, but they are the lawgivers of poets and their construction underlies the structure of every perfect poem."[8] The correctly placed comma here (Whitman actually was very careful about punctuation) only highlights the all-fusing absence of commas earlier in the phrase.

What motivated Whitman to dissolve cultural boundaries in an effort to attract various audiences? He concluded his preface with the declaration, "The proof of a poet is that his country absorbs him as affectionately as he has absorbed it."[9] Where did this desire for complete absorption by his country come from?

Whitman, who once called *Leaves of Grass* "the new Bible," had a messianic view of himself as poetic Answerer come to heal American society. By absorbing and magnifying his culture's best aspects, he believed his poetry could help unify a nation fractured by class conflict and the debate over slavery. The poet, he wrote in his preface, "is the equalizer of his age and land . . . he supplies what wants supplying and checks what wants checking." He offered a recipe for healing: "This is what you shall do . . . read these leaves in the open air every season of every year of your life."

Few of the early readers of the 1855 edition, however, were prepared to follow this advice. Perhaps no work published with such high expectations has ever met so poor a popular reception. The twenty-three known reviews of the first edition, along with Emerson's letter, are reprinted at the end of this volume. As can be seen, with the exception of Emerson's, responses to the book were mixed, sometimes venomous. The book was branded as "a mass of stupid filth" (Rufus Griswold), "reckless and indecent" (Charles A. Dana), "a farrago of rubbish, . . . like the ravings of a drunkard" (*Dublin Review*), "one of the strangest compounds of transcendentalism, bombast, philosophy, folly, wisdom, wit and dullness which it ever entered into the heart of man to conceive" (*Brooklyn Daily Eagle*).[10]

In the face of such attacks, Whitman did what he could to promote his book. He published it in two revised formats within the first six months: one a simplified version of the first edition and the other an inexpensive paperback in pink or light-green paper wrappers. Using his contacts in the press, he published anonymously three long, glowing reviews in periodicals friendly to him. (These self-reviews are included in the Appendix along with the other reviews.) "An American bard at last!" he exclaimed in his first review. "Was he not needed?" he asked, then provided the answer: "You have come in good time, Walt Whitman!"[11] In his other reviews he expanded on the idea that *Leaves of Grass* was a thoroughly American work in which the nation could find itself transformed and improved. Without Emerson's permission, he tactlessly had the Concord sage's letter printed in the *New York Tribune* and put one of Emerson's comments—"I greet you at the beginning of a great career"[12]— on the spine of the 1856 edition.

Privately, however, Whitman was appalled by the poor reception of the volume. In a note he spoke of "Depressions/Every thing I have done seems to me blank and suspicious."[13] In old age, perhaps to highlight his late-won celebrity, he actually exaggerated the negative response to the first edition. "It was tragic—the fate of those books," he said later of the various states of the edition. "None of them were sold— practically none—perhaps one or two, perhaps not even that many."[14] "Nobody would have 'em," he lamented, "for gift or price: nobody: some even returned their copies— editors—others."

The fact that today the 1855 *Leaves of Grass* is widely regarded as the most important American poetry volume ever published and has become a collector's item (a copy was recently offered online for $650,000 by a dealer in rare books) attests to the importance of the volume. The 1855 edition broke ground in many ways: in its relaxed yet heightened style, which prefigured free verse; in its sexual candor; in its images of racial bonding and democratic togetherness; in its philosophical suggestions; in the brash self-confidence of its first-person persona; and in its passionate affirmation of the sanctity of the physical world.

Leaves of Grass was published at the height of the literary period now known as the American Renaissance, which also produced the classics of Melville, Hawthorne, Poe, Dickinson, Thoreau, and Emerson.

Of these writers, only Emerson aroused Whitman's unalloyed enthusiasm. Whitman had once briefly reviewed one of Melville's early novels for a newspaper, but his reaction to Melville's major fiction, if any, is unknown. Understandably, he was unaware of Dickinson, only a handful of whose works were published in her (and his) lifetime. For her part, Dickinson, when asked in 1862 if she had read Whitman's poetry, replied that she hadn't "but was told he was disgraceful."[15] Whitman conceded that Poe was "a star of considerable magnitude" but called him "morbid, shadowy, lugubrious," associated with "abnormal beauty—the sickliness of all technical thought—the abnegation of the perennial or democratic concretes at first hand."[16]

Hawthorne, in Whitman's view, was a "consummate" stylist but finally "monotonous," lacking in experimentation; also, his indifference about slavery made Whitman dismiss him as "a devil of a Copperhead."[17] Whitman saw a healthy "lawlessness" in Thoreau, whom he called "one of the native forces," but was disturbed by what he called Thoreau's "superciliousness," his "disdain for men (for Tom, Dick, and Harry)."[18]

Emerson was a different story. It is fair to say that if Emerson had not been on the cultural scene, *Leaves of Grass* would not have appeared, or, if it had, it would have been a very different volume than it was. Whitman's famous statement to the author John Townsend Trowbridge—"I was simmering, simmering, simmering; Emerson brought me to a boil"—has a ring of truth to it.[19] Reportedly Whitman in the early 1850s took Emerson's essays in his lunch pail when he went off to his carpentry work in Brooklyn. If so, he was manifesting a fascination with Emerson that had dated at least from the mid-1840s, when he glowingly reviewed an Emerson lecture in the *Brooklyn Daily Eagle*.

Emerson's influence permeates the first edition of *Leaves of Grass*. Emerson's insistence on self-reliance and nonconformity is reflected in Whitman's cocksure persona, whose first words are, "I celebrate myself." Emerson's assurance that it is fine to contradict oneself is echoed in Whitman's statement: "Do I contradict myself?/ Very well then . . . . I contradict myself;/ I am large . . . . I contain multitudes."[20] Emerson's belief in the miraculous beauty of even the most ordinary features of the natural world is echoed in Whitman's paeans to grass spears, a mouse, a morning-glory, to name some of the everyday wonders he mentions. Emerson's dismissal of organized religion and his simultaneous admiration of the spirit behind all religions are matched by Whitman's panreligious, ecumenical attitude. Whitman's loosely rhythmic, prose-like lines answered Emerson's caveat, "It is not metres, but a metre-making argument, that makes a poem,—a thought so passionate and alive that, like the spirit of a plant or an animal, it has an architecture of its own, and adorns nature with a new thing."[21] Whitman also fits Emerson's description of the thoroughly democratic poet, surveying with a "tyrannous eye" American life in its dazzling diversity.

Whitman captured this diversity to a degree that even Emerson could not have foreseen. When Emerson first read *Leaves of Grass*, he wondered about its "long foreground."[22] Whitman later would say that it was "useless to attempt reading the book without first carefully tallying that preparatory background."[23]

A way to begin exploring that background is to look at the early draft of some of the verses that survive in a Whitman manuscript dating from the late 1840s or the early 50s. Each page of the soiled manuscript has, on one side, a hand-written draft of lines that would go into the opening poem (later "Song of Myself") and, on the other, jottings about the structure and design of the whole volume.

The manuscript suggests Whitman's original intentions. In it Whitman scribbled working titles for the twelve poems, though he discarded them in the published version. The titles were generally based on the first lines of the poems (e.g., "A child went forth" and "I wander all night"). The most significant title was "Slaves," which Whitman assigned to the poem that later became "I Sing the Body Electric." Not only did Whitman feature slavery in the provisional title, but also he planned to give the poem added importance by placing it at the very end of the volume, as though it was his last word. Although he changed its position in the final arrangement, when we know the original title we see in sharp focus the political force of its lines describing the humanity and nobility of the auctioned slave: "There swells and jets his heart . . . . There all passions and desires . . all reachings and aspirations:/ [...]In him the start of populous states and rich republics."[24]

These words proclaimed that African Americans were fully human, just like whites—a radical message for Whitman's day. Escaping the racism that pervaded white society, Whitman emphasized the humanity of African Americans throughout the 1855 edition. The opening poem contains a long passage in which the "I" takes an escaped slave into his house and washes and feeds him, keeping his rifle ready at the door to fend off possible pursuers. In another passage he actually becomes "the hounded slave," with dogs and men in bloody pursuit. In a third he admires a magnificent black driver, climbing up with him and driving alongside of him. Such passages help explain why his poetry has won favor among African American readers, such as the Abolitionist lecturer Sojourner Truth and the Harlem Renaissance writer Langston Hughes.

Despite Whitman's sympathetic identification with blacks, the 1855 edition shows his effort to embrace not only slaves but also their white owners. Here again the manuscript draft is telling. Among Whitman's handwritten verses were these:

I am the poet of slaves,
  and of the masters of slaves [. . .]

The I go with the slaves of the earth are mine and
The equally with the masters are equally [illegible]
And I will stand between
the masters and the slaves,
  And I Entering into both, and
so that both shall understand
  me alike.[25]

These lines reflect Whitman's moderate position on slavery. On the one hand, he opposed slavery and wanted it to end. On the other hand, he was suspicious of Abolitionism, which he saw as a divisive force that threatened to divide the Union. In the *Eagle* Whitman had called the Abolitionists "foolish red-hot fanatics," an "angry-voiced and silly set."[26] He hated the nullification doctrines of Southern fire-eaters as much as he did the disunionism of the Abolitionists. As editor of the *Brooklyn Daily Eagle* he explained, "Despising and condemning the dangerous and fanatical insanity of 'Abolitionism'—as impracticable as it is wild—the Brooklyn *Eagle* just as much condemns the other extreme from that."[27]

Whitman's solution to the problem of impending disunion was to launch a loving poetic persona who embraced both the North and the South, one who announced a willingness to "stand between the masters and slaves" and "enter into" them as a conciliating presence. In a poem he proclaimed himself "A southerner soon as a northerner, a planter nonchalant and hospitable,/ [. . .] At home on the hills of Vermont or in the woods of Maine or the Texan ranch."[28] In the 1855 preface he assures his readers that the American poet shall "not be for the eastern states more than the western or the northern states more than the southern."[29]

Another social issue addressed in the manuscript drafts and echoed in the 1855 edition was the growing gap between the rich and the poor. America's emerging capitalist economy, unregulated by sound fiscal policy, lurched through boom-and-bust cycles marked by economic panics causing widespread unemployment and working-class resentment against the rich. Social-protest novels by George Lippard and others explored dark "mysteries" of American cities, picturing an idle, pampered "upper ten" as the enemy of the destitute "lower million."

Whitman in his poetry championed the latter. He had emerged from a working-class background. His father had struggled to stay afloat financially as a carpenter and real-estate speculator in Brooklyn. Walt himself drifted through low-paying jobs as a schoolteacher, journalist, newspaper editor, owner of a small stationery store, and carpenter. A city saunterer, he befriended workers and street people. He wanted to give voice to this neglected, oppressed working class. Hence these lines in the manuscript:

> I will not descend among
> professors and capitalists,
> ~~and good society~~ — I will
> turn ~~up~~ the ends of my
> trowsers up around my boots,
> and my cuffs back from
> my wrists and go ~~among~~ with
> ~~the simple~~ drivers and
> boatmen and men ~~who~~ that
> catch fish or ~~hoe corn~~ work in the field.
> I know ~~that~~ they are
> sublime

This working-class perspective governed the 1855 edition. In the preface he sounded like Karl Marx or George Lippard when he instructed readers to "despise riches, give alms to every one that asks, . . . devote your income and labor to others, hate tyrants."[30] In another he jibed a scheming capitalist: "The head of the moneymaker that plotted all day sleeps,/ And the enraged and treacherous dispositions sleep." Elsewhere he repeated the popular charge that the idle rich cruelly appropriated the products of the hard-working poor:

> Many sweating and ploughing and thrashing, and then the chaff for payment
>   receiving,
> A few idly owning, and they the wheat continually claiming.

Whitman does more than express working-class views in the 1855 edition; he actually *inhabits* the working-class sensibility familiar to him from New York street culture. In a draft of a poem he wrote that he alone sang "the young man of Mannahatta, the celebrated rough."[31] In one of the published poems he wrote, "Already a nonchalant breed, silently emerging, appears on the streets," describing the type elsewhere as "Arrogant, masculine, naive, rowdyish/ [. . .]Attitudes lithe and erect, costume free, neck open, of slow movement on foot."[32]

Whitman patterned his 1855 persona after such young men. His memorable frontispiece, showing him grizzled and standing in rumpled, everyday clothes—with shirt open, hand on hip, and head tilted casually—brandished his working-class sympathies. When in the opening poem he describes himself as "Disorderly fleshy and sensual . . . . eating drinking and breeding," he is not giving an accurate account of himself.[33] In real life, he was not disorderly but, by and large, placid. He was not known for overindulgence in "eating drinking." As for "breeding," he did not have children.

If the persona's unrestrained machismo says little about Whitman, it character-ized a roistering type he observed on city streets, the "b'hoy," also called the Bowery Boy or the loafer. The b'hoy was typically a butcher or other worker who spent after-hours running to fires with engines, going on target excursions, or promenading on the Bowery with his "g'hal." The b'hoy clipped his hair short in back, kept his long sidelocks heavily greased with soap (hence his sobriquet "soap-locks"), and perched a stove-pipe hat jauntily on his head. He often had a cigar or chaw of tobacco in his mouth. When featured as a character in popular plays and novels, the b'hoy became a larger-than-life American figure who was irrepressibly pugnacious and given to violent escapades.

Whitman mingled with the workers who made up the b'hoy population. He later recalled going to plays on the Bowery, and "the young shipbuilders, cartmen, butch-ers, firemen (the old-time 'soap-lock' or exaggerated 'Mose' or 'Sikesey,' of Chanfrau's plays,) they, too, were always to be seen in these audiences, racy of the East River and the Dry Dock."[34] In his book on language, *An American Primer*, he recorded several slang expressions used by "the New York Bowery Boy" and praised "the splendid and rugged characters that are forming among these states, or have already formed,—in the cities, the firemen of Mannahatta, and the target excursionist, and Bowery Boy."[35]

One of his goals as a poet was to capture the vitality and defiance of the b'hoy:

> The boy I love, the same becomes a man not through derived
>   power but in his own right,
> Wicked, rather than virtuous out of conformity or fear,
> Fond of his sweetheart, relishing well his steak [. . .]
> Preferring scars and the beard and faces pitted with smallpox over all
>   latherers and those that keep out of the sun.[36]

Whitman's feisty persona, prone to slang and vigorous outbursts, reflected the b'hoy culture, as contemporary readers noted. The very first review placed Whitman in the "class of society sometimes irreverently styled 'loafers.'"[37] Another reviewer declared that Whitman "would well answer equally for a 'Bowery boy,' one of the 'killers,' 'Mose' in the play, 'Bill Sykes after the murder of Nancy,' or the 'B'hoy that runs with the engine,'" adding, "Walt Whitman is evidently the 'representative man' of the 'roughs.'"[38] Another opined that his poems reflected "the extravagance, coarse-ness, and general 'loudness' of Bowery boys," with also their candor and acceptance of the body. Other reviewers referred to him simply as "Walt Whitman the b'hoy poet" and "the 'Bowery Bhoy' in literature."[39]

Some, however, realized that Whitman was a rough with a difference. A reviewer for *Life Illustrated* called him "a *perfect loafer*; yet a thoughtful loafer, an amiable loafer, an able loafer," adding, "The book, perhaps, might be called, American Life, from a Poetical Loafer's Point of View."[40] Charles Eliot Norton in *Putnam's* charac-terized Whitman as "a compound of the New England transcendentalist and the New

York rowdy."[41] The New York *Daily News* chimed in: "Sometimes he is 'Mose'; sometimes almost a Moses."[42]

Actually, Whitman's poems presented an improved version of street types whose tendencies to violence and vulgarity he frowned upon. One of the constant themes of his journalism was that rowdiness and bad habits were all too common among the street toughs of New York and Brooklyn. "Rowdyism Rampant" was the title of an alarmed piece in which he denounced the "law-defying loafers who make the fights, and disturb the public peace"; he prophesied that "some day decent folks will take the matter into their own hands and put down, with a strong will, this rum-swilling, rampant set of rowdies and roughs."[43]

Appalled by squalid forms of urban loafing, he outlined new forms of loafing in his poems. "Walt Whitman, an American, one of the roughs, a kosmos"[44]: this famous self-description in "Song of Myself" uplifts the rough by placing him near words that radiate patriotism ("an American") and mysticism ("a kosmos"). Purposely in his poems Whitman shuttled back and forth between the grimy and the spiritual with the aim of cleansing the quotidian types that sometimes disturbed him.

This improving strategy also governed his response to the political scene. The 1850s was a decade of unprecedented political corruption, a time of vote-buying, wire-pulling, graft, and patronage on all levels of state and national government. The chaos created by the slavery debate caused the collapse of the party system. The Whig Party splintered and disappeared in the early fifties, and the Democratic Party realigned itself around the pro-Southern position. Antislavery groups remained fractious and disunited, even after they gathered under the Republican Party in 1854.

Whitman's disgust with political corruption was more profound than that of any other commentator of the fifties. In his political pamphlet "The Eighteenth Presidency!" he wrote that the parties had become "empty flesh, putrid mouths, mumbling and squeaking the tones of these conventions, the politicians standing back in the shadow, telling lies."[45] Using slashing Gothic imagery, he wrote that many of America's political leaders came "from political hearses, and from the coffins inside, and from the shrouds inside the coffins; from the tumors and abscesses of the land; from the skeletons and skulls in the vaults of the federal almshouses; from the running sores of the great cities."

His wrath against governmental authority figures extended to presidents. The administrations of Millard Fillmore, Franklin Pierce, and James Buchanan eroded his confidence in the executive office. Whitman branded the three presidencies before Lincoln as "our topmost warning and shame," saying they illustrated "how the weakness and wickedness of rulers are just as eligible here in America under republican, as in Europe under dynastic influences." Whitman lambasted the "doughfaced" Pierce, who was from the North but leaned to the South, in scatological metaphors: "The President eats dirt and excrement for his daily meals, likes it, and tries to force it on The States. The cushions of the Presidency are nothing but filth and blood. The pavements of Congress are also bloody."

Whitman's bleak view of contemporary politics is visible throughout the 1855 edition. In the preface he impugns the "swarms of cringers, suckers, doughfaces, lice of politics, planners of sly involutions for their own preferment to city offices or state legislatures or the judiciary or congress or the presidency."[46] Two poems in the volume excoriate political authority. One, later called "A Boston Ballad," recreates a notorious instance of governmental malfeasance: the May 1854 rendition of the black fugitive Anthony Burns to slavery under the guard of federal troops. The tyranny and corruption of the proslavery government are dramatized by the ghosts of alarmed Revolutionary patriots who follow the Burns procession and then, in savage anger, fly to England, exhume the bones of King George, carry them to Boston, and reconstruct the tyrant's skeleton to be put on display as a mock idol for the "President's marshal," "the roarers of Congress," and "the government cannon" to protect. Another politically charged piece in the volume, a revised version of his earlier poem "Resurgemus," lamented the failure of the European revolutions of 1848. Whitman recalls the working class "springing suddenly out of its stale and drowsy lair, the lair of slaves,/ [. . .] Its hands tight to the throats of kings."

As regrettable as was the situation in Europe, Whitman thought it was even worse in America, which had failed to live up to its own ideals. "Of all nations the United States . . . most need poets." *Why* did America need them? Because it preached human equality but enslaved nearly four million African Americans, treated the poor unjustly, and discriminated against people of different ethnicities and religions. Although it was a democracy, rampant corruption often negated the votes of the people.

There were reform groups that addressed such problems—the women's rights movement, labor reform, Abolition, and so on—but Whitman shied away from them because he found them divisive and extreme. He advised, "Be radical, be radical, be radical—be not too damned radical."[47] With all his sympathy for the oppressed, he had a conservative side that stemmed mainly from his undying devotion to the American Union. His hatred of disunionists extended to all "ultraist" reformers, whose extreme stances, he feared, threatened to rip apart America's fragile social fabric.

In the 1855 edition of *Leaves of Grass* he did what he could to repair this fabric. One of his strategies was healing by fiat. Throughout the volume he makes ringing declarations about America and the power of poets, as though social ills could be cured through passionate affirmation. "The union always surrounded by blatherers and always calm and impregnable"[48]—a statement of willed optimism on the part of a writer who saw all too vividly the social tensions that within six years would divide the Union and bring about the bloodiest war in its history.

The poet, in this idealized view, was as "calm and impregnable" as the nation. If presidents were failing America, poets were ready to come to the rescue. He said of the states: "Their Presidents shall not be their common referee so much as their poets shall."

No matter that privately Whitman faced severe family difficulties: the pathetic condition of his younger brother Eddy, retarded since birth; the decline of his possibly alcoholic father, who died shortly before *Leaves of Grass* came out; the marriage of his sister Hannah to a neurotic Vermont artist, Charles Heyde, whom Walt later called "a skunk—a bug, . . . the bed-buggiest man on earth";[49] early signs of mental instability of his older brother Jesse, whom Walt eventually committed to the Kings County Lunatic Asylum; and, perhaps worst of all, the indifference of the whole family (including the "normal" siblings, Jeff, George, and Mary) to his poetic pursuits. "No one of my people," as he put it, appreciated his volume; even his beloved mother was "dead set against the book," viewing it "as a curio of sort."

His private pain notwithstanding, Whitman portrayed the poet as imperturbable in the 1855 edition. He wrote, "Of all mankind the great poet is the equable man. Not in him but off from him things are grotesque or eccentric or fail of their sanity [. . . .] He bestows on every object or quality its fit proportions neither more nor less. He is the arbiter of the diverse and he is the key. He is the equalizer of his age and land."[50]

In his poems he *was* the equalizer of his age and land. The twelve poems of the 1855 edition were a kind of democratic utopia, a place where equality and tolerance were genuine. People of all classes, ethnicities, creeds, and localities came together in Whitman's sweeping, egalitarian vision.

One of his chief democratizing devices was the catalog: the long string of disparate images linked by parallel wording or rhythm. The catalogs forged linguistically a true democracy, one in which all distinctions and boundaries were dissolved. By juxtaposing the president and the prostitute, the lawyer and the prisoner, the white capitalist and the black slave, the Christian and the pagan and the atheist, Whitman reminded readers of every kind that they were linked by a common humanity that made social distinctions artificial.

The crisp images of Whitman's catalogs owed much to the new medium of the daguerreotype, which had been introduced by the Frenchman Louis-Jacques-Mandé Daguerre in 1839 and which achieved a popularity in America unmatched abroad. Whitman once said, "In these *Leaves* [*of Grass*] every thing is literally photographed. Nothing is poeticized."[51] Photography's ability to capture reality was for Whitman its chief attraction. He declared: "The photograph has this advantage: it lets nature have its way: the botheration with the painters is that they don't want nature to have its way."[52] Many moments in the catalogs show Whitman "photographing" scenes from daily life, as though his poetic "I" were a kind of roving camera eye aimed at the world around him.

His democratic portraits of average life were also influenced by the American paintings he loved. An active member of the Brooklyn Art Union, where he befriended many painters, he became so caught up in New York's art-gallery scene that he once wrote a poem, "Pictures," that described his own head as "a little house," in which he kept "many pictures hanging suspended—/ . . . hundreds and thousands,— all the varieties."[53]

Most of the painters he admired strove for a spiritualized realism, one that accorded at once with Whitman's earthly and religious sides. The art exhibits Whitman frequented were filled with life-affirming, nature-affirming works of the Hudson River school and luminist canvases by Fitz Hugh Lane, Frederick Edwin Church, and others. In a magazine article Whitman emphasized "the refining and conservative influence of the fine arts" on society, insisting that "the very stability of good government and the well being of society rest on no surer foundation than when it is cemented by these ties that bind all men in one bond of sentiment and feeling kindled by the admiration excited within them at the glories of art."[54] In the 1855 preface he labeled "a nuisance and revolt" anything that "distorts honest shapes," specifying that in paintings or illustrations or sculptures Americans "shall receive no pleasure from violations of natural models and must not permit them."[55]

In his poems he borrowed from specific paintings. The artistic school he usually tapped was genre painting. American genre painters looked to hearty outdoor types— farmers, hunters, trappers, riverboatmen—portrayed good-humoredly engaged in some form of leisurely, often prankish activity. One whose work Whitman knew well, the Missouri painter George Caleb Bingham, produced popular genre studies of frontier types such as *The Flatboatmen* (1846), which featured a vernacular treatment of frolicking flatboatmen echoed in Whitman's vignettes like these: "The flatboatmen make fast toward dusk near the cottonwood or pekantrees,/ The coon-seekers go now through the regions of the Red river, or through those drained by the Tennessee, or through those of the Arkansas."[56] Whitman reproduced the main scene and characters of Bingham's painting *Shooting for the Beef* (1850) in these lines:

> The western turkey-shooting draws old and young . . . . some lean on their rifles, some sit on logs,
> Out from the crowd steps the marksman and takes his position and levels his piece.

Genre painting was one of the few public arenas in which Indians and blacks were treated with less of the overt racism that permeated nearly every aspect of American society. The humanization of minorities in American art had a strong influence on Whitman. The section of "Song of Myself" picturing the marriage of the trapper and the Indian woman was based on *The Trapper's Bride*, the popular 1837 painting by the Baltimore artist Alfred Jacob Miller. Another of Whitman's scenes of racial harmony, the opening poem about the African American team driver, had precedent in the genre paintings of the Long Island artist William Sidney Mount, whose work Whitman had favorably reviewed as a journalist. Whitman found in Mount an artist who depicted blacks possessing nobility and humanity. Particularly suggestive among Mount's paintings in terms of Whitman's portrayal of blacks is *Farmer's Nooning* (1835), in which a black farmer, highlighted by the sunlight and by his central position among the others, dominates the scene. Whitman evokes a similar spirit in his passage about the black team driver who stands "calm and commanding" on his wagon, his "polished and perfect limbs" gleaming in the sun.

The democracy of Whitman's poems extends beyond the abolishing social and racial barriers to a proclamation of a democratic process in nature itself. Nature becomes a key unifying factor for Whitman. His title, *Leaves of Grass*, not only referred to the "leaves" (pages) of his volume but also brought attention to the earth's most basic form of vegetation, grass. Grass was comprised of individual sprouts that could be admired on their own, as Whitman's persona does when he declares, "I lean and loafe at my ease . . . . observing a spear of summer grass." Also, grass was the earth's ultimate symbol of democracy and human togetherness, for it grew everywhere. As Whitman writes, "Sprouting alike in broad zones and narrow zones,/ Growing among black folks as among white,/ Kanuck, Tuckahoe, Congressman, Cuff, I give them the same, I receive them the same."

Grass also represented nature's eternal cycle of decay and rebirth. Whitman was indebted to contemporary scientists such as the Stockholm chemist Justus Liebig, whose book *Chemistry in Its Application to Physiology and Agriculture* Whitman praised in the *Brooklyn Daily Eagle*. Liebig gave the idea of the cycle of nature validity through the study of transferred chemical compounds. There seemed to be an ongoing resurrection and a democratic exchange of substances inherent in nature. Just as Liebig wrote that "the active state of the atoms of one body has an influence upon the atoms of a body in contact with it," so Whitman announced in the second line of his opening poem that "every atom belonging to me as good belongs to you."[57] If Liebig envisaged an exchange of life forms through decomposition and regrowth, so Whitman fashioned metaphors that vivified the idea of the ceaseless springing of life from death. "Tenderly will I use you curling grass,/ It may be you transpire from the breasts of young men."[58] "The smallest sprout shows there is really no death." "And as to you Corpse I think you are good manure."

Religion and philosophy helped address some of the larger questions left unanswered by science. Whitman generalized that from the start in his poetry "one deep purpose underlay the others, and has underlain it and its execution ever since—and that has been the religious purpose." The poet, in his words, was the "divine literatus" who replaced the priest.[59] America, he constantly stressed, could be rescued from materialism and infidelity only by literature that pointed to the spiritual and moral. He clung to a faith in immortality. "I am not prepared," he told his follower Horace Traubel, "to admit fraud in the scheme of the universe—yet without immortality all would be sham and sport of the most tragic nature."[60] Whitman's Brooklyn friend Helen Price found his "leading characteristic" to be "the *religious sentiment* or feeling. It pervades and dominates his life."[61]

Whitman observed with interest American Protestantism, which was spread by a vigorous, lively brand of preaching that made use of slang and humor, as popularized by two of Whitman's favorite clergymen, the sailors' preacher Edward Thompson Taylor and Brooklyn's Henry Ward Beecher. Participating in the revolution in popular religious style, Whitman coined imaginative religious images in *Leaves of Grass* that in turn fed back into popular religion. Some of them—such as the line "I find letters from God dropped in the street, and every one is signed by God's name"[62]— were picked up by Beecher, the era's leading preacher. Whitman called Beecher "a great absorber of Leaves of Grass," and he said he sometimes met people who, having just heard Beecher preach, told him that "his whole sermon was you, you, you, from top to toe."[63]

In promoting religion in his poetry, Whitman could sound much like a nineteenth-century showman peddling wares: "Magnifying and applying come I,/ Outbidding at the start the old cautious hucksters," as he went on to review all the world religions and then proclaim the miraculous nature of the everyday world.[64] He was conscious from the start about writing a supposedly inspired text. His religious mission was made clear in the 1855 preface, in which he said of the poet, "The time straying toward infidelity and confections and persiflage he withholds by his steady faith."

His religious themes were influenced by two allied popular religious movements, Swedenborgianism and Harmonialism. In a newspaper article he declared that the Swedish mystic Emanuel Swedenborg would have "the deepest and broadest mark upon the religions of future ages here, of any man that ever walked the earth."[65] Like Emerson he found appealing Swedenborg's doctrine of correspondences, which held that every material thing had a spiritual counterpart, or "ultimate." Swedenborg's mysticism was inherently body-specific, as believers thought that the "divine breath," also called the "influx" or "afflatus," was taken in from the spiritual atmosphere through the lungs, which in turn emanated an "efflux" of its own into the atmosphere. Whitman's "I" calls himself the "Partaker of influx and efflux" and declares: "Through me the afflatus surging and surging . . . . through me the current and index."[66] Swedenborg suggested to Whitman how the erotic and the mystical were linked. Whitman told Traubel, "I think Swedenborg was right when he said there was a close connection—a very close connection—between the state we call religious ecstasy and the desire to copulate."[67]

This cultural background of erotic mysticism casts light on the section in "Song of Myself" in which the "I" describes lying with his soul on the grass on a transparent summer morning. The passage begins with a religious statement—"I believe in you my soul"—and leads through rapturous union to an affirmation of the peace and joy and love of God's universe.[68] If Swedenborgians could describe union with God as reception of the divine breath through the head or the chest, so Whitman could imagine the soul plunging its "tongue" to the "barestript heart" and spreading until it embraced the beard and feet.

His treatment of religious matters also had precedent in the Harmonial movement led by the famous "Poughkeepsie Seer," Andrew Jackson Davis, whom Whitman discussed at length with friends. While in a trance state, Davis could accomplish apparently miraculous things, such as reading books through walls, peering inside people's bodies to spot hidden diseases, and traveling mentally to distant places and times, which he called traveling clairvoyance.

Whitman participated in the trend of Harmonial mysticism. In a notebook entry of the period he wrote, "I am in a mystic trance exultation/ Something wild and untamed— half savage."[69] In a later entry he described being "in a trance, yet with all senses alert" and with "the objective world suspended or surmounted for a while, & the powers in exaltation, freedom, vision."[70]

The first edition of *Leaves of Grass* is filled with his versions of traveling clairvoyance. A prominent feature of his poems is their constant shuttling between different times and places. He outdid even Davis in his adventurous gamboling with time and space. He writes: "My ties and ballasts leave me . . . . I travel . . . . I sail . . . . my elbows rest in the sea-gaps,/ I skirt the sierras . . . . my palms cover continents,/ I am afoot with my vision."[71] If the trance writers mentally traversed history and space, so Whitman jumped rapidly between historical events (e.g., "Walking the old hills of Judea with the beautiful gentle God at my side") and distant places ("Speeding through space . . . . speeding through heaven and the stars").

The magnetic "I" at the heart of Whitman's poetry was the ideal Harmonial person, always ready to be absorbed into the mass but always himself—and, above all, in balance. Both spiritually and physically, the "I" is a Harmonial healer. He reassures us that life is "not chaos or death . . . . it is form and union and plan." "I shall be good health to you," he announces, "And filter and fibre your blood." In the poem later called "The Sleepers" the soothing "I" has all the capacities of a Harmonial healer and life-affirmer. The poem moves through disease and social disorder to a sense of Harmonial peace.

It is not surprising, however, that it was the disordered, sometimes bizarre qualities of Whitman's verse that caught the eye of some reviewers, like one who noted that sometimes he ran toward chaos in rhapsodic time-space flights, "as in the rigmarole of trance-speaking mediums, and we are threatened on every hand with a period of mere suggestion in poetry, mere protest against order, and kicking at the old limits of time, space, the horizon, and the sky."[72]

Reviewers inclined to accept the new mystical movements, on the other hand, felt comfortable with Whitman's religious vision. The leading Harmonial journal of the 1850s, the *Christian Spiritualist*, gave a long review of the first edition of *Leaves of Grass*, declaring that it was one of the modern "varieties of Mediumship," "a sign of the times, written as we perceive, under powerful influxes; a prophecy and promise of much that awaits all who are entering with us into the opening doors of a new era."[73]

The distinctive emotional voice of Whitman's poetry was shaped by the performance cultures of acting and music. When Whitman said he spent his young manhood "absorbing theatres at every pore" and seeing "everything, high, low, middling," he revealed his complete identification with the carnivalized culture of antebellum

America.[74] He was especially moved by actors who displayed an intense kind of emotionalism that defined the "American" acting style. The greatest exponent of this style was Junius Brutus Booth, Whitman's favorite actor and the leading tragedian of antebellum America. "His genius," said Whitman, "was to me one of the grandest revelations of my life, a lesson of artistic expression."[75] "He had much to do with shaping me in those early years," he added.

The aspect of Booth that most impressed Whitman was his powerful expression. "I demand that my whole emotional nature be powerfully stirred," Whitman generalized about acting.[76] No one could satisfy this craving more than Booth, who was a key figure in the development of the new acting style. Whitman explained, "The words fire, energy, *abandon*, found in him unprecedented meanings."[77] It was the peaks for which he became known. "When he was in a passion," Whitman wrote, "face, neck, hands, would be suffused, his eye would be frightful—his whole mien enough to scare audience, actors; often the actors *were* afraid of him."[78]

In several senses, Whitman himself was an actor, in daily life and in his poetry. "I have always had a good deal to do with actors: met many, high and low," he said.[79] Obviously they shared trade secrets with him. Not only did he declaim passages from plays on the streets and at the seashore, but he took pride in subtleties of interpretation. His "spouting" of loud Shakespeare passages on the New York omnibuses reflected his participation in the zestful turbulence of American life.

Nowhere did he act so much as in his poetry. When developing his poetic persona in his notebooks, he compared himself to an actor on stage, with "all things and all other beings as an audience at a play-house perpetually and perpetually calling me out from behind the curtain."[80] Few personae in literature are as flexible and adaptable as Whitman's "I." In the opening poem alone he assumes scores of identities: he becomes by turns a hounded slave, a bridegroom, a mutineer, a clock, and so on. He is proud of his role-playing ability: "I do not ask the wounded person how he feels . . . . I myself become the wounded person"; "I become any presence or truth of humanity here."[81]

The theater left an indelible mark on him. In particular, the emotional peaks of the early editions of *Leaves of Grass* seem to reflect the style of the actor he most admired, Junius Brutus Booth. Neither Booth nor Whitman was particularly demonstrative in private. But when performing—Booth on stage, Whitman in his poetry—both were volcanic. Whitman's identification with emotionally charged characters leads him to near-melodramatic peaks. "O Christ! My fit is mastering me!" "That I could forget the mockers and insults! [. . .] That I could look with a separate look on my own crucifixion and bloody crowning!" "Somehow I have been stunned. Stand back!" "You villain touch! what are you doing? . . . . my breath is tight in its throat;/ Unclench your floodgates! you are too much for me." Like the actor who shaped him, Whitman as poetic performer took passionate expression to new heights.

Closely connected with acting was music, another source of Whitman's passionate voice. Surveying all the entertainment experiences of his young manhood, Whitman wrote, "Perhaps my dearest amusement reminiscences are those musical ones."[82] Music was such an important force on him that he saw himself less as a poet than as a singer or bard. "My younger life," he recalled in old age, "was so saturated with the emotions, raptures, up-lifts of such musical experiences that it would be surprising indeed if all my future work had not been colored by them."[83]

Whitman regarded music as a prime agent for unity and uplift in a nation whose tendencies to fragmentation and political corruption appalled him. Music offered a meeting place of aesthetics and egalitarianism. In the 1855 preface to *Leaves of Grass* he mentioned Americans' "delight in music, the sure symptoms of manly tenderness and native elegance of soul."[84] By becoming himself a "bard" singing poetic "songs" he hoped to tap the potential for aesthetic appreciation he saw in Americans' positive responses to their shared musical culture. He was responsive to the simple music of the singing families and the minstrels and was especially inspired by the more sophisticated form of the opera.

In his poems he integrated operatic techniques. "Walt Whitman's method in the construction of his songs is strictly the method of the Italian Opera," he would write in 1860, and to a friend he confided, "But for the opera I could not have written *Leaves of Grass*."[85] As Robert Faner has shown, opera devices run through his poetry.[86] Many of the emotionally expressive, melodic passages follow the slow pattern of the aria. The more expansive, conversational ones follow the looser rhythm of the operatic recitative.

He admired the great opera singers who came to America in the early fifties. Among all the opera stars, the one that shone brightest for him was Marietta Alboni, the great Italian contralto who also sang soprano roles. "For me," he told Traubel, "out of the whole list of stage deities of that period, no one meant so much to me as Alboni, as [Junius Brutus] Booth: narrowing it further, I should say Alboni alone."[87] After several European tours, Alboni toured America in the summer of 1852 to rave reviews, appearing in ten operas and giving twelve concerts of operatic selections in the New York area. Whitman claimed he heard her every time she sang in New York and its vicinity. "She used to sweep me away as with whirlwinds," he said.[88]

In opera history, Alboni is remembered as one of the great representatives of *bel canto*, the flowing, simple line interrupted by vocal scrollwork that has an unearthly, almost orgasmic quality. Whitman's verse often resonates with a *bel canto* feeling. The rapture Alboni inspired in him had more direct ramifications as well, as when he writes, "I hear the trained soprano . . . . she convulses me like the climax of my love-grip;/ The orchestra whirls me wider than Uranus flies,/ It wrenches unnamable ardors from my breast."[89]

As these lines suggest, the feelings Whitman had for music verged on the sexual. But then, so did his feelings about many things. James E. Miller, Jr. aptly describes him as "omnisexual."[90] This brings us to the most controversial aspect of the 1855 edition of *Leaves of Grass*: its treatment of sex. The main reason for the hostile reaction to the volume was its many references to the sexual act, body parts, desire, and so forth.

Whitman, however, maintained that his candid sexual images stood in opposition to what he saw as the degraded, scabrous treatment of sex in popular culture. He was puzzled that some inferred from his poetry that he would take an interest in what he called "all the literature of rape, all the pornograph of vile minds."[91] He sharply distinguished *Leaves of Grass* from this material: "No one would more rigidly keep in mind the difference between the simply erotic, the merely lascivious, and what is frank, free, modern, in sexual behavior, than I would: no one."[92]

When it came to the content of popular literature, he was careful to praise morality and denounce obscenity. Surveying the popular literature of the antebellum period, he said he saw "In the pleantiful [*sic*] feast of romance presented to us, all the novels, all the poems, really dish up only one figure, various forms and preparations of only one plot, namely, a sickly, scrofulous, crude amorousness."[93] He attacked venomously "the perfect cataracts of trash" produced by foreign sensational writers and was dismayed when many American writers of yellow-covered pulp novels followed in the footsteps of the Europeans.[94] Although not explicit by today's standards, antebellum sensational fiction weirdly combined sex and violence and sometimes became daring, particularly in the hands of George Thompson, who churned out nearly a hundred pamphlet novels. Thompson dealt with all kinds of sex: group sex, child sex, sodomy, miscegenation.

Given the popularity of sensational fiction, it is understandable that when Whitman's *Leaves of Grass* was criticized by some for its sexual openness, several of Whitman's defenders were quick to point out its relative purity when compared with the mass literature of the day. His friend William Douglass O'Connor asserted that the eighty or so sexual lines in Whitman did not merit his being lumped with "the anonymous lascivious trash spawned in holes and sold in corners, too witless and disgusting for any notice but that of the police."[95] Similarly, John Burroughs insisted, "Of the morbid, venereal, euphemistic, gentlemanly, club-house lust, which, under thin disguises, is in every novel and most of the poetry of our times, he has not the faintest word or thought—not the faintest whisper."[96]

Indeed, Whitman wrote his poems partly as a response to the popular love plot, with its fast young men and depraved women. "Romances," a popular equivalent of novels in his day, became a word of opprobrium in his lexicon. "Great genius and the people of these states must never be demeaned to romances," he declared in the 1855 preface.[97] He found a powerful weapon against the perfervid sensuality of romances in the natural approach to sex and the body offered by the ascendant science of physiology. Popular physiologists like those associated with the scientific publishing firm of Fowlers & Wells, the distributor of the first edition of *Leaves of Grass* and publisher of the second edition, stridently opposed pornography as one of several unnatural stimulants that threatened to disturb the mind's equilibrium by overexciting the brain's faculty of "amativeness," the phrenological term for heterosexual desire.

Throughout his poetry, Whitman treated sex and the body in a physiological, artistic way as a contrast to what he saw as the cheapened, often perverse forms of sexual expression in popular culture. "Who will underrate the influence of a loose popular literature in debauching the popular mind?" Whitman asked in a magazine article.[98] Directly opposing the often grotesque versions of eroticism appearing in sensational romances, he wrote in the 1855 preface: "Exaggerations will be revenged in human physiology [. . . .] As soon as histories are properly told there is no more need for romances."[99] Priding himself, like the physiologists, on candid acceptance of the body, he announced in his first poem: "Welcome is every organ and attribute of me, and of any man hearty and clean." He sang the naturalness of copulation and the sanctity of the sexual organs with the loving attention of a physiologist or sculptor.

His sexual frankness caused him to be associated with the free love movement of his day. But Whitman hated being associated with the free lovers. True, like them, he saw profound defects in relations between the sexes that he tried to repair by appealing to natural passion and attraction. But the free lovers wanted to abolish marriage, which they viewed as "legalized prostitution" in an age when women, exploited and underpaid, were often forced to marry for the wrong reasons and could not easily escape unhappy marriages due to unfair divorce codes. Whitman, despite his own disinclination to marry and his recognition of flaws in American marriages, always venerated the marriage institution. "When that goes, all goes," he wrote, emphasizing that "the divine institution of the marriage tie lies at the root of the welfare, the safety, the very existence of every Christian nation."[100] When he praised sex in his poetry, he was referring to sex between a man and a wife.

To his frustration, his candid treatment of sex enraged the moral censors of his era. When a British edition of *Leaves of Grass* appeared in 1868, the editors carefully pruned away sexual references, producing an expurgated edition. In 1881 Whitman came into collision with Anthony Comstock, the paunchy, bewhiskered reformer who launched a far-reaching crusade against all forms of pornography. Some of Comstock's cronies prevented the distribution of the 1881 edition of *Leaves of Grass*, published by James R. Osgood of Boston, on the charge that it was obscene literature. Publication was suspended, and Whitman received a long list of poems and images that were considered offensive.

It tells us a lot about sexual mores of the time that these priggish censors complained of even the mildest references to heterosexual sex while finding nothing objectionable in Whitman's images of same-sex love, some of them in the 1855 and 1856 editions and many more in the 1860 edition, which introduced the "Calamus" cluster to *Leaves of Grass*. Amazingly, the censors targeted even the tame "Dalliance of the Eagles" (about the mating of birds) while leaving untouched all but one of the forty-five homoerotic "Calamus" poems—and in that one, "Spontaneous Me," it was a reference to masturbation that was called obscene.

Why were the "Calamus" poems, widely viewed in recent times as homosexual love songs, permitted to stand by these exacting, puritanical readers? The answer would seem to be that same-sex love was not interpreted the same way then as it is now.

Passionate intimacy between people of the same sex was common in pre–Civil War America. The lack of clear sexual categories (homo-, hetero-, bi-) made same-sex affection unself-conscious and widespread. The word "homosexual" was not used in English until 1892, the year of Whitman's death, and was not widely known to Americans until it was used for the first time in the *New York Times* in the mid-1920s. Although Whitman evidently had one or two affairs with women, he was mainly a romantic comrade who had a series of intense relationships with young men, most of whom went on to get married and have children. Whatever the nature of his physical relationships with them, most of the passages of same-sex in his poems were not out of keeping with then-current theories and practices that underscored the healthiness of such love.

Same-sex friends often loved each other passionately. "Lover" had no gender connotation and was used interchangeably with "friend." It was common among both men and women to hug, kiss, and express love for people of the same sex. In hotels and inns, complete strangers often slept in the same bed. Because Whitman was disillusioned with the capitalistic forces that poisoned many heterosexual relationships, producing rampant prostitution as well as so-called "legalized prostitution" in marriage, he wished to glorify the loving friendships he saw around him in working-class life. He said in his notebook that he wanted to find words for the "approval, admiration, friendship" seen "among young men of these States," who he said had "wonderful tenacity of friendship, and passionate fondness for their friends."[101] He wanted to be the one who brought real-life friendship to the printed page. As he wrote in his open letter to Emerson, "as to manly friendship, everywhere observed in These States, there is not the first breath of it to be observed in print."[102]

The phrenological notion of adhesiveness (comradely love) was an important element of his view of comradeship. His friends the Fowlers wrote that when the organ of adhesiveness was well developed, one "loves friends with tenderness" and "will sacrifice almost anything for their sake."[103] Adhesiveness had a personal and social dimension. Privately it caused people of the same sex to be drawn to each other and love each other. Socially, it was a powerful force for cohesion, with the power, as the Fowlers wrote, to "bind mankind together in families, societies, communities, &c." Whitman went so far as to say that comradely love "is one of the United States—it is the quality which makes the states whole—it is their thread—but oh! The significant thread—by which the nation is held together, a chain of comrades . . . I know no country anyhow in which comradeship is so far developed as here—here, among the mechanic classes."[104] Elsewhere he gave his opinion that it was only through "the beautiful and same affection of man for men, latent in all the young fellows, north and south, east and west" that the United States "are to be most effectually welded together, intercalcated, anneal'd into a living union."[105]

Having lost faith in established institutions, Whitman looked to friendship to unify his nation. As he wrote in an 1860 poem, "Affection shall solve everyone of the problems of freedom."[106] Through comradeship,

I will make the continent indissoluble,
I will make the most splendid race the sun ever shone upon,
I will make divine magnetic lands.[107]

His gesture of making his continent "indissoluble" and forging "divine magnetic lands" was the writing of *Leaves of Grass*, which he constantly revised and expanded to the year of his death, 1892. His poetic priorities changed with the times. He welcomed the Civil War, which he viewed as a purifying thunderstorm that would rid the nation of its many social ills, as he had initially hoped his poetry would do. Few people witnessed the war as closely as did Whitman, who spent five years as a volunteer nurse in the Washington war hospitals, visiting over 100,000 patients. After the war, he poeticized the war in his volume *Drum-Taps* and retrospectively idealized the courage and selflessness of both Northern and Southern soldiers. Above all, he cherished the memory of Abraham Lincoln, whose high-minded life and tragic death, Whitman thought, had saved the American Union.

During Reconstruction, Whitman lamented the return—indeed the redoubling—of the kinds of political corruption, cultural materialism, and economic inequity he had originally designed his poetry to combat. But, physically disabled from strokes and well on the road to sanctification as the Good Gray Poet, he was disinclined to resurrect the self-assured, all-absorptive persona of the first edition. His views on some issues—race, especially—stiffened, and the inclusive vision of 1855 was left behind. In some ways, his poetry became more conventional than before, both in content and style. For instance, the innovative ellipses and punctuationless lines of the 1855 edition were replaced by standard grammar and usage.

On a profound level, however, he continued to respect the "ecstasy of statement" that he associated with the first edition. Although he continually tailored the 1855 poems, formalizing their punctuation and changing words here and there, he left them, by and large, close in spirit to the original. To this day, the 1855 pieces, especially "Song of Myself," are beloved by readers around the world. In 1855 Whitman had come closest to fulfilling Emerson's definition of the poet as the person who "traverses the whole scale of experience" from high to low in an omnivorous, creative vision.[108] Without the 1855 poems Whitman would not be "Walt Whitman, an American, one of the roughs, a kosmos."

Has Whitman been absorbed by his country as affectionately as he absorbed it? In a literal sense, no. Today as then, poetry tends to be shoved aside in favor of more diverting or profitable pursuits, and most Americans would rather seek solace in the old Bible than in Whitman's "new Bible." Still, Walt Whitman lingers in the American consciousness—and not just in the shopping malls, schools, bridges, and streets that bear his name. Like Poe's raven, Melville's white whale, and Thoreau's cabin, Whitman's grass leaves float as vague signifiers in the popular mind, ready to appear on any occasion.

Whitman's leaves challenge us in a special way, because they remind us what true democracy is. In Whitman's poems, democracy is like the grass itself—everywhere alike, everywhere individual. More powerfully than any other literary work, the 1855 edition of *Leaves of Grass* reminds all humans of their common identity as fellow-sojourners on this earth At the height of the Cold War, the poet Allen Ginsberg aired the opinion that Whitman's poetry should be read aloud at an international summit meeting to reconcile national tensions. In October 1995 President Bill Clinton welcomed Pope John Paul II to America by addressing His Holiness as follows: "Our great American poet, Walt Whitman, who I know is a favorite of yours, once wrote about America: 'The real and permanent grandeur of these states must be their religion, otherwise there is no real and permanent grandeur.'"[109]

The fact that Whitman could appeal simultaneously to a Jewish homosexual poet, a Democratic president, and the head of the Roman Catholic Church is telling. It suggests that if the spirit of *Leaves of Grass* were universally accepted, tensions caused by differences in creed, class, and nationality would diminish.

Universal acceptance of Whitman's democratic spirit, of course, is far from being realized. Still, it is a goal worth pursuing. There is no better way to start than to read the 1855 edition of *Leaves of Grass* in a format that approximates the original.

Notes

1. W. Whitman, *Leaves of Grass: Comprehensive Reader's Edition*, ed. Harold Blodgett and Sculley Bradley (New York: New York University Press, 1965), p. 729.
2. Horace Traubel, *With Walt Whitman in Camden*, II (1907; rpt., New York: Rowman and Littlefield, 1961): 225.
3. H. Traubel, *With Walt Whitman in Camden,* I (1905; rpt., New York: Rowman and Littlefield, 1961): 194 and H. Traubel, *With Walt Whitman in Camden,* II: 480.
4. H. Traubel, *With Walt Whitman in Camden,* II: 26–7.
5. H. Traubel, *With Walt Whitman in Camden,* VI (Carbondale: Southern Illinois University Press, 1982): 131.
6. W. Whitman, *Notebooks and Unpublished Prose Manuscripts*, ed. Edward F. Grier (New York: New York University Press, 1984), VI: 2147.
7. W. Whitman, *Complete Poetry and Collected Prose* (New York: Library of America, 1982), p. 1327.
8. W. Whitman, *Leaves of Grass* (Brooklyn, 1855), p. vii.
9. W. Whitman, *Leaves of Grass*, p. xii. The quotations in the next paragraphs are on pp. iv and vii, respectively.

10. [Rufus W. Griswold]. *Criterion*, 1 (10 November 1855), 24; [Charles A. Dana]. "New Publications: Leaves of Grass," *New York Daily Tribune*, July 23, 1855; "Notices of Books," *Dublin Review*, 41 (September 1856): 267; and *Brooklyn Daily Eagle,* 15 September 1855.

11. [Walt Whitman], "Walt Whitman and His Poems," *United States Review* 5 (September 1855), 205–12.

12. W. Whitman, *Leaves of Grass: Comprehensive Reader's Edition*, ed. H. Blodgett and S. Bradley, p. 729.

13. W. Whitman, *Notebooks and Unpublished Prose Manuscripts*, ed. E. F. Grier, I: 167.

14. H. Traubel, *With Walt Whitman in Camden,* I: 92. The quotation in the next sentence is in H. Traubel, *With Walt Whitman in Camden,* VI: 289.

15. *The Norton Anthology of American Literature*, ed. Nina Baym et al. (New York: W. W. Norton, 2003), B: 2541.

16. H. Traubel, *With Walt Whitman in Camden,* I: 138 and W. Whitman, *Prose Works, 1892*, ed. Floyd Stovall, I (New York: New York University Press, 1963): 232–33.

17. H. Traubel, *With Walt Whitman in Camden,* I: 111 and VI: 123.

18. H. Traubel, *With Walt Whitman in Camden,* III: (1912; rpt., New York: Rowman and Littlefield, 1961): 374 and *H. Traubel, With Walt Whitman in Camden,* VI: 413 and I: 212.

19. J. T. Trowbridge, "Reminiscences of Walt Whitman," *Atlantic Monthly*, 89 (February 1902): 166.

20. W. Whitman, *Leaves of Grass*, p. 55.

21. R. W. Emerson, "The Poet," in *Norton Anthology of American Literature*, ed. N. Baym et al., B: 1179. The quotation in the next sentence is on p. 1189.

22. W. Whitman, *Leaves of Grass: Comprehensive Reader's Edition*, ed. H. Blodgett and S. Bradley, p. 729.

23. Whitman, *Complete Poetry and Collected Prose*, p. 660.

24. W. Whitman, *Leaves of Grass*, pp. 81–2.

25. The manuscript drafts, along with many other works by and about Whitman, are reproduced on the excellent website "The Walt Whitman Archive" created by Kenneth M. Price and Ed Folsom, at http://www.whitmanarchive.org.

26. *Brooklyn Daily Eagle*, February 23, 1847.

27. *The Uncollected Prose and Poetry of Walt Whitman*, ed. Emory Holloway (Gloucester, MA: Peter Smith, 1972), I: 194.

28. W. Whitman, *Leaves of Grass*, p. 23.

29. W. Whitman, *Leaves of Grass*, p. vii. The quotation in the next sentence is on p. iv.

30. W. Whitman, *Leaves of Grass*, p. vi. The remaining quotations in the paragraph are on pp. 71 and 47, respectively.

31. *Walt Whitman, The Critical Heritage*, ed M. Hindus (London: Routledge K. Paul, 1971), p. 22.

32. Whitman, *Complete Poetry and Collected Prose*, p. 479 and W. Whitman, *Leaves of Grass: A Textual Variorum of the Printed Poems*, ed. Sculley Bradley et al. (New York: New York University Press, 1980), I; 188–89.

33. W. Whitman, *Leaves of Grass*, p. 29.

34. W. Whitman, *Complete Poetry and Collected Prose*, p. 1190.

35. W. Whitman, *Daybooks and Notebooks*, ed. William White (New York: New York University Press, 1978), III: 669, 736.

36. W. Whitman, *Leaves of Grass*, p. 53.

37. [C. Dana]. "New Publications: Leaves of Grass," p. 3.

38. "Notes on New Books," *Washington Daily National Intelligencer,* February 18, 1856, p. 2.

39. *New York Daily News*, February 27, 1856 and *New York Examiner*, January 19, 1882.

40. *Life Illustrated,* July 28, 1855.

41. "Whitman's Leaves of Grass," *Putnam's Monthly: A Magazine of Literature, Science, and Art*, 6 (September 1855): 322.
42. The *New York Daily News*, February 27, 1856.
43. *Brooklyn Daily Times*, February 20, 1858.
44. W. Whitman, *Leaves of Grass*, p. 29.
45. W. Whitman, *Complete Poetry and Collected Prose*, p. 1317. The next quotation in this paragraph is on p. 1313. The quotations in the next paragraph are on pp. 706 and 1310, successively.
46. W. Whitman, *Leaves of Grass*, p. viii. The subsequent quotations in this paragraph are on p. 90 and 87–8, successively. The quotation in the next paragraph is on p. iv.
47. H. Traubel, *With Walt Whitman in Camden*, I: 223.
48. W. Whitman, *Leaves of Grass*, p. iv. The quotation in the next paragraph is also on p. iv.
49. H. Traubel, *With Walt Whitman in Camden*, III: 498. The quotations in the next sentence are in H. Traubel, *With Walt Whitman in Camden*, I: 227 and H. Traubel, *With Walt Whitman in Camden*, IV (1953; Carbondale: Southern Illinois University Press, 1959): 473.
50. W. Whitman, *Leaves of Grass*, p. iv.
51. W. Whitman, *Notebooks and Unpublished Prose Manuscripts*, ed. E. F. Grier, IV: 1524.
52. H. Traubel, *With Walt Whitman in Camden*, IV: 125.
53. W. Whitman, *Leaves of Grass Comprehensive Reader's Edition*, ed. H. Blodgett and S. Bradley, p. 642.
54. *Brooklyn Daily Times*, November 10, 1858.
55. W. Whitman, *Leaves of Grass*, p. ix.
56. W. Whitman, *Leaves of Grass*, p. 23. The next quotation in this paragraph is on p. 22. The quotations in the next two paragraphs are on pp. 19, 13, and 16, successively.
57. J. Liebig, *Organic Chemistry in Its Application to Agriculture and Physiology* (London: Taylor and Walton, 1840), p. 225 and W. Whitman, *Leaves of Grass*, p. 13.
58. W. Whitman, *Leaves of Grass*, p. 16. The quotations in the next two sentences are on pp. 17 and 54, successively.
59. W. Whitman, *Prose Works, 1892*, ed. F. Stovall, II (New York: New York University Press, 1964): 365.
60. H. Traubel, *With Walt Whitman in Camden*, II: 149.
61. *Whitman in His Own Time*, ed. Joel Myerson (Detroit: Omnigraphics, 1991), p. 9.
62. W. Whitman, *Leaves of Grass*, p. 54.
63. H. Traubel, *With Walt Whitman in Camden*, II: 457.
64. W. Whitman, *Leaves of Grass*, p. 45. The quotation in the next sentence is on p. v.
65. *Brooklyn Daily Times*, June 15, 1858.
66. W. Whitman, *Leaves of Grass*, pp. 27, 28.
67. H. Traubel, *With Walt Whitman in Camden*, V (Carbondale: Southern Illinois University Press, 1964): 376.
68. W. Whitman, *Leaves of Grass*, p. 15.
69. W. Whitman, *Notebooks and Unpublished Prose Manuscripts*, ed. E. F. Grier, I: 194.
70. *Walt Whitman's Workshop: A Collection of Unpublished Prose Manuscripts*, ed. Clifton Joseph Furness (New York: Russell & Russell, 1964), p. 191.
71. W. Whitman, *Leaves of Grass*, p. 35. The subsequent quotations in this paragraph are on p. 37. The quotations in the next paragraph are on pp. 55 and 56, successively.
72. *Saturday Press*, June 30, 1860.
73. *Christian Spiritualist* (1856); reprinted in W. Whitman, *Leaves of Grass Imprints* (Boston: Thayer & Eldridge, 1860), pp. 32–6.
74. H. Traubel, *With Walt Whitman in Camden*, I: 455.
75. W. Whitman, *Complete Poetry and Collected Prose*, p. 1192. The quotation in the next sentence paragraph is on p. 1187.
76. H. Traubel, *With Walt Whitman in Camden*, IV: 141.

77. W. Whitman, *Complete Poetry and Collected Prose*, p. 1192.
78. H. Traubel, *With Walt Whitman in Camden*, VII (Carbondale: Southern Illinois University Press, 1992): 295.
79. H. Traubel, *With Walt Whitman in Camden*, IV: 519.
80. W. Whitman, *Notebooks and Unpublished Prose Manuscripts*, ed. E. F. Grier, I: 217.
81. W. Whitman, *Leaves of Grass*, pp. 39, 43. The first four quotations in the next paragraph are on pp. 42–3; the last one is on p. 33.
82. W. Whitman, *Prose Works, 1892*, ed. F. Stovall, II: 592.
83. H. Traubel, *With Walt Whitman in Camden*, II: 174.
84. W. Whitman, *Leaves of Grass*, p. iii.
85. *Saturday Press*, January 7, 1860 and J. T. Trowbridge, "Reminiscences of Walt Whitman," p. 166.
86. Robert D. Faner, *Walt Whitman and the Opera* (Carbondale: Southern Illinois University Press, 1951).
87. H. Traubel, *With Walt Whitman in Camden*, IV: 286.
88. J. Johnston and J. W. Wallace, *Visits to Walt Whitman in 1890–91* (London: G. Allen & Unwin, 1912), p. 162.
89. W. Whitman, *Leaves of Grass*, p. 32.
90. J. E. Miller, Jr., "Whitman's Omnisexual Sensibility," *Études Anglaises*, 45 (July–September 1992), 275–85.
91. H. Traubel, *With Walt Whitman in Camden*, IV: 119.
92. H. Traubel, *With Walt Whitman in Camden*, IV: 388.
93. W. Whitman, *Notebooks and Unpublished Prose Manuscripts*, ed. E. F. Grier, IV: 1604.
94. *Brooklyn Daily Eagle*, July 11, 1846.
95. W. D. O'Connor, *The Good Gray Poet* (1866; reprint in Richard Maurice Bucke, *Walt Whitman* [New York: Johnson Reprint Corporation, 1970]), p. 108.
96. J. Burroughs, *Notes on Walt Whitman, as Poet and Person* (1867; reprint, New York: Haskell House, 1971), p. 27.
97. W. Whitman, *Leaves of Grass*, p. ix.
98. W. Whitman, *I Sit and Look Out: Editorials from the Brooklyn Daily Times*, ed. Emory Holloway and Vernolian Schwartz (New York: AMS Press, 1966), p. 119.
99. *Leaves of Grass*, p. ix. The next two quotations in this paragraph are on pp. 14 and 76, successively.
100. W. Whitman, *I Sit and Look Out*, ed. E. Holloway and V. Schwartz, pp. 113–14.
101. W. Whitman, *Daybooks and Notebooks*, ed. W. White, III: 740–41.
102. W. Whitman, *Complete Poetry and Collected Prose*, p. 1335.
103. Orson Fowler, *Phrenology Proved, Illustrated and Accompanied by a Chart* (New York: Fowlers & Wells, 1842), p. 65. The next quotation in this paragraph is also on p. 65.
104. H. Traubel, *With Walt Whitman in Camden*, IV: 342–43.
105. W. Whitman, *Complete Poetry and Collected Prose*, p. 1011.
106. W. Whitman, *Leaves of Grass: A Textual Variorum of the Printed Poems*, ed. S. Bradley et al., II: 371–72.
107. W.Whitman, *Complete Poetry and Collected Prose*, p. 272.
108. R. W. Emerson, "The Poet," *Norton Anthology of American Literature*, B: 1178.
109. *Associated Press*, October 4, 1995.

Reviews of the 1855 Edition of
Leaves of Grass

1.   [Charles A. Dana]. "New Publications: Leaves of Grass."
     New York Daily Tribune, **23 July 1855, p. 3.**

From the unique effigies of the anonymous author of this volume which graces
the frontispiece, we may infer that he belongs to the exemplary class of society some-
times irreverently styled "loafers." He is therein represented in a garb, half sailor's,
half workman's, with no superfluous appendage of coat or waistcoat, a "wide-awake"
perched jauntily on his head, one hand in his pocket and the other on his hip, with a
certain air of mild defiance, and an expression of pensive insolence in his face which
seems to betoken a consciousness of his mission as the "coming man." This view of
the author is confirmed in the preface. He vouchsafes, before introducing us to his
poetry, to enlighten our benighted minds as to the true function of the American poet.
Evidently the original, which is embodied in the most extraordinary prose since the
"Sayings" of the modern Orpheus, was found in the "interior consciousness" of the
writer. Of the materials afforded by this country for the operations of poetic art we
have a lucid account.

[Extract from preface; c. 160 words:]

"The Americans of all nations at any time upon the earth have probably the
fullest poetical nature.[…]or the bays contain fish or men beget children upon
women."

With veins full of such poetical stuff, the United States, as we are kindly informed,
"of all nations most needs poets, and will doubtless have the greatest and use them
the greatest." Here is a full-length figure of the true poet:

[Extract from preface: c. 280 words]

"Of all mankind the great poet is the equable man[...]he sees eternity in men
and women... he does not see men and women as dreams or dots."

Of the nature of poetry the writer discourses in a somewhat too oracular strain,
especially as he has been anticipated in his "utterances" by Emerson and other mod-
ern "prophets of the soul":

[Extract from preface: c. 260 words]

"The poetic quality is not marshaled in rhyme or uniformity or abstract addresses
to things[…]your very flesh shall be a great poem and have the richest fluency

not only in its words but in the silent lines of its lips and face and between the lashes of your eyes and in every motion and joint of your body."

Such is the poetic theory of our nameless bard. He furnishes a severe standard for the estimate of his own productions. His *Leaves of Grass* are doubtless intended as an illustration of the natural poet. They are certainly original in their external form, have been shaped on no pre-existent model out of the author's own brain. Indeed, his independence often becomes coarse and defiant. His language is too frequently reckless and indecent though this appears to arise from a naive unconsciousness rather than from an impure mind. His words might have passed between Adam and Eve in Paradise, before the want of fig-leaves brought no shame; but they are quite out of place amid the decorum of modern society, and will justly prevent his volume from free circulation in scrupulous circles. With these glaring faults, the *Leaves of Grass* are not destitute of peculiar poetic merits, which will awaken an interest in the lovers of literary curiosities. They are full of bold, stirring thoughts—with occasional passages of effective description, betraying a genuine intimacy with Nature and a keen appreciation of beauty—often presenting a rare felicity of diction, but so disfigured with eccentric fancies as to prevent a consecutive perusal without offense, though no impartial reader can fail to be impressed with the vigor and quaint beauty of isolated portions. A few specimens will suffice to give an idea of this odd genius.

THE LOVER OF NATURE.

[Extract from the poetry; 25 lines]

"I am he that walks with the tender and growing
    night; [...]
Howler and scooper of storms! Capricious and dainty sea!
I am integral with you.... I too am of one phase and of
    all phases."

AFTER A SEA-FIGHT.

[Extract from the poetry; 15 lines]

"Stretched and still lay the midnight,
Two great hulls motionless on the breast of the
    darkness, [...]
These so.... these irretrievable!"

NATURAL IDEALISM.

[Extract from the poetry; 10 lines]

"All doctrines, all politics and civilization exurge from
    you, [...]
It is nearer and further than they."

THE LAST OF EARTH.

[Extract from the poetry; 12 lines]

"When the dull nights are over, and the dull days
    also, [...]
But without eyesight lingers a different living and
    looks curiously on the corpse."

THE HUMAN FACE DIVINE.

[Extract from the poetry; 32 lines]

"Sauntering the pavement or riding the country by-road
    here then are faces, [...]

This face owes to the sexton his dismalest fee,
As unceasing death-bell tolls there."

The volume contains many more "Leaves of Grass" of similar quality, as well as others which cannot be especially commended either for fragrance or form. Whatever severity of criticism they may challenge for their rude ingenuousness, and their frequent divergence into the domain of the fantastic, the taste of not over dainty fastidiousness will discern much of the essential spirit of poetry beneath an uncouth and grotesque embodiment.

2.   *Life Illustrated,* 28 July 1855 [page number unknown].

A curious title; but the book itself is a hundred times more curious. It is like no other book that ever was written, and therefore, the language usually employed in notices of new publications is unavailable in describing it.

It is a thin volume of 95 pages, shaped like a small atlas. On the first page is a portrait of the unknown author. He stands in a careless attitude, without coat or vest, with a rough felt hat on his head, one hand thurst [*sic*] lazily into his pocket and the other resting on his hip. He is the picture of a perfect loafer; yet a thoughtful loafer, an amiable loafer, an able loafer. Then follows a long preface, which most steadygoing, respectable people would pronounce perfect nonsense, but which free-souled persons, here and there, will read and chuckle over with real delight, as the expression of their own best feelings. This remarkable preface is something in the Emersonian manner—that is, it is a succession of independent sentences, many of which are of striking truth and beauty. The body of the volume is filled with "Leaves of Grass," which are lines of rhythmical prose, or a series of utterances (we know not what else to call them), unconnected, curious, and original. The book, perhaps, might be called, American Life, from a Poetical Loafer's Point of View.

The discerning reader will find in this singular book much that will please him, and we advise all who are fond of new and peculiar things to procure it. We may add that the book was printed by the author's own hands, and that he is philosophically indifferent as to its sale. It pleased him to write so, and the public may take it or let it alone, just as they prefer.

3.   [Walt Whitman]. **"Walt Whitman and His Poems."**
      United States Review, 5 (September 1855), 205–12.

An American bard at last! One of the roughs, large, proud, affectionate, eating, drinking, and breeding, his costume manly and free, his face sunburnt and bearded, his posture strong and erect, his voice bringing hope and prophecy to the generous races of young and old. We shall cease shamming and be what we really are. We shall start an athletic and defiant literature. We realize now how it is, and what was most lacking. The interior American republic shall also be declared free and independent.

For all our intellectual people, followed by their books, poems, novels, essays, editorials, lectures, tuitions, and criticism, dress by London and Paris modes, receive what is received there, obey the authorities, settle disputes by the old tests, keep out of rain and sun, retreat to the shelter of houses and schools, trim their hair, shave, touch not the earth barefoot, and enter not the sea except in a complete bathing-dress. One sees unmistakably genteel persons, travelled, college-learned, used to be served by servants, conversing without heat or vulgarity, supported on chairs, or walking through handsomely-carpeted parlors, or along shelves bearing well-bound volumes, and walls adorned with curtained and collared portraits, and china things, and nick-nacks. But where in American literature is the first show of America? Where are the gristle and beards, and broad breasts, and space and ruggedness and nonchalance that the souls of the people love? Where is the tremendous outdoors of these States? Where is the majesty of the federal mother, seated with more than antique grace, calm, just, indulgent to her brood of children, calling them around her regarding the little and the large and the younger and the older with perfect impartiality? Where is the vehement growth of our cities? Where is the spirit of the strong rich life of the American mechanic, farmer, sailor, hunter, and miner? Where is the huge composite of all other nations, cast in a fresher and brawnier matrix, passing adolescence, and needed this day, live and arrogant, to lead the marches of the world?

Self-reliant, with haughty eyes, assuming to himself all the attributes of his country, steps Walt Whitman into literature, talking like a man unaware that there was ever hitherto such a production as a book, or such a being as a writer. Every move of him has the free play of the muscle of one who never knew what it was to feel that he stood in the presence of a superior. Every word that falls from his mouth shows silent disdain and defiance of the old theories and forms. Every phrase announces new laws; not once do his lips unclose except in conformity with them. With light and rapid touch he first indicates in prose the principles of the foundation of a race of poets so deeply to spring from the American people, and become ingrained through them, that their Presidents shall not be the common referees so much as that great race of poets shall. He proceeds himself to exemplify this new school, and set models for their expression and range of subjects. He makes audacious and native use of his own body and soul. He must re-create poetry with the elements always at hand. He must imbue it with himself as he is, disorderly, fleshy, and sensual, a lover of things, yet a lover of men and women above the whole of the other objects of the universe. His work is to be achieved by unusual methods. Neither classic or romantic is he, nor a materialist any more than a spiritualist. Not a whisper comes out of him of the old stock talk and rhyme of poetry—not the first recognition of gods or goddesses, or Greece or Rome. No breath of Europe, or her monarchies, or priestly conventions, or her notions of gentlemen and ladies founded on the idea of caste, seems ever to have fanned his face or been inhaled into his lungs. But in their stead pour vast and fluid the fresh mentality of this mighty age, and the realities of this mighty continent, and the sciences and inventions and discoveries of the present world. Not geology, nor mathematics, nor chemistry, nor navigation, nor astronomy, nor anatomy, nor physiology, nor engineering, is more true to itself than Walt Whitman is true to them. They and the other sciences underlie his whole superstructure. In the beauty of the work of the poet, he affirms, are the tuft and final applause of science.

Affairs then are this man's poems. He will still inject nature through civilization. The movement of his verses is the sweeping movement of great currents of living people, with a general government, and state and municipal governments, courts, commerce, manufactures, arsenals, steamships, railroads, telegraphs, cities with paved streets, and aqueducts, and police and gas—myriads of travellers arriving and departing—newspapers, music, elections and all the features and processes of the nineteenth century in the wholesomest race and the only stable form of politics at present upon the earth. Along his words spread the broad impartialities of the United States. No innovations must be permitted on the stern severities of our liberty and equality. Undecked also is this poet with sentimentalism, or jingle, or nice conceits or flowery similes. He appears in his poems surrounded by women and children, and by young men, and by common objects and qualities. He gives to each just what belongs to it, neither more or less. The person nearest him, that person he ushers hand in hand with himself. Duly take places in his flowing procession, and step to the sounds of the newer and larger music, the essences of American things, and past and present events—the enormous diversity of temperature and agriculture and mines—the tribes of red aborigines—the weather-beaten vessels entering new ports, or making landings on rocky coasts—the first settlements north and south—the rapid stature and impatience of outside control—the sturdy defiance of '76, and the war and peace, and the leadership of Washington, and the formation of the Constitution—the Union always calm and impregnable—the perpetual coming of immigrants—the wharf-hemmed cities and superior marine—the unsurveyed interior—the log-house, and clearings, and wild animals, and hunters, and trappers—the fisheries, and whaling, and gold-digging—the endless gestation of new states—the convening of Congress every December, the members coming up from all climates, and from the utter-most parts—the noble character of the free American workman and workwoman—the fierceness of the people when well-roused—the ardor of their friendships—the large amativeness—the Yankee swap—the New York fireman, and the target excursion—the southern plantation life—the character of the north-east, and of the north-west and south-west—and the character of America and the American people everywhere. For these the old usages of poets afford Walt Whitman no means sufficiently fit and free, and he rejects the old usages. The style of the bard that is waited for is to be transcendent and new. It is to be indirect and not direct or descriptive or epic. Its quality is to go through these to much more. Let the age and wars (he says) of other nations be chanted, and their eras and characters be illustrated, and that finish the verse. Not so (he continues) the great psalm of the republic. Here the theme is creative and has vista. Here comes one among the well-beloved stonecutters, and announces himself, and plans with decision and science, and sees the solid and beautiful forms of the future where there are now no solid forms.

The style of these poems, therefore, is simply their own style, new-born and red. Nature may have given the hint to the author of the *Leaves of Grass*, but there exists no book or fragment of a book, which can have given the hint to them. All beauty, he says, comes from beautiful blood and a beautiful brain. His rhythm and uniformity he will conceal in the roots of his verses, not to be seen of themselves, but to break forth loosely as lilies on a bush, and take shapes compact as the shapes of melons, or chestnuts, or pears.

The poems of the *Leaves of Grass* are twelve in number. Walt Whitman at first proceeds to put his own body and soul into the new versification:

"I celebrate myself, And what I assume you shall assume,
For every atom belonging to me, as good belongs to you."

He leaves houses and their shuttered rooms, for the open air. He drops disguise and ceremony, and walks forth with the confidence and gayety of a child. For the old decorums of writing he substitutes new decorums. The first glance out of his eyes electrifies him with love and delight. He will have the earth receive and return his affection; he will stay with it as the bride-groom stays with the bride. The cool-breathed ground, the slumbering and liquid trees, the just-gone sunset, the vitreous pour of the full moon, the tender and growing night, he salutes and touches, and they touch him. The sea supports him, and hurries him off with its powerful and crooked fingers. Dash me with amorous wet! then he says, I can repay you.

By this writer the rules of polite circles are dismissed with scorn. Your stale modesties, he says, are filthy to such a man as I.

"I believe in the flesh and the appetites,
Seeing, hearing, and feeling are miracles, and each part and tag of me
    is a miracle.
I do not press my finger across my mouth,
I keep as delicate around the bowels as around the head and heart."

No sniveller, or tea-drinking poet, no puny clawback or prude, is Walt Whitman. He will bring poems fit to fill the days and nights—fit for men and women with the attributes of throbbing blood and flesh. The body, he teaches, is beautiful. Sex is also beautiful. Are you to be put down, he seems to ask, to that shallow level of literature and conversation that stops a man's recognizing the delicious pleasure of his sex, or a woman hers? Nature he proclaims inherently pure. Sex will not be put aside; it is a great ordination of the universe. He works the muscle of the male and the teeming fibre of the female throughout his writings, as wholesome realities, impure only by deliberate intention and effort. To men and women he says: You can have healthy and powerful breeds of children on no less terms than these of mine. Follow me and there shall be taller and nobler crops of humanity on the earth.

In the *Leaves of Grass* are the facts of eternity and immortality, largely treated. Happiness is no dream, and perfection is no dream. Amelioration is my lesson, he says with calm voice, and progress is my lesson and the lesson of all things. Then his persuasion becomes a taunt, and his love bitter and compulsory. With strong and steady call he addresses men. Come, he seems to say, from the midst of all that you have been your whole life surrounding yourself with. Leave all the preaching and teaching of others, and mind only these words of mine.

[Extract from the poetry; 23 lines:]

"Long enough have you dreamed contemptible dreams, […]

And I swear I never will translate myself at all, only to him or her who privately stays with me in the open air."

The eleven other poems have each distinct purposes, curiously veiled. Theirs is no writer to be gone through with in a day or a month. Rather it is his pleasure to elude you and provoke you for deliberate purposes of his own.

Doubtless in the scheme this man has built for himself the writing of poems is but a proportionate part of the whole. It is plain that public and private performance, politics, love, friendship, behavior, the art of conversation, science, society, the American people, the reception of the great novelties of city and country, all have their equal call upon him and receive equal attention. In politics he could enter with the freedom and reality he shows in poetry. His scope of life is the amplest of any yet in philosophy. He is the true spiritualist. He recognizes no annihilation, or death, or loss of identity. He is the largest lover and sympathizer that has appeared in literature. He loves the earth and sun, and the animals. He does not separate the learned from the unlearned, the Northerner from the Southerner, the white from the black, or the native from the immigrant just landed at the wharf. Every one, he seems to say, appears excellent to me, every employment is adorned, and every male and female glorious.

[Extract from the poetry; 11 lines:]

"The press of my foot to the earth springs a hundred affections, […]

Not asking the sky to come down to my good will.
Scattering it freely for ever."

If health were not his distinguishing attribute, this poet would be the very harlot of persons. Right and left he flings his arms, drawing men and women with undeniable love to his close embrace, loving the clasp of their hands, the touch of their necks and breasts, and the sound of their voice. All else seems to burn up under his fierce affection for persons. Politics, religion, institutions, art, quickly fall aside before them. In the whole universe, he says, I see nothing more divine than human souls.

[Extract from the poetry; 9 lines:]

"When the psalm sings instead of singer, […]
I intend to reach them my hand and make as much of them as I make of men
    and women."

Who then is that insolent unknown? Who is it, praising himself as if others were not fit to do it, and coming rough and unbidden among writers to unsettle what was settled, and to revolutionize, in fact, our modern civilization? Walt Whitman was born on Long-Island, on the hills about thirty miles from the greatest American city, on the last day of May, 1819, and has grown up in Brooklyn and New York to be thirty-six years old, to enjoy perfect health, and to understand his country and its spirit.

Interrogations more than this, and that will not be put off unanswered, spring continually through the perusal of these *Leaves of Grass:*

If there were to be selected, out of the incalculable volumes of printed matter in existence, any single work to stand for America and her times, should this be the work?

Must not the true American poet indeed absorb all others, and present a new and far more ample and vigorous type?

Has not the time arrived for a school of live writing and tuition consistent with the principles of these poems? consistent with the free spirit of this age, and with the American truths of politics? consistent with geology, and astronomy, and all science and human physiology? consistent with the sublimity of immortality and the direct-ness of common-sense?

If in this poem the United States have found their poetic voice, and taken measure and form, is it any more than a beginning? Walt Whitman himself disclaims singular-ity in his work, and announces the coming after him of great successions of poets, and that he but lifts his finger to give the signal.

Was he not needed? Has not literature been bred in and in long enough? Has it not become unbearably artificial?

Shall a man of faith and practice in the simplicity of real things be called eccen-tric, while the disciple of the fictitious school writes without question?

Shall it still be the amazement of the light and dark that freshness of expression is the rarest quality of all?

You have come in good time, Walt Whitman! In opinions, in manners, in cos-tumes, in books, in the aims and occupancy of life, in associates, in poems, confor-mity to all unnatural and tainted customs passes without remark, while perfect naturalness, health, faith, self-reliance, and all primal expressions of the manliest love and friendship, subject one to the stare and controversy of the world.

4.   [Charles Eliot Norton]. "Whitman's Leaves of Grass." *Putnam's Monthly: A Magazine of Literature, Science, and Art,* 6 (September 1855), 321–3.

Our account of the last month's literature would be incomplete without some no-tice of a curious and lawless collection of poems, called *Leaves of Grass,* and issued in a thin quarto without the name of publisher or author. The poems, twelve in num-ber, are neither in rhyme nor blank verse, but in a sort of excited prose broken into lines without any attempt at measure or regularity, and, as many readers will perhaps think, without any idea of sense or reason. The writer's scorn for the wonted usages of good writing extends to the vocabulary he adopts; words usually banished from polite society are here employed without reserve and with perfect indifference to their effect on the reader's mind; and not only is the book one not to be read aloud to a mixed audience, but the introduction of terms, never before heard or seen, and of slang expressions, often renders an otherwise striking passage altogether laughable. But, as the writer is a new light in poetry, it is only fair to let him state his theory for himself. We extract from the preface:

"The art of art, the glory of expression, is simplicity. Nothing is better than simplicity, and the sunlight of letters is simplicity. Nothing is better than simplicity—nothing can make up for excess, or for the lack of definiteness... To speak in literature, with the perfect rectitude and the insouciance of the movements of animals and the unimpeachableness of the sentiment of trees in the woods, is the flawless triumph of art... The greatest poet has less a marked style, and is more the channel of thought and things, without increase or diminution, and is the free channel of himself. He swears to his art, I will not be meddlesome, I will not have in my writing any elegance, or effect, or originality to hang in the way between me and the rest, like curtains. What I feel, I feel for precisely what it is. Let who may exalt, or startle, or fascinate, or soothe, I will have purposes, as health, or heat, or snow has, and be as regardless of observation. What I experience or portray shall go from my composition without a shred of my composition. You shall stand by my side to look in the mirror with me."

The application of these principles, and of many others equally peculiar, which are expounded in a style equally oracular throughout the long preface,—is made passim, and often with comical success, in the poems themselves, which may briefly be described as a compound of the New England transcendentalist and New York rowdy. A fireman or omnibus driver, who had intelligence enough to absorb the speculations of that school of thought which culminated at Boston some fifteen or eighteen years ago, and resources of expression to put them forth again in a form of his own, with sufficient self-conceit and contempt for public taste to affront all usual propriety of diction, might have written this gross yet elevated, this superficial yet profound, this preposterous yet somehow fascinating book. As we say, it is a mixture of Yankee transcendentalism and New York rowdyism, and, what must be surprising to both these elements, they here seem to fuse and combine with the most perfect harmony. The vast and vague conceptions of the one, lose nothing of their quality in passing through the coarse and odd intellectual medium of the other; while there is an original perception of nature, a manly brawn, and an epic directness in our new poet, which belong to no other adept of the transcendental school. But we have no intention of regularly criticising this very irregular production; our aim is rather to cull, from the rough and ragged thicket of its pages, a few passages equally remarkable in point of thought and expression. Of course we do not select those which are the most transcendental or the most bold:—

[Extract from the poetry; 7 lines:]

"I play not a march for victors only.... I play great marches for conquered and slain persons. [...]

And to all generals that lost engagements, and to all overcome heroes, and the numberless unknown heroes equal to the greatest heroes known."

[Extract from the poetry; 8 lines:]

"I am the mashed fireman, with breast-bone broken.... tumbling
    walls buried me in their debris – [...]

The kneeling crowd fades with the light of the torches."

. . . .

"I tell not the fall of Alamo.... not one escaped to tell the fall of Alamo:
The hundred and fifty are dumb yet at Alamo."

. . . .

"They were the glory of the race of rangers,
Matchless with a horse, a rifle, a song, a supper, or a courtship:
Large, turbulent, brave, handsome, generous, proud and affectionate—
Bearded, sun-burnt, dressed in the free costume of hunters."

. . . .

[Extract from the poetry; 27 lines:]

"Did you read in the books of the old-fashioned frigate fight? [...]

His eyes gave more light to us than our battle-lanterns.
Toward twelve at night, there in the beams of the moon, they surrendered
    to us."

. . . .

[Extract from the poetry; 8 lines:]

"As to you, life, I reckon you are the leavings of many deaths: [...]
Toss to the moaning gibberish of the dry limbs!"

. . . .

[Extract from the poetry; 23 lines:]

"A slave at auction! [...]
They shall be stript, that you may see them. [...]

Within there runs his blood.... the same old blood..... the same
    red running blood—[...]
How do you know who shall come from the offspring of his offspring,
    through the centuries?

. . . .

A woman at auction![...]
    the same old, beautiful mystery."

. . . .

[Extract from the poetry; 9 lines:]

"Behold a woman! [...]
The justified mother of men!"

. . . .

"Old age superbly rising! Ineffable grace of dying days."

. . . .

"Day, full-blown and splendid.... day of the immense sun, and
    action, and ambition, and laughter:
The night follows close, with millions of suns, and sleep, and restoring
    darkness."

As seems very proper in a book of transcendental poetry, the author withholds his name from the title page, and presents his portrait, neatly engraved on steel, instead. This, no doubt, is upon the principle that the name is merely accidental; while the portrait affords an idea of the essential being from whom these utterances proceed. We must add, however, that this significant reticence does not prevail throughout the volume, for we learn on p. 29, that our poet is "Walt Whitman, an American, one of the roughs, a kosmos." That he was an American, we knew before, for, aside from America, there is no quarter of the universe where such a production could have had a genesis. That he was one of the roughs was also tolerably plain; but that he was a kosmos, is a piece of news we were hardly prepared for. Precisely what a kosmos is, we trust Mr. Whitman will take an early occasion to inform the impatient public.

5. "Leaves of Grass—an Extraordinary Book." *Brooklyn Daily Eagle*, 15 September 1855, p. 2.

Here we have a book which fairly staggers us. It sets all the ordinary rules of criticism at defiance. It is one of the strangest compounds of transcendentalism, bombast, philosophy, folly, wisdom, wit and dullness which it ever catered into the heart of man to conceive. Its author is Walter Whitman, and the book is a reproduction of the author. His name is not on the frontispiece, but his portrait, half length, is. The contents of the book form a daguerreotype of his inner being, and the title page bears a representation of its physical tabernacle. It is a poem; but it conforms to none of the rules by which poetry has ever been judged. It is not an epic nor an ode, nor a lyric; nor does its verses move with the measured pace of poetical feet—of Iambic, Trochaic or Anapaestic, nor seek the aid of Amphibrach, of dactyl or Spondee, nor of final or cesural pause, except by accident. But we had better give Walt's own conception of what a poet of the age and country should be. We quote from the preface:

[Extract from the preface; c. 140 words:]

"Other States indicate themselves in their deputies, but the genius of the United States is not best or most in executives or legislatures, [...]—the President's taking off his hat to them, not they to him—these too are unrhymed poetry."

But the poetry which the author contemplates must reflect the nation as well as the people themselves.

[Extracts from the preface; c. 260 words:]

"His spirit responds to his country's spirit; [...] the breadth of above and below is tallied by him. [...]

To him enter the essence of the real things, and past and present events—the large amativeness—the fluid movement of the population, [....]

For such the expression of the American poet is to be transcendent and new."

And the poem seems to accord with the ideas here laid down. No drawing room poet is the author of the *Leaves of Grass;* he prates not of guitar thrumming under ladies' windows, nor deals in the extravagances of sentimentalism; no pretty conceits or polished fancies are tacked together "like orient pearls at random strung;" but we have the free utterance of an untramelled spirit without the slightest regard to established models or fixed standards of taste. His scenery presents no shaven lawns or neatly trimmed arbors; no hot house conservatory, where delicate exotics odorise the air and enchant the eye. If we follow the poet we must scale unknown precipices and climb untrodden mountains; or we boat on nameless lakes, encountering probably rapids and waterfalls, and start wild fowls never classified by Wilson or Audubon; or we wander among primeval forests, now pressing the yielding surface of velvet moss, and anon caught among thickets and brambles. He believes in the ancient philosophy that there is no more real beauty or merit in one particle of matter than another; he appreciates all; every thing is right that is in its place, and everything is wrong that is not in its place. He is guilty, not only of breaches of conventional decorum but treats with nonchalant defiance what goes by the name of refinement and delicacy of feeling and expression. Whatever is natural he takes to his heart; whatever is artificial (in the frivolous sense) he makes of no account. The following description of himself is more truthful than many self-drawn pictures:

[Extract from the poetry; 5 lines:]

"Apart from the pulling and hauling, stands what I am, [...]
Both in and out of the game, and watching and wondering at it."

As a poetic interpretation of nature, we believe the following is not surpassed in the range of poetry:

[Extract from the poetry; 5 lines:]

"A child said, What is grass! fetching it to me with full hands; [...]
Bearing the owner's name someway on the corners, that we
    may see, and remark, and say, Whose?"

We are afforded glimpses of half-formed pictures to tease and tantalize with their indistinctness: like a crimson cheek and flashing eye looking on us through the leaves of an arbor—mocking us for a moment, but vanishing before we can reach them. Here is an example:

[Extract from the poetry; 9 lines:]

"Twenty-eight young men bathe by the shore; [...]
The rest did not see her, but she saw them, &c."

Well, did the lady fall in love with the twenty-ninth bather, or vice versa? Our author scorns to gratify such puerile curiosity; the denouement which novel readers would expect is not hinted at.

In his philosophy justice attains its proper dimensions:

[Extract from the poetry; 7 lines:]

"I play not a march for victors only: I play great marches for [...]
the numberless unknown heroes equal to the greatest heroes known."

The triumphs of victors had been duly celebrated, but surely a poet was needed to sing the praises of the defeated whose cause was righteous, and the heroes who have been trampled under the hoofs of iniquity's onward march.

He does not pick and choose sentiments and expressions fit for general circulation—he gives a voice to whatever is, whatever we see, and hear, and think, and feel. He descends to grossness, which debars the poem from being read aloud in any mixed circle. We have said that the work defies criticism; we pronounce no judgment upon it; it is a work that will satisfy few upon a first perusal; it must be read again and again, and then it will be to many unaccountable. All who read it will agree that it is an extraordinary book, full of beauties and blemishes, such as nature is to those who have only a half formed acquaintance with her mysteries.

6. [Walt Whitman]. "Walt Whitman, a Brooklyn Boy." Brooklyn *Daily Times,* 29 September 1855, p. 2.

To give judgment on real poems, one needs an account of the poet himself. Very devilish to some, and very divine to some, will appear these new poems, the *Leaves of Grass:* an attempt, as they are, of a live, naive, masculine, tenderly affectionate, rowdyish, contemplative, sensual, moral, susceptible and imperious person, to cast into literature not only his own grit and arrogance, but his own flesh and form, un-draped, regardless of foreign models, regardless of modesty or law, and ignorant or silently scornful, as at first appears, of all except his own presence and experience, and all outside of the fiercely loved land of his birth and the birth of his parents, and their parents for several generations before him. Politeness this man has none, and regulation he has none. The effects he produces are no effects of artists or the arts, but effects of the original eye or arm, or the actual atmosphere of grass or brute or bird. You may feel the unconscious teaching of the presence of some fine animal, but will never feel the teaching of the fine writer or speaker.

Other poets celebrate great events, personages, romances, wars, loves, passions, the victories and power of their country, or some real or imagined incident—and polish their work, and come to conclusions, and satisfy the reader. This poet celebrates himself: and that is the way he celebrates all. He comes to no conclusions, and does not satisfy the reader. He certainly leaves him what the serpent left the woman and the man, the taste of the tree of the knowledge of good and evil, never to be erased again.

What good is it to argue about egotism? There can be no two thoughts on Walt Whitman's egotism. That is what he steps out of the crowd and turns and faces them for. Mark, critics! for otherwise is not used for you the key that leads to the use of the other keys to this well enveloped yet terribly in earnest man. His whole work, his life, manners, friendships, writing, all have among their leading purposes, an evident purpose, as strong and avowed as any of the rest, to stamp a new type of character, namely his own, and indelibly fix it and publish it, not for a model but an illustration, for the present and future of American letters and American young men, for the south the same as the north, and for the Pacific and Mississippi country, and Wisconsin and Texas and Canada and Havana, just as much as New York and Boston. Whatever is needed toward this achievement he puts his hand to, and lets imputations take their time to die.

First be yourself what you would show in your poem—such seems to be this man's example and inferred rebuke to the schools of poets. He makes no allusions to books or writers; their spirits do not seem to have touched him; he has not a word to say for or against them, or their theories or ways. He never offers others; what he continually offers is the man whom our Brooklynites know so well. Of pure American breed, of reckless health, his body perfect, free from taint top to toe, free forever from headache and dyspepsia, full-blooded, six feet high, a good feeder, never once using medicine, drinking water only—a swimmer in the river or bay or by the seashore—of straight attitude and slow movement of foot—an indescribable style evincing indifference and disdain—ample limbed, weight one hundred and eighty-five pounds, age thirty-six years (1855)—never dressed in black, always dressed freely and clean in strong clothes, neck open, shirt-collar flat and broad, countenance of swarthy, transparent red, beard short and well mottled with white hair like hay after it has been mowed in the field and lies tossed and streaked—face not refined or intellectual, but calm and wholesome—a face of an unaffected animal—a face that absorbs the sunshine and meets savage or gentleman on equal terms—a face of one who eats and drinks and is a brawny lover and embracer—a face of undying friendship and indulgence toward men and women, and of one who finds the same returned many fold—a face with two grey eyes where passion and hauteur sleep, and melancholy stands behind them—a spirit that mixes cheerfully with the world—a person singularly beloved and welcomed, especially by young men and mechanics—one who has firm attachments there, and associates there—one who does not associate with literary and elegant people—one of the two men sauntering along the street with their arms over each other's shoulders, his companions some boatman or ship joiner, or from the hunting-tent or lumber-raft—one who has that quality of attracting the best out of people that they present to him, none of their meaner and stingier traits, but always their sweetest and most generous traits—a man never called upon to make speeches at public dinners, never on platforms amid the crowds of clergymen or professors or aldermen or congressmen—rather down in the bay with pilots in their pilot boats—or off on a cruise with fishers in a fishing smack—or with a band of laughers and roughs in the streets of the city or the open grounds of the country—fond of New York and Brooklyn—fond of the life of the wharves and great ferries, or along Broadway, observing the endless wonders of that thoroughfare of the world—one whom, if you would meet, you need not expect to meet an extraordinary person—one in whom you will see the singularity which consists in no singularity—whose contact is no dazzling fascination, nor require any difference, but has the easy fascination of what is homely and accustomed—of something you knew before, and was waiting for—of natural pleasures, and well-known places, and welcome familiar faces—perhaps of a remembrance of your brother or mother, or friend away or dead—there you have Walt Whitman, the begetter of a new offspring out of literature, taking with easy nonchalance the chances of its present reception, and, through all misunderstandings and distrusts, the chances of its future reception.

7. [Walt Whitman]. "An English and American Poet" [review of Alfred Tennyson, *Maud*, and other Poems and *Leaves of Grass*]. *American Phrenological Journal*, 22, no. 4 (October 1855), 90–1.

It is always reserved for second-rate poems immediately to gratify. As first-rate or natural objects, in their perfect simplicity and proportion, do not startle or strike, but appear no more than matters of course, so probably natural poetry does not, for all its being the rarest, and telling of the longest and largest work. The artist or writer whose talent is to please the connoisseurs of his time, may obey the laws of his time, and achieve the intense and elaborated beauty of parts. The perfect poet cannot afford any special beauty of parts, or to limit himself by any laws less than those universal ones of the great masters, which include all times, and all men and women, and the living and the dead. For from the study of the universe is drawn this irrefragable truth, that the law of the requisites of a grand poem, or any other complete workmanship, is originality, and the average and superb beauty of the ensemble. Possessed with this law, the fitness of aim, time, persons, places, surely follows. Possessed with this law, and doing justice to it, no poet or any one else will make anything ungraceful or mean, any more than any emanation of nature is.

The poetry of England, by the many rich geniuses of that wonderful little island, has grown out of the facts of the English race, the monarchy and aristocracy prominent over the rest, and conforms to the spirit of them. No nation ever did or ever will receive with national affection any poets except those born of its national blood. Of these, the writings express the finest infusions of government, traditions, faith, and the dependence or independence of a people, and even the good or bad physiognomy, and the ample or small geography. Thus what very properly fits a subject of the British crown may fit very ill an American freeman. No fine romance, no inimitable delineation of character, no grace of delicate illustrations, no rare picture of shore or mountain or sky, no deep thought of the intellect, is so important to a man as his opinion of himself is; everything receives its tinge from that. In the verse of all those undoubtedly great writers, Shakspeare just as much as the rest, there is the air which to America is the air of death. The mass of the people, the laborers and all who serve, are slag, refuse. The countenances of kings and great lords are beautiful; the countenances of mechanics are ridiculous and deformed. What play of Shakspeare, represented in America, is not an insult to America, to the marrow in its bones? How can the tone never silent in their plots and characters be applauded, unless Washington should have been caught and hung, and Jefferson was the most enormous of liars, and common persons, north and south, should bow low to their betters, and to organic superiority of blood? Sure as the heavens envelop the earth, if the Americans want a race of bards worthy of 1855, and of the stern reality of this republic, they must cast around for men essentially different from the old poets, and from the modern succesions of jinglers and snivellers and fops.

English versification is full of these danglers, and America follows after them. Every body writes poetry, and yet there is not a single poet. An age greater than the proudest of the past is swiftly slipping away, without one lyric voice to seize its greatness, and speak it as an encouragement and onward lesson. We have heard, by many grand announcements, that he was to come, but will he come?

"A mighty Poet whom this age shall choose
To be its spokesman to all coming times.
In the ripe full-blown season of his soul,
He shall go forward in his spirit's strength,
And grapple with the questions of all time,
And wring from them their meanings. As King Saul
Called up the buried prophet from his grave
To speak his doom, so shall this Poet-king
Call up the dread past from its awful grave
To tell him of our future. As the air
Doth sphere the world, so shall his heart of love—
Loving mankind, not peoples. As the lake

Reflects the flower, tree, rock, and bending heaven, Shall he reflect
    our great humanity;
And as the young Spring breathes with living breath
On a dead branch, till it sprouts fragrantly
Green leaves and sunny flowers, shall he breathe life
Through every theme he touch, making all Beauty
And Poetry forever like the stars."

                                              (Alexander Smith.)

The best of the school of poets at present received in Great Britain and America is Alfred Tennyson. He is the bard of ennui and of the aristocracy, and their combination into love. This love is the old stock love of playwrights and romancers, Shakspeare the same as the rest. It is possessed of the same unnatural and shocking passion for some girl or woman, that wrenches it from its manhood, emasculated and impotent, without strength to hold the rest of the objects and goods of life in their proper positions. It seeks nature for sickly uses. It goes screaming and weeping after the facts of the universe, in their calm beauty and equanimity, to note the occurrence of itself, and to sound the news, in connection with the charms of the neck, hair, or complexion of a particular female.

Poetry, to Tennyson and his British and American eleves, is a gentleman of the first degree, boating, fishing, and shooting genteelly through nature, admiring the ladies, and talking to them, in company, with that elaborate half-choked deference that is to be made up by the terrible license of men among themselves. The spirit of the burnished society of upper-class England fills this writer and his effusions from top to toe. Like that, he does not ignore courage and the superior qualities of men, but all is to show forth through dandified forms. He meets the nobility and gentry half-way. The models are the same both to the poet and the parlors. Both have the same supercilious elegance, both love the reminiscences which extol caste, both agree on the topics proper for mention and discussion, both hold the same undertone of church and state, both have the same languishing melancholy and irony, both indulge largely in persiflage, both are marked by the contour of high blood and a constitutional aversion to anything cowardly and mean, both accept the love depicted in romances as the great business of a life as a poem, both seem unconscious of the mighty truths of eternity and immortality, both are silent on the presumptions of liberty and equality, and both devour themselves in solitary lassitude. Whatever may be said of all this, it harmonizes and represents facts. The present phases of high-life in Great Britain are as natural a growth there, as Tennyson and his poems are a natural growth of those phases. It remains to be distinctly admitted that this man is a real first-class poet, infused amid all that ennui and aristocracy.

Meanwhile a strange voice parts others aside and demands for its owner that position that is only allowed after the seal of many returning years has stamped with approving stamp the claims of the loftiest leading genius. Do you think the best honors of the earth are won so easily, Walt Whitman? Do you think city and country are to fall before the vehement egotism of your recitative of yourself?

[Extract from *Leaves of Grass*; 10 lines:]

"I am the poet of the body,
And I am the poet of the soul. [...]
I show that size is only development."

It is indeed a strange voice! Critics and lovers and readers of poetry as hitherto written, may well be excused the chilly and unpleasant shudders which will assuredly run through them, to their very blood and bones, when they first read Walt Whitman's poems. If this is poetry, where must its foregoers stand? And what is at once to become of the ranks of rhymesters, melancholy and swallow-tailed, and of all the confectioners and upholsterers of verse, if the tan-faced man here advancing and claiming to speak for America and the nineteenth hundred of the Christian list of years, typifies indeed the natural and proper bard?

The theory and practice of poets have hitherto been to select certain ideas or events or personages, and then describe them in the best manner they could, always with as much ornament as the case allowed. Such are not the theory and practice of the new poet. He never presents for perusal a poem ready-made on the old models, and ending when you come to the end of it; but every sentence and every passage tells of an interior not always seen, and exudes an impalpable something which sticks to him that reads, and pervades and provokes him to tread the half-invisible road where the poet, like an apparition, is striding fearlessly before. If Walt Whitman's premises are true, then there is a subtler range of poetry than that of the grandeur of acts and events, as in Homer, or of characters, as in Shakspeare—poetry to which all other writing is subservient, and which confronts the very meanings of the works of nature and competes with them. It is the direct bringing of occurrences and persons and things to bear on the listener or beholder, to re-appear through him or her; and it offers the best way of making them a part of him and her as the right aim of the greatest poet.

Of the spirit of life in visible forms—of the spirit of the seed growing out of the ground—of the spirit of the resistless motion of the globe passing unsuspected but quick as lightning along its orbit—of them is the spirit of this man's poetry. Like them it eludes and mocks criticism, and appears unerringly in results. Things, facts, events, persons, days, ages, qualities, tumble pell-mell, exhaustless and copious, with what appear to be the same disregard of parts, and the same absence of special purpose, as in nature. But the voice of the few rare and controlling critics, and the voice of more than one generation of men, or two generations of men, must speak for the inexpressible purposes of nature, and for this haughtiest of writers that has ever yet written and printed a book. He is to prove either the most lamentable of failures or the most glorious of triumphs, in the known history of literature. And after all we have written we confess our brain-felt and heart-felt inability to decide which we think it is likely to be.

8.   *Christian Spiritualist* (1856) [full bibliographical data is missing; reprinted in Whitman, *Leaves of Grass Imprints* (Boston: Thayer & Eldridge, 1860), 32–6].

Carlyle represents a contemporary reviewer taking leave of the *Belles-Lettres* department somewhat in this abrupt manner:
    The end having come, it is fit that we end—Poetry having ceased to be read, or published, or written, how can it continue to be reviewed? With your Lake Schools, and Border-Thief Schools, and Cockney and Satanic Schools, there has been enough to do; and now, all these Schools having been burnt or smouldered themselves out, and left nothing but a wide-spread wreck of ashes, dust, and cinders—or perhaps dying embers, kicked to and fro under the feet of innumerable women and children in the magazines, and at best blown here and there into transient sputters, what remains but to adjust ourselves to circumstances? Urge me not, [continues this desperate litterateur] with considerations that Poetry, as the inward Voice of Life, must be perennial; only dead in one form to become alive in another; that this still abundant deluge of Metre, seeing there must needs be fractions of Poetry floating, scattered in it, ought still to be net-fished; at all events, surveyed and taken note of. The survey of English metre, at this epoch, perhaps transcends the human faculties; to hire out the reading of it by estimate, at a remunerative rate per page, would, in a few quarters, reduce the cash-box of any extant review to the verge of insolvency.
    Such is the humorous but essentially truthful picture of the condition and product of the creative faculties during the second quarter of the present century. The great poets, Byron, Shelley, Wordsworth, Goethe, and Schiller, had fulfilled their tasks and gone to other spheres; and all that remained with few exceptions, were weak and feeble echoes of their dying strains, caught up and repeated by numerous imitators and pretenders. And so has it ever been; the visions and perceptions of one man become the creed and superficial life-element of other minds. Swedenborg is worthy to be enrolled among the master minds of the world, because he entered for himself into the Arcana of the profoundest mysteries that can concern human intelligences; his greatest thoughts are revolved, quoted and represented in all "New Church" publications, but very rarely digested and assimilated by those who claim to be his followers. Still more rare is it to find any receiver of "the heavenly doctrines" determined

to enter for himself into the very interiors of all that Swedenborg taught—to see, to the mighty reflections that Swedenborg was able to give of interior realities, but their originals as they stand constellated in the heavens!

But Divine Providence, leading forth the race, as a father the tottering steps of his children, causes the outward form, on which all men are prone to rely, to be forever changing and passing away before their eyes. The seeds of death are ever found luring in the fairest external appearances, till those externals become the mere correspondences and representatives of interior realities, and then, though enduring as the fadeless garments of the blest, they are ever-varying, as those robes of light change with each changing state. The Coming Age will recognize the profoundest truths in the internal thought of the Swedish sage, while his most tenacious adherents will be forced to admit that, in externals, he often erred, and was not unfrequently deceived. But the discovered error will not only wean them from a blind and bigoted reliance upon frail man, but confirm the sincere lovers of truth in loyalty to her standard. So also, the spiritualists are being taught a severe but salutary lesson, that if they will penetrate into the heavenly Arcana of the Inner Life, they must do so by purifying and elevating their own minds, and not by "sitting in circles" or ransacking town and country to find the most "reliable Mediums." Still no step in human progress and development is in vain; even the falls of the child are essential to his discipline. The mistakes and errors of men are needful while in their present imperfect state. They are to the seekers of truth what trials and losses are to those in the pursuit of wealth; they but enhance the value of the prize, and confirm the devotion of the true aspirant as frowns rekindle the ardor of lovers.

Moreover, as man must ever enter into the kingdom of a new unfolding truth with the simplicity and teachableness of little children, it is well that the outer form of the old disappear, that the new may stand alone in its place. It seems also to be a Law that when a change entire and universal is to be outwrought, the means preparatory to its introduction shall be equally widespread, and ultimated to the lowest possible plane. Hence the Spiritual manifestations meet the most external minds; and allow even the unregenerate to know by experience the fact and process of Spiritual inspiration; so that scepticism becomes impossible to the candid and living mind. The second step will be, after such have been convinced that Spiritual intercourse is possible, that they learn that it is worse than useless for the purpose of attaining anything desirable, beyond this conviction—except so far as is orderly and directed, not by the will of man, but of God. But as the old form of poetic inspiration died out with Byron and Shelley, Wordsworth and Goethe, and the miscellaneous Spirit-intercourse itself also as quickly passes away, there will, we apprehend, spring up forms of mediatorial inspiration, of which there will be two permanent types. The first and highest, as it seems to us, will be the opening of the interiors to direct influx to the inspiring sources of love and wisdom. The heavens will flow down into the hearts and lives, into the thought and speech of harmonic natures, as the silent dews impregnate the patient earth. Men will live in heaven, hence they must be inspired by that breath of life that fills its ethereal expanse. A second class of Media will be used for the ultimation, for ends of use and in accordance with Laws of Order, of the creative thoughts and hymns, the Epics and Lyrics, of individual Spirits and societies of Spirits. These will be to the former Media as the youthful artist who copies the work of a master, to the Angelos and Raphaels, who both design and execute their plans, though they themselves, in their deepest interiors, are instructed and sustained from above.

But in the transition period in which we now are, many varieties of Mediumship must be expected. There are those who stand in rapport with the diseased mentalities of the past and present and pour forth as Divine Revelations the froth and scum of a receding age; they are the sponges who absorb the waste and impurities of humanity. They are also like running sores that gather the corrupt humors and drain the body of its most noxious fluids. There are others who come in contact with the outmost portion of the Spirit-life. These give crude, and in themselves, false notions of the state of man after death; yet they prepare the way for more truthful disclosures; if in no other way by stimulating the appetite for more substantial nourishment. There are those who are lifted by genial inspirations to receive influxes from the upper mindsphere of the age. They stand, as it were, on clear mountains of intellectual elevation, and with keenest perception discern the purer forms of new unfolding truths ere they become sufficiently embodied to be manifest to the grosser minds of the race. Of these Ralph Waldo Emerson is the highest-type. He sees the future of truths as our Spirit-seers discern the future of man; he welcomes those impalpable forms, as Spiritualists receive with gladdened minds the returning hosts of Spirit-friends.

There are other mediatorial natures who are in mental and heart-sympathy with man, as he now is, struggling to free himself from the tyranny of the old and effete, and to grasp and retain the new life flowing down from the heavens. And as the kindling rays at first produce more smoke than fire, so their lay is one of promise rather than performance. Such we conceive to be the interior condition of the author of *Leaves of Grass*. He accepts man as he is as to his whole nature, and all men as his own brothers. The lambent flame of his genius encircles the world—nor does he clearly discern between that which is to be preserved, and that which is but as fuel for the purification of the ore from its dross. There is a wild strength, a Spartan simplicity about the man, and he stalks among the dapper gentlemen of this generation, like a drunken Hercules amid the dainty dancers. That his song is highly mediatorial he himself asserts, though probably he is unacquainted with the Spiritual developments of the age.

[Extract from the poetry; 8 lines:]

"Through me [he sings] many long dumb voices, [...]
Voices indecent, by me clarified and transfigured."

We omit much even in this short extract, for the book abounds in passages that cannot be quoted in drawing-rooms, and expressions that fall upon the tympanums of ears polite, with a terrible dissonance. His very gait, as he walks through the world, makes dainty people nervous; and conservatives regard him a social revolution. His style is everywhere graphic and strong, and he sings many things before untouched in prose or rhyme in an idiom that is neither prose nor rhyme, nor yet orthodox blank verse. But it serves his purpose well. He wears strange garb, cut and made by himself, as gracefully as a South American cavalier his poncho. We will continue our quotations.

[Extract from the poetry; several pages:]

Such are the graphic pictures which this new world-painter flings from his easel and dashes upon the moving panorama of life. His night-thoughts are not less striking, as borne by the Muse, he looks into every chamber, and hears the quiet breathing of slumbering humanity.

As the volume advances towards its conclusion, the Spirit of the poet becomes calmer and more serenely elevated. But everywhere his sympathy is with man, and not with conventionalisms.

We cannot take leave of this remarkable volume without advising our friends who are not too delicately nerved, to study the work as a sign of the times, written as we perceive, under powerful influxes; a prophecy and promise of much that awaits all who are entering with us into the opening doors of a new era. A portion of that thought which broods over the American nation, is here seized and bodied forth by a son of the people, rudely, wildly, and with some perversions, yet strongly and genuinely, according to the perception of this bold writer. He is the young Hercules who has seized the serpents that would make him and us their prey; but instead of strangling, he would change them to winged and beautiful forms, who shall become the servants of mankind.

9.   [Rufus W. Griswold]. *Criterion*, 1 (10 November 1855), 24.

An unconsidered letter of introduction has oftentimes procured the admittance of a scurvy fellow into good society, and our apology for permitting any allusion to the above volume in our columns is, that it has been unworthily recommended by a gentleman of wide repute, and might, on that account, obtain access to respectable people, unless its real character were exposed.

Mr. Ralph Waldo Emerson either recognises and accepts these "leaves," as the gratifying results of his own peculiar doctrines, or else he has hastily endorsed them, after a partial and superficial reading. If it is of any importance, he may extricate himself from the dilemma. We, however, believe that this book does express the bolder results of a certain transcendental kind of thinking, which some have styled philosophy.

As to the volume itself, we have only to remark, that it strongly fortifies the doctrines of the Metempsychosists, for it is impossible to imagine how any man's fancy could have conceived such a mass of stupid filth, unless he were possessed of the soul of a sentimental donkey that had died of disappointed love. This poet (?) without wit, but with a certain vagrant wildness, just serves to show the energy which natural imbecility is occasionally capable of under strong excitement.

There are too many persons, who imagine they demonstrate their superiority to their fellows, by disregarding all the politenesses and decencies of life, and, therefore, justify themselves in indulging the vilest imaginings and shamefullest license. But nature, abhorring the abuse of the capacities she has given to man, retaliates upon him, by rendering extravagant indulgence in any direction followed by an insatiable, ever-consuming, and never to be appeased passion.

Thus, to these pitiful beings, virtue and honor are but names. Bloated with self-conceit, they strut abroad unabashed in the daylight, and expose to the world the festering sores that overlay them like a garment. Unless we admit this exhibition to be beautiful, we are at once set down for non-progressive conservatives, destitute of the "inner light," the far-seeingness which, of course, characterize those gifted individuals. Now, any one who has noticed the tendency of thought in these later years, must be aware that a quantity of this kind of nonsense is being constantly displayed. The immodesty of presumption exhibited by these seers; their arrogant pretentiousness; the complacent smile with which they listen to the echo of their own braying, should be, and we believe is, enough to disgust the great majority of sensible folks; but, unfortunately, there is a class that, mistaking sound for sense, attach some importance to all this rant and cant. These candid, these ingenuous, these honest "progressionists;" these human diamonds without flaws; these men that have come, detest furiously all shams; "to the pure, all things are pure;" they are pure, and, consequently, must thrust their reeking presence under every man's nose.

They seem to think that man has no instinctive delicacy; is not imbued with a conservative and preservative modesty, that acts as a restraint upon the violence of passions, which, for a wise purpose, have been made so strong. No! these fellows have no secrets, no disguises; no, indeed! But they do have, conceal it by whatever language they choose, a degrading, beastly sensuality, that is fast rotting the healthy core of all the social virtues.

There was a time when licentiousness laughed at reproval; now it writes essays and delivers lectures. Once it shunned the light; now it courts attention, writes books showing how grand and pure it is, and prophesies from its lecherous lips its own ultimate triumph.

Shall we argue with such men? Shall we admit them into our houses, that they may leave a foul odor, contaminate the pure, healthful air? Or shall they be placed in the same category with the comparatively innocent slave of poverty, ignorance and passion, that skulks along in the shadows of by-ways; even in her deep degradation possessing some sparks of the Divine light, the germ of good that reveals itself by a sense of shame?

Thus, then, we leave this gathering of muck to the laws which, certainly, if they fulfil their intent, must have power to suppress such gross obscenity. As it is entirely destitute of wit, there is no probability that any one would, after this exposure, read it in the hope of finding that; and we trust no one will require further evidence—for, indeed, we do not believe there is a newspaper so vile that would print confirmatory extracts.

In our allusions to this book, we have found it impossible to convey any, even the most faint idea of its style and contents, and of our disgust and detestation of them, without employing language that cannot be pleasing to ears polite; but it does seem that some one should, under circumstances like these, undertake a most disagreeable, yet stern duty. The records of crime show that many monsters have gone on in impunity, because the exposure of their vileness was attended with too great indelicacy. "Peccatum illud horribile, inter Christianos non nominandum."

10. **"Studies among the Leaves: The Assembly of Extremes" [Review of**
     Leaves of Grass **and Tennyson's** *Maud*]. *Crayon*, **3 (January 1856), 30–2.**

A subtle old proverb says, "extremes meet," and science, Art, and even morality, sometimes testify to the truth of the proverb; and there are some curious problems involved in the demonstration of it. The loftiest attainment of the wisdom and worth of age only reaches to the simplicity and fervor of childhood, from which we all start, and returning to which we are blessed. Art makes the same voyage round its sphere, holding ever westward its way into new and unexplored regions, until it does what Columbus would have done, had his faith and self-denial been greater, reaches the east again. If the individual, Columbus, failed to accomplish the destiny, the class, Columbus, fails never. And so in Art, what no one does, the many accomplish, and finally the cycle is filled.

We see this most forcibly in the comparison of two late poems, as unlike, at first thought, as two could be, and yet in which the most striking likenesses prevail, *Maud,* and *Leaves of Grass;* the one as refined in its Art as the most refined, delicate in its structure, and consummate in its subtlety of expression, the other rude and rough, and heedless in its forms—nonchalant in everything but its essential ideas. The one comes from the last stage of cultivation of the Old World, and shows evidence of morbid, luxurious waste of power, and contempt of mental wealth, from inability longer to appreciate the propriety of subjects on which to expend it; as, to one who has overlived, all values are the same, because nothing, and indifferent; while the other, from among the "roughs," is morbid from overgrowth, and likewise prodigal of its thought-treasure, because it has so much that it can afford to throw it away on everything, and considers all things that are, as equally worth gilding. The subject of *Maud* is nothing—a mere common-place incident, but artistically dealt with—a blanched, decayed sea-shell, around which the amber has gathered; and that of the newer poem is equally nothing, blades of sea-grass amber-cemented. Both are characterized by the extreme of affectation of suggestiveness—piers of thought being given, over which the reader must throw his own arches. Both are bold, defiant of laws which attempt to regulate forms, and of those which should regulate essences. *Maud* is irreligious through mental disease, produced by excess of sentimental action—*Leaves of Grass,* through irregularly-developed mental action and insufficiency of sentiment. A calmer perception of Nature would have corrected in Tennyson that feeling which looks upon sorrow as the only thing poetic, and serenity and holy trust, as things to which Love has no alliance, while a higher seeing of Nature would have shown Walt Whitman that all things in Nature are not alike beautiful, or to be loved and honored by song.

Although it is mainly with the Art of the two poems that we have to deal, the form rather than the motive, yet so entirely does the former arise from the latter that the criticism passed on the one must lie upon the other. In the mere versification, for instance, of both, see what indifference to the dignity of verse (while there is still the extorted homage to its forms), arising in both cases, it would seem, from an overweening confidence in the value of what is said, as in the following passages:

"Long have I sighed for a calm; God grant I may find it at last!
It will never be broken by Maud, she has neither savor nor salt,
But a cold, clear, cut face, as I found when her carriage past,
Perfectly beautiful: let it be granted her: where is the fault?"

Maud, Sec. ii., St. 1.

"Do you suspect death? If I were to suspect death, I should die now.
Do you think I could walk pleasantly and well-suited toward annihilation?
Pleasantly and well-suited I walk,
Whither I walk I cannot define, but I know it is good.
The whole universe indicates that it is good.
The past and present indicates that it is good."

Leaves of Grass, p. 69.

All Tennyson's exquisite care over his lines produces no other impression than that which Whitman's carelessness arrives at; viz., nonchalance with regard to forms. In either case, it is an imperfection, we are bold to say, since we do not love beauty and perfection of form for nothing, nor can the measure of poetic feeling be full when we do not care for the highest grace and symmetry of construction. It is an impertinence which says to us, "my ideas are so fine that they need no dressing up," even greater than that which says, "mine are so fine that they cannot be dressed as well as they deserve." The childlike instinct demands perfect melody as an essential to perfect poetry, and more than that, the melodious thought will work out its just and adequate form by the essential law of its spiritual organization—when the heart sings, the feet will move to its music. An unjust measure in verse is prima facie evidence of a jarring note in the soul of the poem, and studied or permitted irregularity of form proves an arrogant self-estimation or irreverence in the poet; and both these poems are irreverent, irreligious, in fact. *Maud* commences, singularly enough, with the words, "I hate," and the whole sentiment of the poem ignores the nobler and purer feelings of humanity—it is full of hatred and morbid feeling, diseased from pure worldliness. This is well enough for one whom the world calls a laureate, but the true poet seeks a laurel that the world cannot gather, growing on mountains where its feet never tread, he lives with beauty and things holy, or, if evil things come to him, it is that they may be commanded behind him. *Maud* rambles and raves through human love and human hate, and the hero lives his life of selfish desire and selfish enjoyment, and then through the bitterness of selfish regret and despair, without one thought of anything better, nobler than himself—the summit of creation. He worships nothing, even reverences nothing, his love is only passion, and his only thought of God one of fear. In his happiness, he is a cynic, in his unhappiness, a madman.

"For the drift of the Maker is dark, an Isis hid by the veil.
Who knows the ways of the world, how God will bring them
     about?
Our planet is one, the suns are many, the world is wide.
Shall I weep if a Poland fail? shall I shriek if a Hungary fail?
Or an infant civilization be ruled with rod or with knout?
I have not made the world, and He that made it will guide.

Be mine a philosopher's life in the quiet woodland ways,
Where if I cannot be gay let a passionless peace be my lot,
Far off from the clamor of liars belied in the hubbub of lies;
From the long-neck'd geese of the world that are ever hissing
     dispraise
Because their natures are little, and, whether he heed it or not,
Where each man walks with his head in a cloud of poisonous
     flies."

. . . .

"Dead, long dead,
Long dead!
And my heart is a handful of dust,
And the wheels go over my head,
And my bones are shaken with pain,

For into a shallow grave they are thrust,
Only a yard beneath the street,
And the hoofs of the horses beat, beat,
The hoofs of the horses beat,
Beat into my scalp and my brain,
With never an end to the stream of passing feet,
Driving, hurrying, marrying, burying,
Clamor and rumble, and ringing and clatter,
And here beneath it is all as bad,
For I thought the dead had peace, but it is not so;
To have no peace in the grave, is that not sad?
But up and down and to and fro,
Ever about me the dead men go;
And then to hear a dead man chatter
Is enough to drive one mad.

Wretchedest age, since Time began,
They cannot even bury a man;
And tho' we paid our tithes in the days that are gone,
Not a bell was rung, not a prayer was read;
It is that which makes us loud in the world of the dead;
There is none that does his work, not one;
A touch of their office might have sufficed,
But the churchmen fain would kill their church,
As the churches have kill'd their Christ.

See, there is one of us sobbing,
No limit to his distress;
And another, a lord of all things, praying
To his own great self, as I guess;
And another, a statesman there, betraying
His party-secret, fool, to the press;
And yonder a vile physician, blabbing
The case of his patient—all for what?
To tickle the maggot born in an empty head,
And wheedle a world that loves him not,
For it is but a world of the dead."

Leaves of Grass is irreligious, because it springs from a low recognition of the nature of Deity, not, perhaps, so in intent, but really so in its result. To Whitman, all things are alike good—no thing is better than another, and thence there is no ideal, no aspiration, no progress to things better. It is not enough that all things are good, all things are equally good, and, therefore, there is no order in creation; no better, no worse—but all is a democratic level from which can come no symmetry, in which there is no head, no subordination, no system, and, of course, no result. With a wonderful vigor of thought and intensity of perception, a power, indeed, not often found, *Leaves of Grass* has no ideality, no concentration, no purpose—it is barbarous, undisciplined, like the poetry of a half-civilized people, and, as a whole, useless, save to those miners of thought who prefer the metal in its unworked state. The preface of the book contains an inestimable wealth of this unworked ore—it is a creed of the material, not denying the ideal, but ignorant of it.

[Extracts from the preface; c. 450 words:]

"The greatest poet hardly knows pettiness or triviality[....] Who troubles himself about his ornaments or fluency is lost." [...]

"The greatest poet has less a marked style, [...] You shall stand by my side, and look in the mirror with me."

[Extracts from the poetry; 28 lines:]

"I am of old and young, of the foolish as much as the wise, [...]

A prisoner, fancy-man, rowdy, lawyer, physician or priest."

. . . .

"I am he attesting sympathy; [...]
My gait is no fault-finder's or rejecter's gait,
I moisten the roots of all that has grown."

In other words, according to Whitman's theory, the greatest poet is he who performs the office of camera to the world, merely reflecting what he sees—art is merely reproduction.
    Yet it cannot be denied that he has felt the beauty of the material in full measure, and sometimes most felicitously.

[Extracts from the poetry; 52 lines:]

"A child said, What is the grass? fetching it to me with full hands; [...]

And now it seems to me the beautiful uncut hair of graves."

. . . .

"The big doors of the country-barn stand open and ready, [...]
And roll head over heels, and tangle my hair full of wisps."

. . . .

"I think I could turn and live awhile with the animals.... they are so placid and self-contained, [...]
They bring me tokens of myself.... they evince them plainly in
    their possession."

. . . .

"When the dull nights are over, and the dull days also, [...]
But without eyesight lingers a different living and looks curiously on the corpse."

. . . .

"I knew a man.... he was a common farmer..... he was the father of fivesons.... and in them were the fathers of sons.... and in them were the fathers of sons. [...]
You would wish long and long to be with him... you would wish
    to sit by him in the boat that you and he might touch each
    other."

It is not possible to compare the feverish, dying sentiment of Tennyson, dying from false indulgence, to the rude, vigorous, and grand if chaotic thought of Whitman, imperfect only from want of development—the poems are alike maimed, but one from loss of parts, the other from not yet having attained its parts. But still they are the extremes—truth lies between them always. What if Columbus had sailed round the world, and made its extremes meet! He would only have been back in Spain again—the true end of his voyage was midway.

11. Edward Everett Hale. *North American Review*, 83 (January 1856), 275–7.

Everything about the external arrangement of this book was odd and out of the way. The author printed it himself, and it seems to have been left to the winds of heaven to publish it. So it happened that we had not discovered it before our last number, although we believe the sheets had then passed the press. It bears no publisher's name, and, if the reader goes to a bookstore for it, he may expect to be told at first, as we were, that there is no such book, and has not been. Nevertheless, there is such a book, and it is well worth going twice to the bookstore to buy it. Walter Whitman, an American,—one of the roughs,—no sentimentalist,—no stander above men and women, or apart from them,—no more modest than immodest,—has tried to write down here, in a sort of prose poetry, a good deal of what he has seen, felt, and guessed at in a pilgrimage of some thirty-five years. He has a horror of conventional language of any kind. His theory of expression is, that, "to speak in literature with the perfect rectitude and insouciance of the movements of animals, is the flawless triumph of art." Now a great many men have said this before. But generally it is the introduction to something more artistic than ever,—more conventional and strained. Antony began by saying he was no orator, but none the less did an oration follow. In this book, however, the prophecy is fairly fulfilled in the accomplishment. "What I experience or portray shall go from my composition without a shred of my composition. You shall stand by my side and look in the mirror with me."

So truly accomplished is this promise,—which anywhere else would be a flourish of trumpets,—that this thin quarto deserves its name. That is to say, one reads and enjoys the freshness, simplicity, and reality of what he reads, just as the tired man, lying on the hill-side in summer, enjoys the leaves of grass around him,—enjoys the shadow,—enjoys the flecks of sunshine,—not for what they "suggest to him," but for what they are.

So completely does the author's remarkable power rest in his simplicity, that the preface to the book—which does not even have large letters at the beginning of the lines, as the rest has—is perhaps the very best thing in it. We find more to the point in the following analysis of the "genius of the United States," than we have found in many more pretentious studies of it.

> Other states indicate themselves in their deputies, but the genius of the United States is not best or most in its executives or legislatures, nor in its ambassadors or authors or colleges or churches or parlors, nor even in its newspapers or inventors;—but always most in the common people. Their manners, speech, dress, friendships;—the freshness and candor of their physiognomy, the picturesque looseness of their carriage, their deathless attachment to freedom, their aversion to everything indecorous or soft or mean, the practical acknowledgment of the citizens of one State by the citizens of all other States, the fierceness of their roused resentment, their curiosity and welcome of novelty, their self-esteem and wonderful sympathy, their susceptibility to a slight, the air they have of persons who never knew how it felt to stand in the presence of superiors, the fluency of their speech, their delight in music (the sure symptom of manly tenderness and native elegance of soul), their good temper and open-handedness, the terrible significance of their elections, the President's taking off his hat to them, not they to him,—these too are unrhymed poetry. It awaits the gigantic and generous treatment worthy of it.

The book is divided into a dozen or more sections, and in each one of these some thread of connection may be traced, now with ease, now with difficulty,—each being a string of verses, which claim to be written without effort and with entire abandon. So the book is a collection of observations, speculations, memories, and prophecies, clad in the simplest, truest, and often the most nervous English,—in the midst of which the reader comes upon something as much out of place as a piece of rotten wood would be among leaves of grass in the meadow, if the meadow had no object but to furnish a child's couch. So slender is the connection, that we hardly injure the following scraps by extracting them.

[Extracts from the poetry; 20 lines:]

"I am the teacher of Athletes; [...]
He that by me spreads a wider breast than my own, proves the width
   of my own;
Preferring scars, and faces pitted with small-pox, over all
   latherers and those that keep out of the sun."

     . . . .

"Here is the story of the gallant seaman who rescued the passengers on the
   San Francisco:—[...]
I am the man, I suffered, I was there."

Claiming in this way a personal interest in every thing that has ever happened in the world, and, by the wonderful sharpness and distinctness of his imagination, making the claim effective and reasonable, Mr. "Walt Whitman" leaves it a matter of doubt where he has been in this world, and where not. It is very clear, that with him, as with most other effective writers, a keen, absolute memory, which takes in and holds every detail of the past,—as they say the exaggerated power of the memory does when a man is drowning,—is a gift of his organization as remarkable as his vivid imagination. What he has seen once, he has seen for ever. And thus there are in this curious book little thumb-nail sketches of life in the prairie, life in California, life at school, life in the nursery,—life, indeed, we know not where not,—which, as they are unfolded one after another, strike us as real,—so real that we wonder how they came on paper.

For the purpose of showing that he is above every conventionalism, Mr. Whitman puts into the book one or two lines which he would not address to a woman nor to a company of men. There is not anything, perhaps, which modern usage would stamp as more indelicate than are some passages in Homer. There is not a word in it meant to attract readers by its grossness, as there is in half the literature of the last century, which holds its place unchallenged on the tables of our drawing-rooms. For all that, it is a pity that a book where everything else is natural should go out of the way to avoid the suspicion of being prudish.

12. "Notes on New Books." *Washington Daily National Intelligencer,* 18 February 1856, p. 2.

Such is the curt and undescriptive title of a prose poem which has created some remark in certain literary circles. It is in every way a singular volume: singular in its form, singular in its arrangement, singular in its style, and most singular of all in its rhapsodical fancies. Its title-page, as will be seen, bears upon it the name of no author, and the book is ushered into the world without the patronage of any publisher to give it currency and protection. Of "complimentary copies" for the press, none, so far as we are aware, have been vouchsafed by the writer. Ostrich-like, he has laid his egg in the sand and left it to quicken or not, according to that time and chance which, as the wise man says, happen to all things. We are not left, however, in the body of the work, wholly ignorant of the writer's name, profession, or age—"Walt Whitman, an American, one of the roughs, a kosmos, disorderly, fleshly, and sensual, no senti-mentalist, no stander above men or women or apart from them, no more modest than immodest," is the odd fish who avows himself as the father of this odd volume. Walt Whitman is a printer by trade, whose punctuation is as loose as his morality, and who no more minds his *ems* than his p's and q's. He tells us that he was born on the last day of May, and "passed from a babe in the creeping trance of three summers and three winters to articulate and walk," all which he thinks "wonderful;" while that he "grew six feet high and became a man thirty-six years old in 1855, and that he is [I am] here any how," are facts which he pronounces equally "wonderful" in the won-der-world of his philosophy.

Though Walt Whitman has modestly withheld his name from the title-page of his production, he has favored us with his likeness by way of frontispiece to the volume. If the artist has faithfully depicted his effigy, Walt is indeed "one of the roughs;" for his picture would answer equally well for a "Bowery boy," one of the "killers," "Mose" in the play, "Bill Sykes after the murder of Nancy," or the "B'hoy that runs with the engine," much as we have known certain "portraits taken from life" compelled to do duty in pictorial newspapers as the true likeness of half a dozen celebrated criminals. Walt Whitman is evidently the "representative-man" of the "roughs."

The avowed object of Walter in the loose quarto before us is to "celebrate" him-self; and as the pastoral muse of Virgil "meditated" on a slender oat straw, so Mr. Whitman "leans and loafes" at his ease, "observing a spear of summer grass." Holy Writ informs us that "all flesh is grass," which, according to quaint old Sir Thomas Browne, is just as true literally as metaphorically; for all the adipose matter depos-ited in the human body from roast beef and mutton is, after all, at the bottom of the account only grass taking upon itself a coat of flesh, for grass forms the ox and roast beef forms the physical man; ergo, the most carnivorous gastronome, no less than the most immaculate vegetarian, is nothing but grass at the last chemical analysis of his constituents. Hence it will be seen that "grass" is what Mr. Whitman calls a "uniform hieroglyphic" of the whole human family, and as such deserves to be scanned by the minute philosopher.

A handful of grass fetched by a child to Walter Whitman inspires him with myste-rious thoughts which he vainly essays to grasp, and hints intrusive questionings which he vainly endeavors to answer. At first he guesses that blades of grass "must be the flag of his disposition, out of hopeful green stuff woven," and anon he guesses they are the "handkerchief of the Lord," designedly dropped from above "as scented gifts and remembrancers." He next guesses that "the grass itself is a child, the produced babe of the vegetation," and now he exclaims, in the next breath, "it seems to me the beautiful uncut hair of graves," and hence he feels like caressing it, and breaks out in the following address to the "curling grass:"

[Extracts from the poetry; 12 lines:]

"It may be you transpire from the breasts of young men; [...]
And here you are the mother's lap."

. . . .

"What do you think has become of the young and old men? [...]
I hasten to inform him or her that it is just as lucky to die, and
  I know it."

The reader who has proceeded only thus far begins already to discover that Walter Whitman is a pantheist. Without, perhaps, ever having read Spinoza, he is a Spinozist. Without, perhaps, much deep insight into Plato the divine, he is a Platonist "in the rough," and believes profoundly in the "immanence of all in each," without ever once mouthing that grand phrase of the Greek philosopher. With-out knowing how to chop the formal logic of the schools, he is a necessitarian and fatalist, with whom "whatever is is right." The world as he finds it, and man as he is, good or bad, high or low, ignorant or learned, holy or vicious, are all alike good enough for Walter Whitman, who is in himself a "kosmos," and whose emotional nature is at once the sensorium of humanity and the sounding board which catches up and intones each note of joy or sorrow in the "gamut of human feeling."

He represents himself as being alike of the old and the young, of the foolish as much as the wise; maternal in his instincts as well as paternal; a child as well as a man; a Southerner as soon as a Northerner; a planter, nonchalant and hospitable; a Yankee, bound his own way and ever ready for a swap; a Kentuckian, walking the trail of the Elkhorn with deerskin leggings; a boatman over the lakes or bays or along coasts; a Hoosier, a Badger, a Wolverine, a Buckeye, a Louisianian, a "poke-easy" from sandhills and pines: at home equally on the hills of Vermont, or in the woods of Maine, or the Texas ranch; a learner with the simplest, a teacher of the thoughtfulest, a farmer, mechanic, or artist, a gentleman, sailor, lover, or quaker, a prisoner, fancy-man, rowdy, lawyer, physician, or priest. He rejoices to feel that he is "not stuck up and is in his place," for

> "The moth and the fish eggs are in their place:
> The suns I see and the suns I cannot see are in their place;
> The palpable is in its place and the impalpable is in its place."

So fully has the world-spirit possessed the soul of Walter that he thinks he could turn and live awhile with the animals; "they are so placid and self-contained" that he sometimes "stands and looks at them half the day long."

> "They do not sweat and whine about their condition;
> They do not lie awake in the dark and weep for their sins;
> They do not make me sick discussing their duty to God."

Mr. Whitman's philosophy, it will be seen, is somewhat different from Blaise Pascal's, and we hope we shall not hurt Mr. W's feelings if we venture to give to the devout Jansenist a slight precedence over him. Pascal, the poor man, having no better guides than his own august reason and the oracles of divine inspiration, in his profound speculations on the greatness and misery of man, came to the conclusion that man's consciousness of his misery was one of the most signal and primary proofs of his greatness. These anxious longings of the soul as for an unknown good were to his mind the indication of slumbering capacities not yet developed, and revealed that power of introspection and self-scrutiny which is at once the attribute of consciousness and the attestation of human responsibility. The man who degrades himself to the level of the brutes, or sinks even lower than they, does yet by his very nature rise above them in that he is conscious of his degradation. At least so thought Pascal, and so think still all those who find in man's consciousness the proof of his dignity and of his elevation above the brute creation.

Mr. Whitman thinks, however, he would like to turn and live awhile with the animals. Well, one's associates should certainly be determined according to one's tastes. Every one to his liking, as remarked the venerable dame in the proverb when she kissed her cow. *De gustibus*, &c. Mr. Whitman, it is true, can plead royal example and ancient precedent in defence of his "passional attraction" towards the dumb animals. King Nebuchadnezzar, many years before him, consorted with the oxen of the field and went to graze after the most approved style of the bovine quadruped. We do not read, however, that his majesty greatly relished this species of out door life [...] because, "unlike one of the roughs," he failed to remark how "placid and self-contained" were his companions of the herd. Nebuchadnezzar too, it is to be feared, lacked the proper pantheistic instincts to permit his entering fully into the sublime mysteries of Serapis and Anubis. If his life-experiences had been the same as "Walt Whitman's" before undergoing his change, he might have managed better to enjoy his new society.

In the "Golden Ass" of Apuleius we have also another record of life among the animals. We need not repeat the story of Fotis's ill-starred lover and his magical transformation into an ass, with the long series of misfortunes, the cudgellings and flayings which, sad to tell, befell him in that condition. Are they not all written in the "golden" book aforesaid?—a book which Mr. Whitman, we are sure, would find very much after his own heart in its freedom from anything like sentimental refinement or prudish delicacy, while it is to be hoped that its faithful portraiture of life among the *graminivors* [grass eaters] would cure him of his disposition to herd awhile with the quadrupeds, and render him willing to content himself with his present advantages in the privilege of "standing and looking at them half the day long." It behooves him also to bear in mind that according to all accounts the condition of the Irish peasantry is not greatly elevated over "the rest of mankind" by their hereditary custom of assigning to the "placid" porker and domestic cow a cozy corner in the cabin along with its other inmates. If much good was to be expected from turning and living with the animals, Ireland would have convinced the world of it long before Mr. Whitman's day, and if he had properly studied her history we question whether he would have considered it a matter worth boasting of that he feels himself—

"Stucco'd with quadrupeds and birds all over."

As we do not wish, however, to press Mr. Whitman too hard upon this point, and seek to exhibit rather the philosophy of his teachings than his *petits ridicules*, we append in this same connection the following lyrical outburst of the true pantheistic spirit:

[Extract from the poetry; 7 lines:]

"How beautiful and perfect are the animals! How perfect is my soul! [...]
The trees have, rooted in the ground; the weeds of the sea have;
    the animals!"

It is quite possible that, owing to some radical and congenital defect of our mental organization, we have never been able to penetrate "within the veil" in the Pantheon of the transcendentalists and of the Emersonian school in general. Mr. Emerson, we understand, greatly admires the present work; indeed, we have read a published letter of his in which he tenders to Mr. Whitman his thanks for the *Leaves of Grass*. When we read that eulogy we were satisfied that this volume would prove to us a sealed book, and that its hieroglyphs would be as unintelligible to our ken as was the inscription around the sacred ibex to the erudite Mr. [George Robins] Gliddon. Still we determined to read it, in the humble but earnest hope of endeavoring occasionally to catch its esoteric meaning in a few at least of those passages, which we are assured from Mr. Emerson's enjoyment of them must contain a hidden significance which nothing less potent than the magic salve of the dervise of Balsora can open our eyes to behold; and in default of which we must be content with such a poor comprehension of these Sibylline leaves as falls to the lot of common readers.

No one, we may say, however, in all candor, can read this singular prose-poem without being struck by the writer's wonderful powers of description and of word-painting. His memory seems as retentive of its treasures as his imagination is opulent in its creations. He writes like one who has but to prick his mind and forthwith it gushes out in a perennial flow of "thoughts which have tarried in its inner chambers." It is only when we are balked in our attempt to trail his transcendental sinuosities of thought that we feel ourselves at fault, and then we are reminded of Longfellow's description of the Emersonian philosophy, which he likened to some of the roads in our great West, which at first open very fair and wide, and are shaded on both sides by the towering giants of the primeval forest, but which before long become narrower and narrower and at last dwindle to a squirrel path and run up a tree.

13. **The New York *Daily News*, 27 February 1856, p. 1. *Leaves of Grass*. Entered according to Act of Congress, by Walter Whitman, &c., &c. Brooklyn.**

A new edition, we believe, of the famous Whitman's poems, which made such a flutter among the "gray goose quills" of this city and "other quarters of the globe" some time ago. Of the poem which occupies the ninety-five pages of this folio, we have before briefly spoken. Upon examining it a second time, and pondering its aims and expressions, we feel constrained to say that it is certainly the strangest, most extraordinary production we have ever attempted to peruse. Still, like the rest of our countrymen, we are by no means either averse to extraordinary things or afraid of them. We enjoy enterprise in speech and writing as thoroughly as in steam vessels, revolving rifles or new-found Nicaraguas. Therefore we shall not quarrel with Mr. Whitman for being odd. Oddness is the normal condition of some natures—of the freshest and best, perhaps—at least when it means frankness and opposition to solemn propriety, alias humbug and red tape.

Mr. Whitman's preface is what the hum-drum world calls "queer" as entirely perhaps as his poem, yet we think a great deal of it both finely and bravely uttered as well as true. None can, more than we do, entirely hate that cant which always ascribes this or that kind of writing to this or the other "school," as if the young author had necessarily in every instance copied some model; as if two similarly constituted minds may not naturally seek similar expression! It is precisely this stupid, stereotyped classification adopted by indolent or clique-led reviewers, that has produced so many abortions in literature through the straining after at least the appearance of total originality, but to give future readers of this book some indication of its style, ere they have opened it, we will say that it is Germanic and Carlylean—even Emersonian—sometimes in the strain of Martin Farquhar Tupper, although far stronger and more pointed than the latter.

The poem exhibits undoubted and striking evidence of genius and power. But the author reasoning that the spirit of the American people, nay, of any people is chiefly represented by its uncultivated though, perhaps, naturally intelligent classes, falls into the error of mistaking their frequent uncouthness as a fair revelation of that spirit, and the bathos often produced in some of his finest passages by the presence of this idea defaces his work and repels hundreds of candid minds who would be eager to acknowledge his claims, but are thus prevented from reading enough to recognize them.

In glancing rapidly over the "Leaves of Grass" you are puzzled whether to set the author down as a madman or an opium eater; when you have studied them you recognize a poet of extraordinary vigor, nay even beauty of thought, beneath the most fantastic possible garments of diction. If Hamlet had gone mad, in Ophelia's way, as well as in his own, and in addition to his own vein of madness, he might, when transported to our own age and country, have talked thus.

In a crush hat and red shirt open at the neck, without waistcoat or jacket, one hand on his hip and the other thrust into his pocket, Walt Whitman the b'hoy poet, on his muscle, writes sentences like these:

> "A child said, What is grass?—fetching it to me with
> full hands.
> How could I answer the child....I do not know what it
> is any more than he."
>
> . . . .

> "And now it seems to me the beautiful uncut hair of
> graves."
>
> . . . .

> "This grass is very dark to be from the white heads of
> old mothers.
> Darker than the colorless bears of old men,
> Dark to come from under the faint red roofs of mouths.
> Oh I perceive, after all, so many uttering tongues!
> And I perceive they do not come from the roofs of mouths
> for nothing."

Again:

> "Press close, bare bosomed night! Press close
> magnetic nourishing night!
> Night of South winds! Night of the large few stars!
> Still nodding night! Mad naked Summer night!"
>
> . . . .

> "Sea breathing broad and convulsive breaths!
> Sea of the brine of life! Sea of unshovelled and always ready
> graves!"

His own picture:

> "Walt Whitman, an American, one of the roughs, a Kosmos,
> Disorderly, fleshy, sensual....eating, drinking and breeding,
> No sentimentalist....no stander above men and women or
> apart from the,....no more modest than immodest."

Yet, he is a sentimentalist! Read the lines beginning

> "I believe a leaf of grass is no less than the journey
> work of the stars, &c.—"

He is a painter, carver and sculptor:

"A gigantic beauty of a stallion, fresh and responsive to my
    caresses,
Head high in the forehead and between the ears,
Limbs glossy and supple, tail dusting the ground,
Eyes well apart and full of sparkling wickedness....ears
    finely cut and flexibly moving."

He is a genuine "rough"—a male muse in horse-blanket and boots. Sometimes he
is "Mose;" sometimes almost a Moses.

He enjoys "he-festivals with blackguard jibes, and ironical license, and bull dances,
and drinking, and laughter." Then he is

"Pleased with primitive tunes of the choir of the white-
    washed church,"

And then you see him

"Walking the old hills of Judea with the beautiful gentle
    god by his side."

Now, with him, we

"Visit the orchards of God, and look at quintillions green."

Or

"Go hunting polar furs and the seal....leaping chasms
    with a pike-pointed staff....clinging to topples
    of brittle and blue.["]

Read this noble passage:

[Extract from the poetry; 5 lines:]

"How the skipper saw the crowded and rudderless wreck [...]
How the silent old-faced infants, and the lifted sick, and the
    sharp-lipped unshaven men."

We are tempted to quote many strophes from this remarkable collection of genius
inebriated with its own overflowing fountains of fancy, but must conclude with the
following fine lines, referring to past struggles for freedom, and predicting a future:

[Extract from the poetry; 17 lines:]

"Meanwhile corpses lie in new-made graves....bloody corpses
    of young men: [...]
He will soon return....his messengers come anon."

For the sum of 75 cents any reader may accompany Whitman through a poetic chaos—bright, dark, splendid, common, ridiculous and sublime—in which are floating the nebulae and germs of matter for a starry universe of organized and harmonious systems that may yet revolve, in all the magnificence of artistic order, through the highest heaven of fame!

As proof that whatever may be the merits or demerits of this singular production, we may state that very many thousand copies have been sold and the demand is still increasing.

14.   [William Howitt? or William J. Fox?]. London *Weekly Dispatch*, 9 March 1856, p. 6.

We have before us one of the most extraordinary specimens of Yankee intelligence and American eccentricity in authorship, it is possible to conceive. It is of a *genus* so peculiar as to embarrass us, and has an air at once so novel, so audacious, and so strange as to verge upon absurdity, and yet it would be an injustice to pronounce it so, as the work is saved from this extreme by a certain mastery over diction not very easy of definition. What Emerson has pronounced to be good must not be lightly treated, and before we pronounce upon the merits of this performance it is but right to examine them. We have, then, a series of pithy prose sentences strung together—forming twelve grand divisions in all, but which, having a rude rhythmical cadence about them admit of the designation poetical being applied. They are destitute of rhyme, measure of feet, and the like, every condition under which poetry is generally understood to exist being absent; but in their strength of expression, their fervor, hearty wholesomeness, their originality, mannerism, and freshness, one finds in them a singular harmony and flow, as if by reading, they gradually formed themselves into melody, and adopted characteristics peculiar and appropriate to themselves alone. If, however, some sentences be fine, there are others altogether laughable; nevertheless, in the bare strength, the unhesitating frankness of a man who "believes in the flesh and the appetites," and who dares to call simplest things by their plainest names, conveying also a large sense of the beautiful, and with an emphasis which gives a clearer conception of what manly modesty really is than any thing we have, in all conventional forms of word, deed, or act so far known of, that we rid ourselves, little by little, of the strangeness with which we greet this bluff new-comer, and, beginning to understand him better, appreciate him in proportion as he becomes more known. He will soon make his way into the confidence of his readers, and his poems in time will become a pregnant text-book, out of which quotation as sterling as the minted gold will be taken and applied to every form and phase of the "inner" or the "outer" life; and we express our pleasure in making the acquaintance of Walt Whitman, hoping to know more of him in time to come.

15.   "Leaves of Grass." *Saturday Review*, 1 (15 March 1856), 393–4.

We have received a volume, bound in green, and bearing the above title, under rather singular circumstances. Not only does the donor send us the book, but he favours us with hints—pretty broad hints—towards a favourable review of it. He has pasted in the first page a number of notices extracted with the scissors from American newspapers, and all magnificently eulogistic of Leaves of Grass. So original a proceeding merits an exceptional course; and therefore we shall confine ourselves to laying before our readers, first, the opinions of the American reviewers, and next giving specimens of the work reviewed. The relation of the two classes of extracts is curiously illustrative of contemporary American criticism.

The first panegyrist is not a newspaper writer, but the "Representative Man," Ralph Waldo Emerson:—

[Emerson's letter here reprinted:]

"DEAR SIR,—I am not blind to the worth of the wonderful gift of Leaves of Grass. […] It has the best merits, namely, of fortifying and encouraging.

R. W. EMERSON."

From the Brooklyn *Daily Times* we take a description of Mr. Walt Whitman, the author of *Leaves of Grass*:—

[Extract from Whitman's self-review in the *Daily Times*, above; c. 180 words:]

"He never offers others; […] meets savage or gentleman on equal terms."

The *American Phrenological Journal* contrasts the poet of *Leaves of Grass* with Tennyson:—

[Extracts from Whitman's self-review in this periodical, above; c. 190 words:]

"The best of the school of poets at present received in Great Britain and America is Alfred Tennyson. […] and to sound the news, in connexion with the charms of the neck, hair, or complexion of a particular female......"

"Not a borrower from other lands, […] and he is fain to say,—

I too am not a bit tamed—I too am untranslatable;
I sound my barbaric yawp over the roofs of the world."

The *United States Review* discovers in Mr. Whitman the founder of an indigenous school of American poetry:—

[Extract from Whitman's self-review in this periodical, above; c. 320 words:]

"Self-reliant, with haughty eyes, assuming to himself all the attributes of his country, […] In the beauty of the work of the poet, he affirms, are the tuft and final applause of science."

Now for the pieces justificatives. The exordium of *Leaves of Grass* is as follows:—

[Extract from the poetry; 13 lines:]

"I celebrate myself, […]
I am mad for it to be in contact with me."

A little further on, the poet describes the subject of his poem, viz., himself:—

[Extract from the poetry; 7 lines:]

"Walt Whitman, an American, one of the roughs, a kosmos, […]
And whatever I do or say I also return."

The title of the poem is explained at page 16:—

[Extract from the poetry; 12 lines:]

"A child said, What is the grass? fetching it to me with
full hands; […]

And now it seems to me the beautiful uncut hair of graves."

Mr. Whitman speculates on Humanity:—

[Extract from the poetry; 11 lines:]

"What is a man anyhow? What am I? and what are you? […]
and found no sweeter fat than sticks to my own bones."

Shortly afterwards the poet applies his theory of humanity to himself:—

[Extract from the poetry; 7 lines:]

"I know I am august, […]
And if each and all be aware I sit content."

Our last extract embodies Mr. Whitman's theological creed:—

[Extract from the poetry; 10 lines:]

"And I call to mankind, Be not curious about God, […]
And I leave them where they are, for I know that others
will punctually come for ever and ever."

   After poetry like this, and criticism like this, it seems strange that we cannot rec-
ommend the book to our readers' perusal. But the truth is, that after every five or six
pages of matter such as we have quoted, Mr. Whitman suddenly becomes exceed-
ingly intelligible, but exceedingly obscene. If the *Leaves of Grass* should come into
anybody's possession, our advice is to throw them instantly behind the fire.

16. *Examiner*, 22 March 1856, 180–1.

We have too long overlooked in this country the great poet who has recently arisen in America, of whom some of his countrymen speak in connection with Bacon and Shakespeare, whom others compare with Tennyson,—much to the disadvantage of our excellent laureate,—and to whom Mr Emerson writes that he finds in his book "incomparable things, said incomparably well." The book he pronounces "the most extraordinary piece of wit and wisdom that America has yet contributed;" at which, indeed, says Mr Emerson in the printed letter sent to us,—"I rubbed my eyes a little, to see if this sunbeam were no illusion."

No illusion truly is Walt Whitman, the new American prodigy, who, as he is himself candid enough to intimate, sounds his barbaric yawp over the roofs of the world. He is described by one of his own local papers as "a tenderly affectionate, rowdyish, contemplative, sensual, moral, susceptible, and imperious person," who aspires to cast some of his own grit, whatever that may be, into literature. We have ourselves been disposed to think there is in literature grit enough, according to the ordinary sense, but decidedly Walt Whitman tosses in some more. The author describes himself as "one of the roughs, a kosmos;" indeed, he seems to be very much impressed with the fact that he is a kosmos, and repeats it frequently. A kosmos we may define, from the portrait of it on the front of the book, as a gentleman in his shirt-sleeves, with one hand in a pocket of his pantaloons, and his wide-awake cocked with a dammee-sir air over his forehead.

On the other hand, according to an American review that flatters Mr Whitman, this kosmos is "a compound of the New England transcendentalist and New York rowdy."

But as such terms of compliment may not be quite clear to English readers, we must be content, in simpler fashion, to describe to them this Brooklyn boy as a wild Tupper of the West. We can describe him perfectly by a few suppositions. Suppose that Mr Tupper had been brought up to the business of an auctioneer, then banished to the backwoods, compelled to live for a long time as a backwoodsman, and thus contracting a passion for the reading of Emerson and Carlyle? Suppose him maddened by this course of reading, and fancying himself not only an Emerson but a Carlyle and an American Shakespeare to boot when the fits come on, and putting forth his notion of that combination in his own self-satisfied way, and in his own wonderful cadences? In that state he would write a book exactly like Walt Whitman's *Leaves of Grass*.

[Four extracts from "Song of Myself," totaling 67 lines:]

We must be just to Mr Whitman in allowing that he has one positive merit. His verse has a purpose. He desires to assert the pleasure that a man has in himself, his body and its sympathies, his mind (in a lesser degree, however) and its sympathies. He asserts man's right to express his delight in animal enjoyment, and the harmony in which he should stand, body and soul, with fellow men and the whole universe. To express this, and to declare that the poet is the highest manifestation of this, generally also to suppress shams, is the purport of these *Leaves of Grass*. Perhaps it might have been done as well, however, without being always so purposely obscene, and intentionally foul-mouthed, as Mr Whitman is.

[10-line extract from "Song of Myself"]

The fit being very strong indeed upon him, our Wild Tupper of the West thus puts into words his pleasure at the hearing of an overture:

[15-line extract from "Song of Myself"]

In the construction of our artificial Whitman, we began with the requirement that a certain philosopher should have been bred to the business of an auctioneer. We must add now, to complete the imitation of Walt Whitman, that the wild philosopher and poet, as conceived by us, should be perpetually haunted by the delusion that he has a catalogue to make. Three-fourths of Walt Whitman's book is poetry as catalogues of auctioneers are poems. Whenever any general term is used, off the mind wanders on this fatal track, and an attempt is made to specify all lots included under it. Does Mr Whitman speak of a town, he is at once ready with pages of town lots. Does he mention the American country, he feels bound thereupon to draw up a list of barns, waggons, wilds, mountains, animals, trees, people, "a Hoosier, a Badger, a Buckeye, a Lousianian, or Georgian, a poke-easy from sandhills and pines," &c. &c. We will give an illustration of this form of lunacy. The subject from which the patient starts off is equivalent to things in general, and we can spare room only for half the catalogue. It will be enough, however, to show how there arises catalogue within catalogue, and how sorely the paroxysm is aggravated by the incidental mention of any one particular that is itself again capable of subdivision into lots.

[31-line extract from "A Song for Occupations"]

Now let us compare with this a real auctioneer's catalogue. We will take that of Goldsmith's chambers, by way of departing as little as we can from the poetical. For, as Mr Whitman would say (and here we quote quite literally, prefixing only a verse of our own, from "A Catalogue of the Household Furniture with the select collection of scarce, curious, and valuable books of Dr Goldsmith, deceased, which, by order of the admr, will be sold by auction, &c., &c.)"—
[...]
After all, we are not sure whether the poetry of that excellent Mr Good, the auctioneer who, at his Great Room, No. 121 Fleet street, sold the household furniture of Oliver Goldsmith in the summer of 1774, does not transcend in wisdom and in wit "the most extraordinary piece of wit and wisdom that" (according to Mr Emerson) "America has yet contributed."

17.   *Critic* [London], 15 (1 April 1856), 170–1.

We had ceased, we imagined, to be surprised at anything that America could produce. We had become stoically indifferent to her Woolly Horses, her Mermaids, her Sea Serpents, her Barnums, and her Fanny Ferns; but the last monstrous importation from Brooklyn, New York, has scattered our indifference to the winds. Here is a thin quarto volume without an author's name on the title-page; but to atone for which we have a portrait engraved on steel of the notorious individual who is the poet presumptive. This portrait expresses all the features of the hard democrat, and none of the flexile delicacy of the civilised poet. The damaged hat, the rough beard, the naked throat, the shirt exposed to the waist, are each and all presented to show that the man to whom those articles belong scorns the delicate arts of civilisation. The man is the true impersonation of his book—rough, uncouth, vulgar. It was by the merest accident that we discovered the name of this erratic and newest wonder; but at page 29 we find that he is—

"Walt Whitman, an American, one of the roughs, a Kosmos,
Disorderly, fleshly, and sensual."

The words "an American" are a surplusage, "one of the roughs" too painfully apparent; but what is intended to be conveyed by "a Kosmos" we cannot tell, unless it means a man who thinks that the fine essence of poetry consists in writing a book which an American reviewer is compelled to declare is "not to be read aloud to a mixed audience." We should have passed over this book, *Leaves of Grass*, with indignant contempt, had not some few Transatlantic critics attempted to "fix" this Walt Whitman as the poet who shall give a new and independent literature to America—who shall form a race of poets as Banquo's issue formed a line of kings. Is it possible that the most prudish nation in the world will adopt a poet whose indecencies stink in the nostrils? We hope not; and yet there is a probability, and we will show why, that this Walt Whitman will not meet with the stern rebuke which he so richly deserves. America has felt, oftener perhaps than we have declared, that she has no national poet—that each one of her children of song has relied too much on European inspiration, and clung too fervently to the old conventionalities. It is therefore not unlikely that she may believe in the dawn of a thoroughly original literature, now there has arisen a man who scorns the Hellenic deities, who has no belief in, perhaps because he has no knowledge of, Homer and Shakspere; who relies on his own rugged nature, and trusts to his own rugged language, being himself what he shows in his poems. Once transfix him as the genesis of a new era, and the manner of the man may be forgiven or forgotten. But what claim has this Walt Whitman to be thus considered, or to be considered a poet at all? We grant freely enough that he has a strong relish for nature and freedom, just as an animal has; nay, further, that his crude mind is capable of appreciating some of nature's beauties; but it by no means follows that, because nature is excellent, therefore art is contemptible. Walt Whitman is, as unacquainted with art, as a hog is with mathematics. His poems—we must call them so for convenience—twelve in number, are innocent of rhythm, and resemble nothing so much as the war-cry of the Red Indians. Indeed, Walt Whitman has had near and ample opportunities of studying the vociferations of a few amiable savages. Or rather perhaps, this Walt Whitman reminds us of Caliban flinging down his logs, and setting himself to write a poem. In fact Caliban, and not Walt Whitman, might have written this:

"I too am not a bit tamed—I too am untranslatable.
I sound my *barbaric yawp* over the roofs of the world."

Is this man with the "barbaric yawp" to push Longfellow into the shade, and he meanwhile to stand and "make mouths" at the sun? The chance of this might be formidable were it not ridiculous. That object or that act which most develops the ridiculous element carries in its bosom the seeds of decay, and is wholly powerless to trample out of God's universe one spark of the beautiful. We do not, then, fear this Walt Whitman, who gives us slang in the place of melody, and rowdyism in the place of regularity. The depth of his indecencies will be the grave of his fame, or ought to be if all proper feeling is not extinct. The very nature of this man's compositions excludes us from proving by extracts the truth of our remarks; but we, who are not prudish, emphatically declare that the man who wrote page 79 of the *Leaves of Grass* deserves nothing so richly as the public executioner's whip. Walt Whitman libels the highest type of humanity, and calls his free speech the true utterance of *a man*: we, who may have been misdirected by civilisation, call it the expression of *a beast*.

The leading idea of Walt Whitman's poems is as old as the hills. It is the doctrine of universal sympathy which the first poet maintained, and which the last on earth will maintain also. He says:

> "Not a mutineer walks handcuffed to the jail but I am
>   handcuffed to him and walk by his side,
> Not a cholera patient lies at the last gasp but I also
>   lie at the last gasp."

To show this sympathy he instances a thousand paltry, frivolous, and obscene circumstances. Herein we may behold the difference between a great and a contemptible poet. What Shakspere—mighty shade of the mightiest bard, forgive us the comparison!—expressed in a single line,

> One touch of nature makes the whole world kin,

this Walt Whitman has tortured into scores of pages. A single extract will show what we mean. This miserable spinner of words declares that the earth has "no themes, or hints, or provokers," and never had, if you cannot find such themes, or hints, or provokers in

[18-line extract from "A Song for Occupations"]

Can it be possible that its author intended this as a portion of a poem? Is it not more reasonable to suppose that Walt Whitman has been learning to write, and that the compositor has got hold of his copy-book? The American critics are, in the main, pleased with this man because he is self-reliant, and because he assumes all the attributes of his country. If Walt Whitman has really assumed those attributes, America should hasten to repudiate them, be they what they may. The critics are pleased also because he talks like a man unaware that there was ever such a production as a book, or ever such a being as a writer. This in the present day is a qualification exceedingly rare, and *may* be valuable, so we wish those gentlemen joy of their GREAT UNTAMED.

We must not neglect to quote an unusual passage, which may be suggestive to writers of the Old World. To silence our incredulous readers, we assure them that the passage may be found at page 92:—

[Extract from the poetry; 5 lines:]

> "Is it wonderful that I should be immortal? [...]
>   anyhow, are all equally wonderful."

The transformation and the ethereal nature of Walt Whitman is marvellous to us, but perhaps not so to a nation from which the spirit-rappers sprung.

"I depart as air, I shake my white locks at the runaway
I effuse my flesh in eddies, and drift it in lacy jags;
I bequeath myself to the dirt, to grow from the grass love.
If you want me again, look for me under your boot-soles."

Here is also a sample of the man's slang and vulgarity:

[10-line extract from "Song of Myself"]

And here a spice of his republican insolence, his rank Yankeedom, and his audacious trifling with death:

[11-line extract from "A Boston Ballad"]

We will neither weary nor insult our readers with more extracts from this notable book. Emerson *has praised it*, and called it the "most extraordinary piece of wit and wisdom America has yet contributed." Because Emerson has grasped substantial fame, he can afford to be generous; but Emerson's generosity must not be mistaken for justice. If this work is really a work of genius—if the principles of those poems, their free language, their amazing and audacious egotism, their animal vigour, be real poetry and the divinest evidence of the true poet—then our studies have been in vain, and vainer still the homage which we have paid the monarchs of Saxon intellect, Shakspere, and Milton, and Byron. This Walt Whitman holds that his claim to be a poet lies in his robust and rude health. He is, in fact, as he declares, "the poet of the body." Adopt this theory, and Walt Whitman is a Titan; Shelley and Keats the merest pigmies. If we had commenced a notice of *Leaves of Grass* in anger, we could not but dismiss it in grief, for its author, we have just discovered, is conscious of his affliction. He says, at page 33,

I am given up by traitors;
I talk wildly, I am mad.

18. **[George Eliot].** *Westminster and Foreign Quarterly Review*, **N.S. 9 [London] (1 April 1856), 625–50.**

[In the first pages of this essay Eliot treats a variety of works, ranging from John Ruskin's *Modern Painters* and Adolf Stahr's study of Greek sculpture to a collection of tales by Wilkie Collins and a translation of Homer's *Iliad*. It is only at the end of the essay that she makes the following comments regarding *Leaves of Grass*.]
... We have still said nothing of Mr. Ernest Jones's war strains; of a new poem by the American poet, Mr. Buchanan Reade—a gracefully rhymed, imaginative story; or of another American production which, according to some Transatlantic critics, is to initiate a new school of poetry. This is a poem called "Leaves of Grass," and, instead of criticizing it, we will give a short extract, typical in every respect, except that it contains none of the very bold expressions by which the author indicates his contempt for the "prejudices" of decency.

[Extract from the poetry; 12 lines:]

"A child said, What is the grass? fetching it to me with full
    hands; [...]
And now it seems to me the beautiful uncut hair of graves."

. . . .

[Extract from the poetry; 8 lines:]

"I think I could turn and live awhile with the animals . . . . they are so placid
    and self-contained, [...]
Not one is respectable or industrious over the whole earth."

19.   **Fanny Fern. "Fresh Fern Leaves: Leaves of Grass."** *New York Ledger,* **10
    May 1856, p. 4.**

Well baptized: fresh, hardy, and grown for the masses. Not more welcome is their
natural type to the winter-bound, bed-ridden, and spring-emancipated invalid. *Leaves
of Grass* thou art unspeakably delicious, after the forced, stiff, Parnassian exotics for
which our admiration has been vainly challenged.

Walt Whitman, the effeminate world needed thee. The timidest soul whose wings
ever drooped with discouragement, could not choose but rise on thy strong pinions.

"Undrape—you are not guilty to me, nor stale nor discarded;
I see through the broadcloth and gingham whether or no."

"O despairer, here is my neck,
You shall *not* go down! Hang your whole weight upon me."

Walt Whitman, the world needed a "Native American" of thorough, out and out
breed—enamored of *women* not *ladies, men* not *gentlemen*; something beside a mere
Catholic-hating Know-Nothing; it needed a man who dared speak out his strong,
honest thoughts, in the face of pusillanimous, toadeying, republican aristocracy; dic-
tionary-men, hypocrites, cliques and creeds; it needed a large-hearted, untainted, self-
reliant, fearless son of the Stars and Stripes, who disdains to sell his birthright for a
mess of pottage; who does

"Not call one greater or one smaller,
That which fills its period and place being equal to any;"

who will

"Accept nothing which all cannot have their counterpart
    of on the same terms."

Fresh *Leaves of Grass!* not submitted by the self-reliant author to the fingering of
any publisher's critic, to be arranged, rearranged and disarranged to his circumscribed
liking, till they hung limp, tame, spiritless, and scentless. No. It were a spectacle worth

seeing, this glorious Native American, who, when the daily labor of chisel and plane was over, him-self, with toil-hardened fingers, handled the types to print the pages which wise and good men have since delighted to endorse and to honor. Small critics, whose contracted vision could see no beauty, strength, or grace, in these *Leaves*, have long ago repented that they so hastily wrote themselves down shallow by such a premature confession. Where an Emerson, and a Howitt have commended, my woman's voice of praise may not avail; but happiness was born a twin, and so I would fain share with others the unmingled delight which these "Leaves" have given me.

I say unmingled; I am not unaware that the charge of coarseness and sensuality has been affixed to them. My moral constitution may be hopelessly tainted or—too sound to be tainted, as the critic wills, but I confess that I extract no poison from these *Leaves*—to me they have brought only healing. Let him who can do so, shroud the eyes of the nursing babe lest it should see its mother's breast. Let him look carefully between the gilded covers of books, backed by high-sounding names, and endorsed by parson and priest, lying unrebuked upon his own family table; where the asp of sensuality lies coiled amid rhetorical flowers. Let him examine well the paper dropped weekly at his door, in which virtue and religion are rendered disgusting, save when they walk in satin slippers, or, clothed in purple and fine linen, kneel on a damask *"prie-dieu."*

Sensual!—No—the moral assassin looks you not boldly in the eye by broad daylight; but Borgia-like takes you treacherously by the hand, while from the glittering ring on his finger he distils through your veins the subtle and deadly poison.

Sensual? The artist who would inflame, paints you not nude Nature, but stealing Virtue's veil, with artful artlessness now conceals, now exposes, the ripe and swelling proportions.

Sensual? Let him who would affix this stigma upon *Leaves of Grass*, write upon his heart, in letters of fire, these noble words of its author:

> "In woman I see the bearer of the great fruit, which is
>   immortality.... the good thereof is not tasted by
>   *roues*, and never can be.
>
>   . . . .
>
> Who degrades or defiles the living human body is cursed,
> Who degrades or defiles the body of the dead is not more
>   cursed."

Were I an artist I would like no more suggestive subjects for my easel than Walt Whitman's pen has furnished.

> "The little one sleeps in its cradle,
> I lift the gauze and look a long time, and silently
>   brush away flies with my hand.
> The farmer stops by the bars of a Sunday and looks at
>   the oats and rye."
>
>   . . . .
>
> "Earth of the slumbering and liquid trees!
> Earth of departed Sunset,

Earth of the mountain's misty topt!
Earth of the vitreous pour of the full moon just tinged
      with blue!
Earth of shine and dark mottling the tide of the river!
Earth of the limpid grey of clouds brighter and clearer
      for my sake!
Far swooping elbowed earth! Rich apple-blossomed earth!
      Smile, for your lover comes!"

I quote at random, the following passages which appeal to me:

"A morning glory at my window, satisfies me more than
      the metaphysics of books."

          . . . .

"Logic and sermons never convince.
The damp of the night drives deeper into my soul."

Speaking of animals, he says:

"I stand and look at them sometimes half the day long.
They do not make me sick, discussing their duty to God."

          . . . .

"Whoever walks a furlong without sympathy, walks to his
 own funeral dressed in his shroud."

          . . . .

"I hate him that oppresses me,
I will either destroy him, or he shall release me."

          . . . .

"I find letters from God dropped in the street, and every
      one is signed by God's name,
And I leave them where they are, for I know that others
      will punctually come forever and ever."

          . . . .

"Under Niagara, *the cataract falling like a veil over my
      countenance.*"

Of the grass he says:

"It seems to me *the beautiful uncut hair of graves.*"

I close the extracts from these *Leaves*, which it were easy to multiply, for one is more puzzled what to leave unculled, than what to gather, with the following sentiments; for which, and for all the good things included between the covers of his book Mr. Whitman will please accept the cordial grasp of a woman's hand:

> "The wife—and she is not one jot less than the
>   husband,
> The daughter—and she is just as good as the son,
> The mother—and she is every bit as much as the
>   father."

20. **"Transatlantic Latter-Day Poetry."** *Leader*, **7** (7 June 1856), 547–2 [*sic*, should be 548].

—"Latter-day poetry" in America is of a very different character from the same manifestation in the old country. Here, it is occupied for the most part with dreams of the middle ages, of the old knightly and religious times: in America, it is employed chiefly with the present, except when it travels out into the undiscovered future. Here, our latter-day poets are apt to whine over the times, as if Heaven were perpetually betraying the earth with a show of progress that is in fact retrogression, like the backward advance of crabs: there, the minstrels of the stars and stripes blow a loud note of exultation before the grand new epoch, and think the Greeks and Romans, the early Oriental races, and the later men of the middle centuries, of small account before the onward tramping of these present generations. Of this latter sect is a certain phenomenon who has recently started up in Brooklyn, New York—one Walt Whitman, author of *Leaves of Grass*, who has been received by a section of his countrymen as a sort of prophet, and by Englishmen as a kind of fool. For ourselves, we are not disposed to accept him as the one, having less faith in latter-day prophets than in latter-day poets; but assuredly we cannot regard him as the other. Walt is one of the most amazing, one of the most startling, one of the most perplexing, creations of the modern American mind; but he is no fool, though abundantly eccentric, nor is his book mere food for laughter, though undoubtedly containing much that may most easily and fairly be turned into ridicule.

The singularity of the author's mind—his utter disregard of ordinary forms and modes—appears in the very title-page and frontispiece of his work. Not only is there no author's name (which in itself would not be singular), but there is no publisher's name—that of the English bookseller being a London addition. Fronting the title is the portrait of a bearded gentleman in his shirt-sleeves and a Spanish hat, with an all-pervading atmosphere of Yankee-doodle about him; but again there is no patronymic, and we can only infer that this roystering blade is the author of the book. Then follows a long prose treatise by way of Preface (and here once more the anonymous system is carried out, the treatise having no heading whatever); and after that we have the poem, in the course of which, a short autobiographical discourse reveals to us the name of the author.

A passage from the Preface, if it may be so called, will give some insight into the character and objects of the work. The dots do not indicate any abbreviation by us, but are part of the author's singular system of punctuation:—

[Extract from the preface; c. 215 words:]

Other states indicate themselves in their deputies [...] these too are unrhymed poetry. It awaits the gigantic and generous treatment worthy of it.

This "gigantic and generous treatment," we presume, is offered in the pages which ensue. The poem is written in wild, irregular, unrhymed, almost unmetrical "lengths," like the measured prose of Mr. Martin Farquhar Tupper's *Proverbial Philosophy*, or of some of the Oriental writings. The external form, therefore, is startling, and by no means seductive, to English ears, accustomed to the sumptuous music of ordinary metres; and the central principle of the poem is equally staggering. It seems to re-solve itself into an all-attracting egotism—an eternal presence of the individual soul of Walt Whitman in all things, yet in such wise that this one soul shall be presented as a type of all human souls whatsoever. He goes forth into the world, this rough, devil-may-care Yankee; passionately identifies himself with all forms of being, sentient or inanimate; sympathizes deeply with humanity; riots with a kind of Bacchanal fury in the force and fervour of his own sensations; will not have the most vicious or aban-doned shut out from final comfort and reconciliation; is delighted with Broadway, New York, and equally in love with the desolate backwoods, and the long stretch of the uninhabited prairie, where the wild beasts wallow in the reeds, and the wilder birds start upwards from their nests among the grass; perceives a divine mystery wherever his feet conduct or his thoughts transport him; and beholds all beings tend-ing towards the central and sovereign Me. Such, as we conceive, is the key to this strange, grotesque, and bewildering book; yet we are far from saying that the key will unlock all the quirks and oddities of the volume. Much remains of which we confess we can make nothing; much that seems to us purely fantastical and prepos-terous; much that appears to our muddy vision gratuitously prosaic, needlessly plain-speaking, disgusting without purpose, and singular without result. There are so many evidences of a noble soul in Whitman's pages that we regret these aberrations, which only have the effect of discrediting what is genuine by the show of something false; and especially do we deplore the unnecessary openness with which Walt reveals to us matters which ought rather to remain in a sacred silence. It is good not to be ashamed of Nature; it is good to have an all-inclusive charity; but it is also good, sometimes, to leave the veil across the Temple.

That the reader may be made acquainted with the vividness with which Walt can paint the unhackneyed scenery of his native land, we subjoin a panorama:—

[24-line extract from "Song of Myself"]

21. **"Notices of Books."** *Dublin Review*, 41 (September 1856), 267–8.

We have glanced through this book with disgust and astonishment;—astonish-ment that anyone can be found who would dare to print such a farrago of rubbish,—lucubrations more like the ravings of a drunkard, or one half crazy, than anything which a man in his senses could think it fit to offer to the consideration of his fellow men. Where these bald, confused, disjointed, caricatures of blank verse have any meaning, it is generally indecent; several times execrably profane. We should not have bestowed one line of notice upon such an insult to common sense and common propriety, as this book but that, to our unspeakable surprise, we find bound up with it extracts from various American papers highly laudatory of this marvellous production: and we think it right to call the attention of our American readers to the fact, that any (even of the meanest) of their literary critics, should be mistaken enough to lend a sanction to such trash as this.

22.   **D.W. [from review of W. Edmondstoune Aytoun, *Bothwell:*
      A Poem in Six Parts and *Leaves of Grass*]. *Canadian Journal*, n.s. 1
      (November 1856), 541–51.**

In the works named above we have two not unmete representatives of the extremes of the Old and of the New World poetic ideal: *Bothwell*, the product of the severely critical, refined, and ultra-conservative author of the *Lays of the Scottish Cavaliers*; and *Leaves of Grass*, the wild, exuberant, lawless offspring of Walt Whitman, a Brooklyn Boy, "One of the Roughs!"
                                    [...]
In contrast with this we have named the effusions of the Brooklyn Bard. If the accredited author of "Firmilian" has now shown us what a poem ought to be, assuredly Walt Whitman is wide of the mark. Externally and internally he sets all law, decorum, prosody and propriety at defiance. A tall, lean, sallow, most republican, and Yankee-looking volume, is his *Leaves of Grass*; full of egotism, extravagance, and spasmodic eccentricities of all sorts; and heralded by a sheaf of double-columned extracts from Reviews—not always the least curious of its singular contents. Here, for example, is a protest against the intrusion of the British muse on the free soil of the States of the Union, which must surely satisfy the most clamant demand for native poetics and republican egotism:

"What very properly fits a subject of the British crown, may fit very ill an American freeman. No fine romance, no inimitable delineation of character, no grace of delicate illustrations, no rare picture of shore or mountain or sky, no deep thought of the intellect, is so important to a man as his opinion of himself is; everything receives its tinge from that. In the verse of all those undoubtedly great writers, *Shakespeare, just as much as the rest*, there is the air which to America is the air of death. The mass of the people, the laborers and all who serve, are slag, refuse. The countenances of kings and great lords are beautiful; the countenances of mechanics are ridiculous and deformed. What play of Shakespeare represented in America, is not an insult to America, to the marrow in its bones? How can the tone—never silent in their plots and characters—be applauded, unless Washington should have been caught and hung, and Jefferson was the most enormous of liars, and common persons, North and South, should bow low to their betters, and to organic superiority of blood? Sure as the heavens envelop the earth, if the Americans want a race of bards worthy of 1855, and of the stern reality of this republic, they must cast around for men essentially different from the old poets, and from the modern successions of jinglers and snivellers and fops."

—and here accordingly is something essentially different from all poets, both old and new.

The poet, unnamed on his title page, figures on his frontispiece, and unmistakeably utters his own poem:

"I celebrate myself,
And what I assume, you shall assume;
For every atom belonging to me as good belongs to you.
I loafe, and invite my soul;
I lean and loafe at my ease—
Observing a spear of Summer grass."

Such is the starting point of this most eccentric and republican of poets; of whom the republican critic above quoted, after contrasting with him Tennyson, as "The bard of ennui, and the aristocracy and their combination into love, the old stock love of playwrights and romancers, Shakespeare, the same as the rest."—concludes by confessing his inability to decide whether Walt Whitman is "to prove the most lamentable of failures, or the most glorious of triumphs, in the known history of literature."

Assuredly, the Brooklyn poet is no commonplace writer. That he is startling and *outré*, no one who opens his volume will doubt. The conventionalities, and proprieties, and modesties, of thought, as well as of language, hold him in no restraint; and hence he has a vantage ground from which he may claim such credit as its licence deserves. But, apart from this, there are unmistakeable freshness, originality, and true poetic gleams of thought, mingled with the strange incoherencies of his boastful rhapsody. To call his *Leaves* poems, would be a mistake; they resemble rather the poet's first jottings, out of which the poem is to be formed; the ore out of which the metal is to be smelted; and, in its present form, with more of dross than sterling metal in the mass.

To find an extractable passage is no easy task. Here a fine suggestive fancy ends in some offensive pruriency; there it dwindles into incomprehensible aggregations of words and terms, which—unless Machiavelli was right in teaching that words were given us to conceal our thoughts,—are mere clotted nonsense! Were we disposed to ridicule: our selections would be easy enough; or gravely to censure: abundant justification is at hand. We rather cull—not without needful omissions—the thoughts that seem to have suggested the quaint title of *Leaves of Grass*.

[Extracts from the poetry; 34 lines:]

"Loafe with me on the grass...... loose the stop from
     your throat, [...]
Only the lull I like, the hum of your valved voice."

. . . .

"I know that the hand of God is the elderhand of my own, [...]
And limitless are leaves, stiff or drooping in the
     fields."

. . . .

"A child said, what is the Grass? fetching it to me with
     full hands; [...]

And now it seems to me the beautiful uncut hair of
    graves."

. . . .

"All truths wait in all things, […]
The damp of the night drives deeper into my soul."

. . . .

"I believe a leaf of grass is no less than the
    journeywork of the stars, […]
And a mouse is miracle enough to stagger sextillions of
    infidels."

This passage is far from being the most characteristic of the poem, and even in it we have stopped abruptly for one line more, and........ Yet this will show that the punctuation is as odd as any other feature of the work; for the whole is full of conceits which speak fully as much of coarse vain-glorious egotism as of originality of genius. Any man may be an original, whether in the fopperies of the dress he puts on himself or on his poem. We are not, therefore, disposed to rate such very high, or to reckon Walt Whitman's typographical whims any more indicative of special genius, than the shirt-sleeves and unshaven chin of his frontispiece. If they indicate any thing specially, we should infer that he is a compositor by trade, and, for all his affectations of independence, could not keep "the shop" out of his verse. But that he sets all the ordinary rules of men and poets at defiance is visible on every page of his lank volume; and if readers judge thereby that he thinks himself wiser than all previous men and poets—we have no authority to contradict them. That some of his thoughts are far from vain or common place, however, a few gleanings may suffice to prove; culled in the form, not of detached passages but of isolated ideas—line, or fragments of lines:—

[Extracts from the poetry; 11 lines:]

"The friendly and flowing savage.... Who is he?
Is he waiting for civilization or past it and mastering
    it?"

. . . .

"The welcome ugly face of some beautiful soul."

. . . .

"The clock indicates the moment.... but what does
    eternity indicate?"

. . . .

"Afar down I see the huge first Nothing, […]
And took my time.... and took no hurt from the foetid
    carbon."

. . . .

"See ever so far.... there is limitless space outside of
    that, [...]

Our rendezvous is fitly appointed.... God will be there
    and wait till we come."

These doubled and quadrupled points, let us add, pertain to the original, whatever
their precise significance may be. Here again is a grand idea, not altogether new; and
rough in its present setting, as the native gold still buried in Californian beds of
quartz and debris. Nevertheless it is full of suggestive thought, and like much else in
the volume—though less than most,—only requires the hand of the artist to cut, and
polish, and set, that it may gleam and sparkle with true poetic lustre:—

[Extract from the poetry:]

"A slave at auction! [...]
Who might you find you have come from yourself?"

"Great is life..and real and mystical..wherever and
    whoever, [...]
after they merge in the light, death is greater than life."

Such are some of the "Leaves of Grass," of the Brooklyn poet who describes
himself in one of them as:

"Walt Whitman, an American, one of the roughs, a
Kosmos!"

But if the reader—recognising true poetry in some of these,—should assume such
a likeness running through the whole as pertains to the blades of Nature's Grass, we
disclaim all responsibility if he find reason to revise his fancy. In the two very di-
verse volumes under review it seems to us that we have in the one the polish of the
artist, which can accomplish so much when applied to the gem or rich ore; in the
other we discern the ore, but overlaid with the valueless matrix and foul rubbish of
the mine, and devoid of all the unveiling beauties of art. Viewed in such aspects these
poems are characteristic of the age. From each we have striven to select what ap-
peared most worthy of the space at command, and best calculated to present them to
the reader in the most favorable point of view consistent with truth. And so we leave
the reader to his own judgment, between the old-world stickler for authority, prece-
dent, and poetical respectability, and the new-world contemner of all authorities,
laws, and respectabilities whatsoever. Happily for us, all choice is not necessarily
limited to these. The golden mean of poesie does not, we imagine, lie between such
extremes. There are not a few left, both in England and in America, for whom old
Shakspeare is still respectable enough, and poetical enough,—aye and free enough
too, in spite of all the freedom which has budded and bloomed since that year 1616,
when his sacred ashes were laid beneath the chancel stone whose curse still guards

them from impious hands. Nevertheless we have faith in the future. We doubt not even the present. When a greater poet than Shakespeare does arrive we shall not count him an impossibility.

23. Frank Leslie's *Illustrated Newspaper*, 20 December 1856, p. 42.

We find upon our table (and shall put into the fire) a thin octavo volume, handsomely printed and bound, with the above curious title. We shall not aid in extending the sale of this intensely vulgar, nay, absolutely beastly book, by telling our readers where it may be purchased. The only review we shall attempt of it, will be to thus publicly call the attention of the grand jury to a matter that needs presentment by them, and to mildly suggest that the author should be sent to a lunatic asylum, and the mercenary publishers to the penitentiary for pandering to the prurient tastes of morbid sensualists. Ralph W. Emerson's name appears as an indorser of these (so-called) poems (?)—God save the mark! We can only account for this strange fatuity upon the supposition that the letter is a forgery, that Mr. E. has not read some passages in the book, or that he lends his name to this vile production of a vitiated nature or diseased imagination, because the author is an imitator of his style, and apes him occasionally in his transcendentalisms. Affectation is as pitiful an ambition in literature as alliteration, and never has it been more fully exhibited during the present century than in the case of Thomas Carlyle, a man with an order of intellect approaching genius, but who for a distinguishing mark to point like a finger-board to himself, left a very terse and effective style of writing to adopt a jargon filled with new-fangled phrases and ungrammatical super-superlative adjectives—Mr. Carlyle buried himself for a long time in German universities and German philosophy, and came forth clothed in a full "old clothes" suit of transcendentalism worthy of the Chatham street embodiments of that pseudo-philosophy, Kant and Spinosa [*sic*]—Carlyle by this operation became a full-fledged Psyche from the chrysalis, and sported in the sunshine of popularity, whereupon a young gentleman ambitious of making New England an umbra of Scottish-Germanic glory, one Ralph Waldo Emerson, suddenly transforms himself into a metaphysical transcendentalist and begins talking about "Objective and Subjective," the "Inner and Outer," the "Real and Ideal," the "God-heads and God-tails," "Planes," "Spheres," "Finite, Infinite," "Unities," and "Dualities," "Squills, Ipecac," "Cascading and Cavorting," &c., &c. And lo! another appeared after this Mr. Emerson, one Walt Whitman, who kicked over the whole bucket of the Milky Way, and deluged the world with the whey, curds and bonny-clabber of Brooklyn—which has resulted from the turning of the milk of human kindness in a "b'hoy's" brains to the cream of Tartar—and a delicious dish of the same is now furnished under cover of Leaves of Grass, and indorsed by the said Emerson, who swallows down Whitman's vulgarity and beastliness as if they were curds and whey. No wonder the Boston female schools are demoralized when Emerson, the head of the moral and solid people of Boston, indorses Whitman, and thus drags his slimy work into the sanctum of New England firesides.

Letters

Emerson, LETTER TO WHITMAN

DEAR SIR—I am not blind to the worth of the wonderful gift of "LEAVES OF GRASS." I find it the most extraordinary piece of wit and wisdom that America has yet contributed. I am very happy in reading it, as great power makes us happy. It meets the demand I am always making of what seemed the sterile and stingy nature, as if too much handiwork, or too much lymph in the temperament, were making our western wits fat and mean.

I give you joy of your free and brave thought. I have great joy in it. I find incomparable things said incomparably well, as they must be. I find the courage of treatment which so delights us, and which large perception only can inspire.

I greet you at the beginning of a great career, which yet must have had a long foreground somewhere, for such a start. I rubbed my eyes a little, to see if this sunbeam were no illusion; but the solid sense of the book is a sober certainty. It has the best merits, namely, of fortifying and encouraging.

I did not know until I last night saw the book advertised in newspaper that I could trust the name as real and available for a post-office. I wish to see my benefactor, and have felt much like striking my tasks, and visiting New York to pay you my respects.

R. W. EMERSON
Concord, Massachusetts, 21 July, 1855

Whitman, LETTER TO EMERSON
BROOKLYN, August, 1856.

HERE are thirty-two Poems, which I send you, dear Friend and Master, not having found how I could satisfy myself with sending any usual acknowledgment of your letter. The first edition, on which you mailed me that till now unanswered letter, was twelve poems—I printed a thousand copies, and they readily sold; these thirty-two Poems I stereotype, to print several thousand copies of. I much enjoy making poems. Other work I have set for myself to do, to meet people and The States face to face, to confront them with an American rude tongue; but the work of my life is making poems. I keep on till I make a hundred, and then several hundred—perhaps a thousand. The way is clear to me. A few years, and the average annual call for my Poems is ten or twenty thousand copies—more, quite likely. Why should I hurry or compromise? In poems or in speeches I say the word or two that has got to be said, adhere to the body, step with the countless common footsteps, and remind every man and woman of something.

Master, I am a man who has perfect faith. Master, we have not come through centuries, caste, heroisms, fables, to halt in this land today. Or I think it is to collect a ten-fold impetus that any halt is made. As nature, inexorable, onward, resistless, impassive amid the threats and screams of disputants, so America. Let all defer. Let all attend respectfully the leisure of These States, their politics, poems, literature, manners, and their free-handed modes of training their own offspring. Their own comes, just matured, certain, numerous and capable enough, with egotistical tongues, with sinewed wrists, seizing openly what belongs to them. They resume Personality, too long left out of mind. Their shadows are projected in employments, in books, in the cities, in trade; their feet are on the flights of the steps of the Capitol; they dilate, a larger, brawnier, more candid, more democratic, lawless, positive native to The States, sweet-bodied, completer, dauntless, flowing, masterful, beard-faced, new race of men.

Swiftly, on limitless foundations, the United States too are founding a literature. It is all as well done, in my opinion, as could be practicable. Each element here is in condition. Every day I go among the people of Manhattan Island, Brooklyn, and other cities, and among the young men, to discover the spirit of them, and to refresh myself. These are to be attended to; I am myself more drawn here than to those authors, publishers, importations, reprints, and so forth. I pass coolly through those, understanding them perfectly well, and that they do the indispensable service, outside of men like me, which nothing else could do. In poems, the young men of The States shall be represented, for they out-rival the best of the rest of the earth.

The lists of ready-made literature which America inherits by the mighty inheritance of the English language—all the rich repertoire of traditions, poems, historics, metaphysics, plays, classics, translations, have made, and still continue, magnificent preparations for that other plainly signified literature, to be our own, to be electric, fresh, lusty, to express the full-sized body, male and female—to give the modern meanings of things, to grow up beautiful, lasting, commensurate with America, with all the passions of home, with the inimitable sympathies of having been boys and girls together, and of parents who were with our parents.

What else can happen The States, even in their own despite? That huge English flow, so sweet, so undeniable, has done incalculable good here, and is to be spoken of for its own sake with generous praise and with gratitude. Yet the price The States have had to lie under for the same has not been a small price. Payment prevails; a nation can never take the issues of the needs of other nations for nothing. America, grandest of lands in the theory of its politics, in popular reading, in hospitality, breadth, animal beauty, cities, ships, machines, money, credit, collapses quick as lightning at the repeated, admonishing, stern words, Where are any mental expressions from you, beyond what you have copied or stolen? Where the born throngs of poets, literats, orators, you promised? Will you but tag after other nations? They struggled long for their literature, painfully working their way, some with deficient languages, some with priest-craft, some in the endeavor just to live—yet achieved for their times, works, poems, perhaps the only solid consolation left to them through ages afterward of shame and decay. You are young, have the perfectest of dialects, a free press, a free government, the world forwarding its best to be with you. As justice has been strictly done to you, from this hour do strict justice to yourself. Strangle the singers who will not sing you loud and strong. Open the doors of The West. Call for new great masters to comprehend new arts, new perfections, new wants. Submit to the most robust bard till he remedy your barrenness. Then you will not need to adopt the heirs of others; you will have true heirs, begotten of yourself, blooded with your own blood.

With composure I see such propositions, seeing more and more every day of the answers that serve. Expressions do not yet serve, for sufficient reasons; but that is getting ready, beyond what the earth has hitherto known, to take home the expressions when they come, and to identify them with the populace of The States, which is the schooling cheaply procured by any outlay any number of years. Such schooling The States extract from the swarms of reprints, and from the current authors and editors. Such service and extract are done after enormous, reckless, free modes, characteristic of The States. Here are to be attained results never elsewhere thought possible; the modes are very grand too. The instincts of the American people are all perfect, and tend to make heroes. It is a rare thing in a man here to understand The States.

All current nourishments to literature serve. Of authors and editors I do not know how many there are in The States, but there are thousands, each one building his or her step to the stairs by which giants shall mount. Of the twenty-four modern mammoth two-double, three-double, and four-double cylinder presses now in the world, printing by steam, twenty-one of them are in These States. The twelve thousand large and small shops for dispensing books and newspapers—the same number of public libraries, any one of which has all the reading wanted to equip a man or woman for American reading—the three thousand different newspapers, the nutriment of the imperfect ones coming in just as usefully as any—the story papers, various, full of strong-flavored romances, widely circulated—the one-cent and two-cent journals— the political ones, no matter what side—the weeklies in the country—the sporting and pictorial papers—the monthly magazines, with plentiful imported feed—the sentimental novels, numberless copies of them—the low-priced flaring tales, adventures, biographies—all are prophetic; all waft rapidly on. I see that they swell wide, for reasons. I am not troubled at the movement of them, but greatly pleased. I see plying shuttles, the active ephemeral myriads of books also, faithfully weaving the garments of a generation of men, and a generation of women, they do not perceive or know. What a progress popular reading and writing has made in fifty years! What a progress fifty years hence! The time is at hand when inherent literature will be a main part of These States, as general and real as steam-power, iron, corn, beef, fish. First-rate American persons are to be supplied. Our perennial materials for fresh thoughts, histories, poems, music, orations, religions, recitations, amusements, will then not be disregarded, any more than our perennial fields, mines, rivers, seas. Certain things are established, and are immovable; in those things millions of years stand justified. The mothers and fathers of whom modern centuries have come, have not existed for nothing; they too had brains and hearts. Of course all literature, in all nations and years, will share marked attributes in common, as we all, of all ages, share the common human attributes. America is to be kept coarse and broad. What is to be done is to withdraw from precedents, and be directed to men and women—also to The States in their federalness; for the union of the parts of the body is not more necessary to their life than the union of These States is to their life.

A profound person can easily know more of the people than they know of themselves. Always waiting untold in the souls of the armies of common people, is stuff better than anything that can possibly appear in the leadership of the same. That gives final verdicts. In every department of These States, he who travels with a coterie, or with selected persons, or with imitators, or with infidels, or with the owners of slaves, or with that which is ashamed of the body of a man, or with that which is ashamed of the body of a woman, or with any thing less than the bravest and the

openest, travels straight for the slopes of dissolution. The genius of all foreign litera-
ture is clipped and cut small, compared to our genius, and is essentially insulting to
our usages, and to the organic compacts of These States. Old forms, old poems,
majestic and proper in their own lands here in this land are exiles; the air here is very
strong. Much that stands well and has a little enough place provided for it in the
small scales of European kingdoms, empires, and the like, here stands haggard,
dwarfed, ludicrous, or has no place little enough provided for it. Authorities, poems,
models, laws, names, imported into America, are useful to America today to destroy
them, and so move disencumbered to great works, great days.

Just so long, in our country or any country, as no revolutionists advance, and are
backed by the people, sweeping off the swarms of routine representatives, officers in
power, book-makers, teachers, ecclesiastics, politicians, just so long, I perceive, do
they who are in power fairly represent that country, and remain of use, probably of
very great use. To supersede them, when it is the pleasure of These States, full provi-
sion is made; and I say the time has arrived to use it with a strong hand. Here also the
souls of the armies have not only overtaken the souls of the officer, but passed on,
and left the souls of the officers behind out of sight many weeks' journey; and the
souls of the armies now go en-masse without officers. Here also formulas, glosses,
blanks, minutiæ, are choking the throats of the spokesmen to death. Those things
most listened for, certainly those are the things least said. There is not a single His-
tory of the World. There is not one of America, or of the organic compacts of These
States, or of Washington, or of Jefferson, nor of Language, nor any Dictionary of the
English Language. There is no great author; every one has demeaned himself to
some etiquette or some impotence. There is no manhood or life-power in poems;
there are shoats and geldings more like. Or literature will be dressed up, a fine gentle-
man, distasteful to our instincts, foreign to our soil. Its neck bends right and left
wherever it goes. Its costumes and jewelry prove how little it knows Nature. Its flesh
is soft; it shows less and less of the indefinable hard something that is Nature. Where
is any thing but the shaved Nature of synods and schools? Where is a savage and
luxuriant man? Where is an overseer? In lives, in poems, in codes of law, in Con-
gress, in tuitions, theatres, conversations, argumentations, not a single head lifts it-
self clean out, with proof that it is their master, and has subordinated them to itself,
and is ready to try their superiors. None believes in These States, boldly illustrating
them in himself. Not a man faces round at the rest with terrible negative voice, refus-
ing all terms to be bought off from his own eye-sight, or from the soul that he is, or
from friendship, or from the body that he is, or from the soil and sea. To creeds,
literature, art, the army, the navy, the executive, life is hardly proposed, but the sick
and dying are proposed to cure the sick and dying. The churches are one vast lie; the
people do not believe them, and they do not believe themselves; the priests are con-
tinually telling what they know well enough is not so, and keeping back what they
know is so. The spectacle is a pitiful one. I think there can never be again upon the
festive earth more bad-disordered persons deliberately taking seats, as of late in These
States, at the heads of the public tables—such corpses' eyes for judges—such a ras-
cal and thief in the Presidency.

Up to the present, as helps best, the people, like a lot of large boys, have no
determined tastes, are quite unaware of the grandeur of themselves, and of their des-
tiny, and of their immense strides—accept with voracity whatever is presented them
in novels, histories, newspapers, poems, schools, lectures, every thing. Pretty soon,

through these and other means, their development makes the fibre that is capable of itself, and will assume determined tastes. The young men will be clear what they want, and will have it. They will follow none except him whose spirit leads them in the like spirit with themselves. Any such man will be welcome as the flowers of May. Others will be put out without ceremony. How much is there anyhow, to the young men of These States, in a parcel of helpless dandies, who can neither fight, work, shoot, ride, run, command—some of them devout, some quite insane, some castrated— all second-hand, or third, fourth, or fifth hand—waited upon by waiters, putting not this land first, but always other lands first, talking of art, doing the most ridiculous things for fear of being called ridiculous, smirking and skipping along, continually taking off their hats—no one behaving, dressing, writing, talking, loving, out of any natural and manly tastes of his own, but each one looking cautiously to see how the rest behave, dress, write, talk, love—pressing the noses of dead books upon themselves and upon their country—favoring no poets, philosophs, literats here, but dog-like danglers at the heels of the poets, philosophs, literats, of enemies' lands—favoring mental expressions, models of gentlemen and ladies, social habitudes in These States, to grow up in sneaking defiance of the popular substratums of The States? Of course they and the likes of them can never justify the strong poems of America. Of course no feed of theirs is to stop and be made welcome to muscle the bodies, male and female, for Manhattan Island, Brooklyn, Boston, Worcester, Hartford, Portland, Montreal, Detroit, Buffalo, Cleaveland, Milwaukee, St. Louis, Indianapolis, Chicago, Cincinnati, Iowa City, Philadelphia, Baltimore, Releigh, Savannah, Charleston, Mobile, New Orleans, Galveston, Brownsville, San Francisco, Havana, and a thousand equal cities, present and to come. Of course what they and the likes of them have been used for, draws toward its close, after which they will all be discharged, and not one of them will ever be heard of any more.

America, having duly conceived, bears out of herself offspring of her own to do the workmanship wanted. To freedom, to strength, to poems, to personal greatness, it is never permitted to rest, not a generation or part of a generation. To be ripe beyond further increase is to prepare to die. The architects of These States laid their foundations, and passed to further, spheres. What they laid is a work done; as much more remains. Now are needed other architects, whose duty is not less difficult, but perhaps more difficult. Each age forever needs architects. America is not finished, perhaps never will be; now America is a divine true sketch. There are Thirty-Two States sketched—the population thirty millions. In a few years there will be Fifty States. Again in a few years there will be A Hundred States, the population hundreds of millions, the freshest and freest of men. Of course such men stand to nothing less than the freshest and freest expression.

Poets here, literats here, are to rest on organic different bases from other countries; not a class set apart, circling only in the circle of themselves, modest and pretty, desperately scratching for rhymes, pallid with white paper, shut off, aware of the old pictures and traditions of the race, but unaware of the actual race around them—not breeding in and in among each other till they all have the scrofula. Lands of ensemble, bards of ensemble! Walking freely out from the old traditions, as our politics has walked out, American poets and literats recognize nothing behind them superior to what is present with them—recognize with joy the sturdy living forms of the men and women of These States, the divinity of sex, the perfect eligibility of the female with the male, all The States, liberty and equality, real articles, the different trades, mechanics, the young fellows of Manhattan Island, customs, instincts, slang, Wisconsin, Georgia, the noble Southern heart, the hot blood, the spirit that will be nothing less than master, the filibuster spirit, the Western man, native-born perceptions, the eye for forms, the perfect models of made things, the wild smack of freedom, California, money, electrictelegraphs, free-trade, iron and the iron mines—recognize without demur those splendid resistless black poems, the steam-ships of the seaboard states, and those other resistless splendid poems, the locomotives, followed through the interior states by trains of rail-road cars.

A word remains to be said, as of one ever present, not yet permitted to be acknowledged, discarded or made dumb by literature, and the results apparent. To the lack of an avowed, empowered, unabashed development of sex, (the only salvation for the same,) and to the fact of speakers and writers fraudulently assuming as always dead what every one knows to be always alive, is attributable the remarkable non-personality and indistinctness of modern productions in books, art, talk; also that in the scanned lives of men and women most of them appear to have been for some time past of the neuter gender; and also the stinging fact that in orthodox society today if the dresses were changed, the men might easily pass for women and the women for men.

Infidelism usurps most with foetid polite face; among the rest infidelism about sex. By silence or obedience the pens of savans, poets, historians, biographers, and the rest, have long connived at the filthy law, and books enslaved to it, that what makes the manhood of a man, that sex, womanhood, maternity, desires, lusty animations, organs, acts, are unmentionable and to be ashamed of, to be driven to skulk out of literature with whatever belongs to them. This filthy law has to be repealed—it stands in the way of great reforms. Of women just as much as men, it is the interest that there should not be infidelism about sex, but perfect faith. Women in These States approach the day of that organic equality with men, without which, I see, men cannot have organic equality among themselves. This empty dish, gallantry, will then be filled with something. This tepid wash, this diluted deferential love, as in songs, fictions, and so forth, is enough to make a man vomit; as to manly friendship, everywhere observed in The States, there is not the first breath of it to be observed in print. I say that the body of a man or woman, the main matter, is so far quite unexpressed in poems; but that the body is to be expressed, and sex is. Of bards for These States, if it come to a question, it is whether they shall celebrate in poems the eternal decency of the amativeness of Nature, the motherhood of all, or whether they shall be the bards of the fashionable delusion of the inherent nastiness of sex, and of the feeble and querulous modesty of deprivation. This is important in poems, because the whole of the other expressions of a nation are but flanges out of its great poems. To me, henceforth, that theory of any thing, no matter what, stagnates in its vitals, cowardly and rotten, while it cannot publicly accept, and publicly name, with specific words, the things on which all existence, all souls, all realization, all decency, all health, all that is worth being here for, all of woman and of man, all beauty, all purity, all sweetness, all friendship, all strength, all life, all immortality depend. The courageous soul, for a year or two to come, may be proved by faith in sex, and by disdaining concessions.

To poets and literats—to every woman and man, today or any day, the conditions of the present, needs, dangers, prejudices, and the like, are the perfect conditions on which we are here, and the conditions for wording the future with undissuadable words. These States, receivers of the stamina of past ages and lands, initiate the outlines of repayment a thousand fold. They fetch the American great masters, waited for by old worlds and new, who accept evil as well as good, ignorance as well as erudition, black as soon as white, foreign-born materials as well as home-born, reject none, force discrepancies into range, surround the whole, concentrate them on present periods and places, show the application to each and any one's body and soul, and show the true use of precedents. Always America will be agitated and turbulent. This day it is taking shape, not to be less so, but to be more so, stormily, capriciously, on native principles, with such vast proportions of parts! As for me, I love screaming, wrestling, boiling-hot days.

Of course, we shall have a national character, an identity. As it ought to be, and as soon as it ought to be, it will be. That, with much else, takes care of itself, is a result, and the cause of greater results. With Ohio, Illinois, Missouri, Oregon—with the states around the Mexican sea—with cheerfully welcomed immigrants from Europe, Asia, Africa—with Connecticut, Vermont, New Hampshire, Rhode Island—with all varied interests, facts, beliefs, parties, genesis—there is being fused a determined character, fit for the broadest use for the freewomen and freemen of The States, accomplished and to be accomplished, without any exception whatever—each indeed free, each idiomatic, as becomes live states and men, but each adhering to one enclosing general form of politics, manners, talk, personal style, as the plenteous varieties of the race adhere to one physical form. Such character is the brain and spine to all, including literature, including poems. Such character, strong, limber, just, open-mouthed, American-blooded, full of pride, full of ease, of passionate friendliness, is to stand compact upon that vast basis of the supremacy of Individuality—that new moral American continent without which, I see, the physical continent remained incomplete, may-be a carcass, a bloat—that newer America, answering face to face with The States, with ever-satisfying and ever-unsurveyable seas and shores.

Those shores you found. I say you have led The States there—have led Me there. I say that none has ever done, or ever can do, a greater deed for The States, than your deed. Others may line out the lines, build cities, work mines, break up farms; it is yours to have been the original true Captain who put to sea, intuitive, positive, rendering the first report, to be told less by any report, and more by the mariners of a thousand bays, in each tack of their arriving and departing, many years after you.

Receive, dear Master, these statements and assurances through me, for all the young men, and for an earnest that we know none before you, but the best following you; and that we demand to take your name into our keeping, and that we understand what you have indicated, and find the same indicated in ourselves, and that we will stick to it and enlarge upon it through These States.

WALT WHITMAN.